SEVEN BONES

Two wives, two violent murders, a fight for justice...

Big Sky Publishing Pty Ltd

PO Box 303, Newport, NSW 2106, Australia

Phone: (61 2) 9918 2168

Fax: (61 2) 9918 2396

Email: info@bigskypublishing.com.au

Web: www.bigskypublishing.com.au

Cover design and typesetting: Think Productions

National Library of Australia Cataloguing-in-Publication entry

Author: Seymour, Peter.

Title: Seven bones : two wives, two violent murders, a fight for justice / Peter Seymour & Jason K. Foster.

ISBN: 9781921941146 (pbk.)

Subjects: Keir, Thomas Andrew.
Strachan, Jean Angela.
Canonizado, Rosalina.
Murder--New South Wales--Case studies.
Murder--Investigation--New South Wales.
Murder victims--New South Wales.
Trials (Murder)--New South Wales--Sydney.

Other Authors/Contributors: Foster, Jason K.

Dewey Number: 364.152309944

SEVEN BONES

Two Wives, Two Violent Murders, A Fight For Justice...

BIG SKY PUBLISHING
www.bigskypublishing.com.au

PETER SEYMOUR & JASON K. FOSTER

CONTENTS

FOREWORD

By Jane Hansen

A cold-blooded killer sat in front of me, eyes downcast, shoulders slumped, body stiff. He knew he was a killer, I knew he was a killer, but his desperate attempts to convince the world of his concocted innocence had pulled a thread, and the camera was rolling on it. Thomas Keir was many things, but innocent he was not. His guilt seeped so heavily from his pores you could almost smell it under the harsh camera lights.

Getting away with murder is quite a clever thing, and Thomas Keir thought he was smarter than everyone else, including the police. He had carefully fabricated what he thought was a believable story that explained the disappearance of his young wife Jean, who had not been seen since 10 February 1988. He was the last person to see her, and with no body, he thought his 'my wife ran off with another man' theory was holding with the police and the media. It may have held longer had his second wife, Rosalie, not been found strangled and burnt to death on their marital bed just three years later. Keir was the last one to see her alive too.

It was 1991, and Keir played distraught husband in the media, where he wrote a tearful letter which he subsequently dropped around the local neighbourhood in an 'attempt' to find her killer. His 'unlucky in love' victim line was played to the hilt, even though human bones other than Rosalie's had been discovered in a search of his backyard. Everyone had their suspicions. He was charged with Rosalie's murder, but was acquitted in 1993, much to the surprise, and disappointment, of everyone.

DNA technology was at that time simply not up to the task of extracting an identity from the seven small bones. Police knew they had their man, but it would be a waiting game. In the meantime, his fabricated media existence was about to pull a thread.

In 1994, I ran a story on Channel Seven's *Real Life* about Asian brides being over-represented in murder statistics, and ran a list of names where the husband was implicated in the crimes. I ran Rosalie's name in that list and Thomas Keir sent us several letters of protest threatening to sue. It was not until the Executive Producer Gerald Stone received a call from Keir demanding to see a separate, inconsequential story we ran a few weeks later that our ears pricked. Keir said he had seen his missing wife Jean in the background of the file footage taken on Bribie Island. He wanted to show us.

By now, Stone thought the man was acting very strangely. We did our homework. Here was a man who had virtually stalked his first wife from age fifteen, whose possessiveness included lopping photos in half if they showed too much of his wife's leg and demands to his mother-in-law Christine to alter her daughter's swimsuits to reveal less breast and leg.

Christine told me she knew what a mother knows in her heart – that her daughter was dead and that her son-in-law was to blame, but she had to play the game for the sake of her grandson, Jean's little boy. She knew what police knew too, but no-one could risk another acquittal, and that meant waiting.

We treated Keir's dealings with us at Channel Seven as a case of 'him doth protest too much' and invited him in to show us his missing wife in the footage. She wasn't there, of course; he was mistaken.

Then I conducted an interview that said so much on so many levels, and his non-verbal communication spoke volumes. In fact, Keir refused to look me in the eye at all, and when I asked him why, he said, 'Oh, I've got a crook neck!' It was pathetic.

Like a scene from CSI, we had the tape assessed by a forensic psychologist, who pointed out that Keir had never actually denied killing Jean. When asked if he'd killed Jean in a jealous fit of rage, he replied, 'It didn't happen like that.'

However, he would not elaborate on how it had happened. Indeed, when I confronted him about the extraordinary coincidence that *both* his wives had ended up dead, he merely put it down to 'sheer bad luck.'

To kill someone is a very significant event. To cover it up and live a lie must have been exhausting for Keir, and he felt compelled to test whether his fabricated innocence was still holding, but the human body is a lousy vessel. Guilt eventually seeps out one way or another, but *looking* guilty is not a crime, or grounds for a conviction.

Seeking justice through the correct channels would prove an exercise in fortitude, patience and resilience for the dedicated police involved and Jean's family, all of whom endured three long court cases.

There has never been any justice for Rosalie.

PROLOGUE

The Homecoming

Fear.

It was an all-to-familiar feeling for Jean Angela Keir, but she'd never known it like this, as it hungrily devoured the only part of her soul she still possessed. She shook. She shivered. The butterflies gnawed away at the insides of her stomach; anywhere else would have been better than here. *He'd* created that fear and she hated him for it. No, she despised him. How had her life come to this? What was she talking about: it wasn't her life any more - it was *his*. No single aspect remained beyond his control. Her identity had totally vanished, lost in his psychopathic jealously.

'Who am I?' She'd always ask herself this question, but it never seemed to have an answer. Whenever she looked in the mirror, the reflection staring back at her was a ghost, an emaciated and thin stranger, an unrecognisable version of herself. Her delicate, porcelain skin had turned a pale grey, and her long, brunette curls had lost their shine and lustre. Her eyes had changed from a deep brown to a fiery red from an eternity of tears. They'd become hollow somehow. Her smile, her beautiful smile, had evaporated. Everyone, her mum, her dad, her friends, had all told her that her special sparkle had disappeared.

He was responsible. *He* was literally driving her crazy. Possessive, resentful, he always teetered on the brink of insanity. Brutality was something she knew like a lifelong friend; even wearing revealing shorts or a bikini resulted in him flying into fits of rage laced with an anger that knew no limits. She bathed with her own son…he beat her. She played around with her cousin….he beat her. She wrestled with friends…he beat her.

He'd always said, 'I'll cut you up and feed you to the dogs if you ever leave me or touch another man.' Visions of him laughing as he tossed scraps of her to his beloved greyhounds raced through her head. How could she go into her house? How could she be left alone with *him*?

Freedom. She'd tasted it for the first time in years. The man sitting next to her had given her something that her husband never could. Staring blankly out the passenger-side window, she regained her composure and turned to her lover. 'Carl,' she said, 'I don't want to go in. I'm scared of him. He'll kill me.'

'You have to. He's your husband, and you guys need to sort this out.'

'But I'm in love with you.'

'I know. I'm sorry. There's nothing I can do. You guys are married.'

Terror engulfed her as she stepped out of the red Renault station wagon and saw *him* standing on the veranda. Moving towards the front gate, her breathing became shallow and short, as though a python was constricting her chest.

'I go to face the Devil. My life's in God's hands,' she thought to herself as she walked straight past her husband keeping her head bowed, too afraid to make eye contact.

Thomas Andrew Keir had been waiting for hours. With each passing minute, his anger and resentment grew. He could feel the fury frothing and bubbling deep down in the recesses of his soul and, for what felt like an eternity, he stared out the window searching for any sign of his wife and the man who'd stolen her. Finally, he watched the Renault as it came down the street.

'She'd told me it was over,' he thought to himself. 'She was a liar; a filthy liar. I let her have the week with her sister and her sister's boyfriend at the caravan park in Culburra,' he thought, 'but she doesn't belong there. She belongs at home with me.'

Two days earlier, he'd driven down there and dragged her, kicking and screaming, into the car. On the way home, they'd stopped at a service station at Casula. Jean had gone to the toilet, escaped out the window and hitchhiked to her lover's flat in Bondi. He knew she wouldn't escape again; she'd pay for her infidelity. She was his: no-one else was going to have her, ever.

Tom opened the front door of his home in Wilkes Crescent, Tregear. His face carried a strained smile as he walked down the footpath, but deep inside the fires of rage burned brightly upon seeing his wife seated next to her lover. He watched her as she walked past him, head down, and then turned his attention to the car. When he reached it, he bent down and looked inside. 'Do you want to come in?' he asked.

'Nah, mate, you guys work it out. Work this out for yourself.'

'Righto, see you later then.'

Carl waited until Tom was inside before turning the ignition. The motor sparked into life, and a strange feeling of uneasiness, as if the world had tilted from its axis, came over him. He drove off. His unease stayed with him through the night and, to entirely remove himself from the situation, he moved out of his flat the next morning.

Inside the house, Jean sat on the couch waiting, hoping. Maybe, Carl would come in, tell Tom she was his and take her away with him - forever. She looked up expectantly at the sound of heavy, thudding footsteps. *He* was standing there staring at her with an arctic gaze. Slowly, meticulously, he moved closer. With his head bowed, he lingered over every step, like an animal stalking its prey. She looked up in trepidation. She knew he was unpredictable. She knew she could never be sure which way his temper would turn. He stopped a few feet in front of her. The icy words left his lips slowly as he repeated what he'd said when he'd first found out about the affair. 'How could you, Jean? We're married.'

'I didn't mean for it to happen. It just…did,' she stammered desperately.

'You're *my* wife!' Tom spat through clenched teeth. 'That means you belong to *me!*'

Jean put her head into her hands. 'I'm sorry,' she sobbed. 'It won't happen again.'

'Too bloody right it won't! I told you before that if you ever had an affair I'd cut you up and feed you to the dogs!'

'Tom, I'm sorry. Please forgive me!' she begged as she stood and moved to embrace him, but he was having none of it.

'Get away from me! I don't even want to know you at the moment! You're just a whore!'

'Tom, I said I was sorry and I won't do it again. What more do you want from me?'

'Nothing, that's what! Nothing! You're a dirty slut.'

Suddenly something inside her snapped. Years of pent-up anger and repression exploded from her mouth like bullets from a gun. 'This is all your fault, anyway! You treat me like shit! You never let me do anything! You never let me leave the house! You even have your friends follow me! You don't *own* me, Tom. I'm not a possession! Besides, if you were a better husband, I wouldn't have needed to have an affair!'

The last word of her tirade had barely left her lips when the back of his right hand smashed into the side of her cheek, jerking her head sideways. She tasted the blood pooling in the corner of her mouth, put her hand to her lips and, seeing the blood on her fingers, spat back at him, 'That's right! Beat the crap out of me! That's your solution to everything. I've had enough! I'm leaving you forever, and I'm taking my son with me! I don't care what you say!'

With that, she moved towards her three-year-old son's bedroom, picking up some of his toys and clothes as she went, but now something inside Tom snapped. 'How dare she threaten to take his child! How dare she defy him!' He exploded.

Taking on a life of their own, his fists pounded her, again and again and again, until eventually she fell to the floor. With weak and trembling arms, she struggled to raise herself. Her hair hung down over her face, hiding the merging streams of blood and tears, and she strained to speak. 'I'm sorry, Tom. I'm sorry. I swear I won't do it again. I just want my mum. Please stop! Please.'

'You're a liar! You'll never do this again! You'll never see Carl again. I'll make sure of that!' He gave her a hefty kick with his boot and took sick satisfaction in hearing the breath forced from her lungs and the cracking of her ribs. She slumped back onto the floor with a heavy thud. She rolled herself over, trying to force some air back into her body but, as she tried to rise once more, he was instantly on top of her. As she lay beneath him, she mustered the last of her strength, kicking and struggling, but her tiny body was no match for his emotional rage, and her strength soon faded as his huge hands wrapped around her throat, his fingers clenching together like a vice, squeezing tighter and tighter. Leaning in close, he whispered his last words to her. 'If I can't have you, no-one will.' Moments later, her essence escaped her.

Tom Keir continued to shake his wife's lifeless body again and again to make sure the job was done, and then crawled across the lounge room floor as he tried to regain his breath. He climbed onto the sofa and sat pensively, a thousand thoughts rushing through his mind as he stared at his wife's body; first and foremost, how to dispose of it? Cutting her up and feeding her to the dogs had always been his plan, but there wasn't time for that. He had to get rid of her quickly, because he knew her mother could come over at any minute, or that his son could wake up. So, what to do with her?

He'd buried things in the yard before, blocks of concrete, car panels, fencing panels, a car engine and a forty-four-gallon drum, and they hadn't taken him that long. He'd already buried so much junk, she would be just one more piece.

Rising from the sofa, he roughly picked up his wife's battered corpse and tossed it over his shoulder, knowing that dragging her through the house would only wake his infant son. He gently put the body down when he reached the back door and crept silently out into the backyard to check if his actions had aroused suspicion from the neighbours, but they hadn't. The neighbourhood remained quiet and peaceful.

He looked up at the sky, breathing a sigh of relief that there wasn't a full moon. What light it was giving off was dimmed by the thick, dark clouds. Making his way back inside, he picked the body up and tossed it over his shoulder once more. He carried it out into the yard and made straight for the chosen spot. He knew exactly where he was going to put her. After hurriedly hiding the body under the house, between the foundations on the western side, he went to fetch his tools.

Several crickets chirped as he crept quietly across the lawn to the garage. He slowly opened the door, grimacing as it creaked. Freezing, he slowly looked around once more, certain that someone must have heard, but no-one had.

'What's the best tool for the hard ground?' he thought to himself as he scanned the walls of his garage.

Gently lifting a crowbar and shovel off the wall, he carried them outside and slowly crept back to the side of the house. As he rounded the corner, his pulse quickened. There was movement near the body! His son must have woken up, come out to the yard. 'Get out of it,' he said, as softly as he could.

His German Shepherd stopped sniffing Jean's body and gave a slight yelp when Tom tapped it with the crowbar. The dog ran off, and Tom, lying as flat as he could, began scratching in the dirt. As the soil loosened, he picked it up with the shovel, until a small pile soon developed next to his wife's body.

The ground was harder than he'd expected, and it was slow going. Beads of sweat had formed on his forehead, and he'd barely excavated more than a few centimetres. The faster he dug, the more the sweat dripped from his brow, and he struggled to wipe it away with his sleeve. After a few minutes, he slid out from under the house and scanned his surroundings. Nothing. Resuming his digging, his mind was awash.

'She made me do this,' he said to himself. 'I had no choice. If only she'd done what she was supposed to! How dare she mouth off at me like that! Dopey bitch had to go and have an affair. Well, this taught her a lesson. Shit! What am I going to say to everyone?...I'll tell them she ran off with Carl. Yeah, they'll believe that.'

Pleased with his ruse, he dug quicker and quicker and the hole became deeper and deeper. By the time it reached a suitable depth, he was almost completely exhausted.

'Thank God she's only short,' he thought to himself as he carefully slid Jean's body into the hole. Due to the short distance between the ground and the floor of the house, he had to bend her body to ease it into the deep, narrow hole, where it would stand upright, but it proved to be a perfect fit. Silently and methodically, he began to shovel the dirt back into the hole around the body. When the last of it was in place, he patted the soil down. 'This is the last place anyone will think to look for her,' he thought as he made his way back across the yard. In the garage, he took extra care to make sure the tools were returned to the wall *exactly* as they had been. Pausing at the door, he allowed himself a smile, satisfied with his evening's work.

He was barely halfway across the lawn on his way back to the house when he heard the phone ring. 'Dammit, that'll be her mum. I have to answer it, or she'll know something's up.' Sprinting inside, he got to the phone on the twelfth ring. 'Hello?' he gasped, out of breath.

'Where were you?' said Jean's mother, curious as to why Tom was breathless at this time of night.

'I…was down the back…feeding the dog.'

'Is Jean back yet?'

'No, not yet.'

'Okay. I'll ring back later.'

The words had barely left her lips before he snapped the phone back onto the receiver. When he did, he remembered the dirt and blood on his hands, so he headed into the laundry and scrubbed and scrubbed until the last of it was gone. When he'd finished, he went and sat in the lounge room to finish calculating his deception.

At eleven o'clock, the phone rang again.

'Hello?'

'It's Christine. Are they back yet?'

'No.'

At twelve o'clock, she called again.

'Hello?'

'It's Christine again. Are they back yet?'

'Yes, they arrived a few minutes ago.'

'Would you put Jean on the phone? I want to talk with her.'

'No, she doesn't want to talk to you. She was very tired. She's gone to sleep.'

'Alright, I'm coming over.'

'No, no, don't do that, because you're only going to have a quarrel. She doesn't want to talk to you. She's tired.'

'Okay, tell her I'll see her tomorrow after work.' She hung up reluctantly.

'No you won't,' Tom thought smugly to himself, 'because I've just committed the perfect crime.'

CHAPTER 1

Beginnings

Jean Angela Keir.

The first time I heard her name was when I was handed a Missing Persons file back in 1989. I had no idea that, from the moment that brief was put in my hand, my life and that of my family would be completely and utterly turned upside down. My partner Mick Lyons and I would be launched into a bizarre investigation for which, truthfully, we were not prepared. Over the next decade, it would consume my life almost entirely; eventually threatening to tear my family apart.

It began in Mt Druitt, in the west of Sydney. The 'Druitt' and the surrounding suburbs like Blackett, Emerton, Lethbridge Park and Tregear are undoubtedly some of the toughest areas of the city. It is a very low socio-economic area, with high unemployment, alcohol, drugs, domestic violence and racial tension. It was, and still is, a real hotbed, which meant there was always something on the boil. However, mixed in amongst the pockets of shit (the druggies, the wife-beaters and the dole bludgers) there was a spattering of people who, despite their lower social position, took great pride in their personal appearance and that of their homes. These were your truly genuine, hardworking Aussies. They were the salt of the earth with good, warm hearts.

Some coppers might have complained about being in a difficult area, but not me. I was always happy about being there. From my first posting to Blacktown as a trainee constable I'd wanted to be in the thick of the action.

My Dad was very proud when I graduated from the Academy in 1980 and he always told me it was better to go somewhere busy so I could learn as much as I could. Some precincts can be fairly routine but the Druitt was one of those places where you walked in each morning with no idea what to expect or what was going to be thrown your way. It was sink or swim. Even the Uniforms and the Ds got on well which was not always the case elsewhere. The Uniform guys wouldn't flick a job to the Ds because they didn't feel like doing it. Instead, they'd pitch in, help out and ask for advice when needed. I really did like working there.

One day, I was in the Detectives' Office struggling with our antiquated photocopier.

'Stupid machine!' I cursed as it jammed for the umpteenth time. It wasn't my usual style but I started screaming profanities as I became stroppier and stroppier. All I was trying to do was put together a simple brief but every time I pressed the 'copy' button the thing would start beeping and flashing with those little red circles indicating a paper jam. I'd pull it all apart, take the paper out and then close everything. It'd warm up and the little green light would flash telling me it was good to go. I'd press 'copy' and, sure enough, the red lights would start flashing again and the whole process would have to be repeated.

'Time-saving devices and paperless age my arse!' I muttered to myself as I slammed my fist down on the copier. I was just readying myself to give it a hefty kick when someone called out:

'Pete! Boss wants you in his office!'

The photocopier was not getting off that easily. I kicked it, hard, before making my way to the boss's office.

My boss was Detective Senior Sergeant Mick O'Connell. He was your true old-school cop, like someone from a seventies TV detective show. I got on with him extremely well, probably because I'd made my decision to become a detective whilst watching *Homicide* with my Dad as a kid. I really identified with Leonard Teale's character, Senior Detective David 'Mac' Mackay. Like Mackay, Mick had seen and done it all. He never took a backward step, and commanded respect from all around him. He wasn't one for fancy or flashy clothes and always wore an open-necked collared shirt. His attire pretty much reflected his attitude towards police work: everything stripped down to its simplest form: no nonsense and no bull. His brown hair was parted and flipped over to the left. He always wore his sunnies either hanging from the pocket of his short-sleeved shirt or from the buttons which sometimes struggled to do their job as Mick had the build of a man who enjoyed a few beers. He hated wearing ties and I only ever remember seeing him wear one when he went to court. He was a pretty jovial character who loved a laugh and had been a detective for most of his time in the force. Mick was a dead-set rough diamond and one of the best things about him was that you knew that as long as you did your job properly he'd always be there to back you up. He fondly referred to us as his 'boys' and in return for his support he had the fellas' loyalty one hundred per cent. If anyone ever unfairly criticised one of his 'boys' he'd be up them like a rat up a drainpipe.

'You wanted to see me, Boss?' I said when I got to his door. True to character, Mick was studying the form guide intently, his eyes not deviating as he spoke.

'Having trouble with that bloody photocopier, are you? We should chuck it down the stairs and make the bastards buy us another one. Take a seat, mate. I'll be with you in a tick.'

I sat down and looked at my ink-stained hands while listening to Mick muttering about the next 'friggin' donkey' that had better run a good race or he'd make sure it ended up at the glue factory. He circled the last of his selections, put the form guide down and swivelled around on his chair. It creaked and squeaked as he rustled through the paper tray on the right-hand corner of his desk before retrieving a file and handing it to me.

'Mate, seeing how you're on late shift this arvo do you reckon you could have a look at this Missing Persons file? The sheila disappeared last year and everything points to her pissin' off with another bloke. Just go around and have a chat to her husband and see if there's anything more he can tell us about it. If there's bugger-all to it just fill in the report and send it back to Missing Persons.'

'Yeah, no dramas,' I said, 'I'll check it out later on tonight.' I took a quick peek at the cover of the file: *Missing Person – Jean Angela Keir.*

'Thanks, mate. Have a good one,' Mick said as he swivelled his chair to face the window and returned to his form guide.

Later, another D and I went around to the Keir household in Wilkes Crescent, Tregear. When we arrived I paused out the front to take a good look around. It was your typical suburban Australian home, a white-panelled place with a metre and a half high mesh fence enclosing the front yard. A deep-green Colorbond fence separated the front yard from the back. On that same side there was a double gate leading through to a side access driveway to a rear garage which appeared to be detached from the main house. We walked through the gate of the mesh fence and up the front path. We knocked on the door but there was no-one home. Over the next few weeks, we went there again and again, but still no-one answered. Every time we knocked and waited, I felt an irresistible pull to search around the house; something just felt totally wrong. A few weeks later, we were patrolling in the area so we decided to give it another go. It was approaching ten o'clock at night by the time we turned into the street and the closer we came to the house the more uncomfortable I felt but, to be honest, I didn't really expect much. This was a routine 'tick and flick' and, in reality, we had more important cases to attend to. We pulled up outside the house and something immediately struck me.

'Hey, Dave. Bloody hell, mate!' I said to my partner. 'There's actually a light on; looks like we might get lucky.'

We hopped out of the car, and as soon as I set foot inside the property I stopped. There *was* something wrong. I knew this house was keeping a dark secret, so I began looking around like someone who's lost something but doesn't know where to begin.

'Are you coming?' Dave asked as he leapt up onto the raised concrete veranda.

'Yep,' I said, making my way up the path.

'What were you doing?' he asked.

'I don't know, mate, but as soon as I walked through the gate something felt wrong. I dunno; must be going mad.' Dave just shook his head and knocked on the door.

We heard heavy footsteps and then the door opened and a man in his early thirties appeared. I couldn't see him clearly through the flyscreen, but the outside light was just strong enough to reveal some of his features. He had thick, dark hair that was beginning to grey a little, and one bushy eyebrow that stretched across his forehead. I remember thinking that he looked a little like Animal, or Sam the Eagle from *The Muppet Show*.

'Good evening, sir. We're from Mt Druitt Detectives,' I said as I held up my I.D. 'Are you Thomas Keir?'

'Yes.'

'Mr Keir, I've got a Missing Persons file in relation to your wife, Jean Angela Keir. I understand she went missing about a year ago. We're just following up on her disappearance and checking with her family to see if there is any further information that may assist us in locating her.'

With that, Keir opened the screen door and stepped outside. Straightaway, his actions struck me as a little odd. He took a quick, almost imperceptible glance to the right and made a point of positioning himself between us and that side of the house. I looked past him to try to see what he'd been looking at, but seeing nothing out of the ordinary, I turned my attention back to him. His face was as blank as that of a statue, and when he opened his mouth to speak he was calm and clear, a little too much so I thought, like he'd rehearsed his answer or said it a hundred times.

'No, I've told the police everything I know,' he said. 'Jeannie took off with some bloke, and I haven't seen her since. I've spoken to her on the phone a couple of times, but that's about it.'

I started taking notes. 'What about the rest of your family and friends? Has anyone else heard from her?' I said.

'No. Nobody.'

'This bloke's not fair dinkum,' I thought to myself. 'If she's run off with another bloke and he's spoken to her, then why is there a Missing Persons report? If he, and the family knew she was alive and okay, then what the bloody hell am I doing here?'

I was just preparing to press him for clarification when there was a sudden loud bang behind us. Dave and I spun around to see that a car had run squarely up the back-end of ours. The bloke in the passenger seat got out and, after staggering around for a bit, started calling out to his mate. 'Damn it! That's all we bloody need!' Dave grumbled as he launched himself off the veranda and set off down the footpath.

'Excuse me for a minute, Mr Keir, while we sort this out,' I said as I leapt off the veranda and followed Dave.

The passenger was now yelling incoherently as he staggered across the street. 'Hey, mate, you just hit the back of a police car!' Dave called to him. 'Where do you think you're going?' He stopped dead in his tracks and turned around and signalled to his mate, who immediately jumped out of the driver's seat and started doing a runner.

I quickly set off in pursuit. He was obviously pissed, but was still pretty quick, and I had to sprint a good hundred metres up the road before eventually catching up with him. I'm a tall but pretty thin bloke, and physical confrontation isn't my style, so I always try to avoid it if at all possible, but I'd played a fair bit of footy for the coppers' team as a winger and full-back, and so I brought him down from behind like I was making a last-ditch try-saving tackle. He hit the ground pretty hard, and I thought I'd knocked the wind out of him, but he managed to get up and take a swing at me. Fortunately, I was able to duck out of the way. I went to give him an uppercut, but my feet slipped on the gravel driveway and my intended knockout blow simply glanced off his chin.

Suddenly, he belted me in the right eye, which dazed me a bit and later produced a bloody good shiner, but it wasn't enough to stop me. I drove my right shoulder into his chest and we both fell to the ground, with me landing on top of him and pinning him down. 'Keep going, mate, and there's only going to be one winner out of this, and it won't be you,' I said as I pressed his face down onto the ground.

'Alright, mate, I'll stop,' he said, realising that he had nowhere to go, and deciding that enough was enough. He'd given me his best shot, and I was still standing.

I released my grip on him and he got to his feet, still hunched over as he tried to regain his breath. I grabbed both his hands and held them tightly behind his back, then whacked the cuffs on and marched him back down the street. As I neared the car, I realised that Dave was having troubles of his own. The scuffle had spilled back into Keir's property and, as I watched them wrestling with each other, Dave was smashed into the Colorbond fence. I heard him let out a pained grunt, and knew he'd buggered his shoulder.

Rather than deterring Dave, however, it just pissed him off even more, and now he found the extra strength needed to overwhelm the bloke and cuff him. We chucked the two of them in the back of our Ford Falcon and I leant back on the bonnet with my hands resting on my knees as I tried to regain my breath, while Dave got on the radio and called for a Uniform car. The Uniforms turned up as quick as a flash, and before long the two jokers were in the back of a paddy wagon, later to be charged with drink-driving, assaulting police and resisting arrest. I watched the paddy wagon drive off with my left eye while I held my palm up to my right. All I could think about was how I was going to explain to my wife that I'd copped *another* shiner. I felt alright, but I certainly didn't look the best. My wife would later tell me that when I came home all battered and bruised, it was one of the scariest moments she'd had in all the time I was in the Force.

'Dave, mate, are you alright?' I eventually asked.

'Yeah, mate, me shoulder's a bit sore, but no dramas.'

CHAPTER 1

'Do you guys want me to give a statement?' we heard a voice say. 'I saw the whole thing.'

Dave and I turned around to see Keir leaning with his elbows on the mesh fence across the front of his house. 'Yeah, that'd be great,' I said. 'We'll be in touch.'

It was a bloody good thing he was there, because Keir's testimony meant we were able to secure convictions.

SEVEN BONES

CHAPTER 2
Questions

Two years later, I was called back to Wilkes Crescent.

It was a beautifully sunny afternoon, and I was out the back playing with my three-year-old daughter Ashleigh. I was watching her running around, and started to think how much work was beginning to intrude more and more into my family life. It was something I struggled with constantly, never really leaving work at work. I tried to enjoy time spent with my family, but cases and criminals always consumed my thoughts.

'No, I don't have to be at work for a few hours yet. I'm going to enjoy my time with my daughter,' I thought as I watched Ashleigh walking towards my German Shepherd, Khan, who didn't notice her, too concerned with chomping on the remnants of last night's dinner. Ashleigh moved closer and closer and then, sure enough, gave Khan a few pats and made off with his lamb bone. He didn't move. He was a good-tempered dog, and he and I both watched as Ashleigh wandered off with long strings of juicy slobber sliding off the bone and onto her hand. Deciding that the bone wasn't for her after all, Ash dropped it and continued on her merry way. Khan watched for a bit and, when he was happy she was far enough away, walked over, plonked himself down and resumed chewing on the bone.

I felt more relaxed than I could remember as I leant back in my deckchair. I was finally letting go of work, even if just for a few moments. I was basking in the sun's warmth when suddenly a cold shiver shot straight up my spine.

I sat bolt upright as I was gripped by a severe sense of dejà vu, feeling like I'd been transported somewhere else. I was still sitting in a backyard, but it looked different. Behind me, there was an oddly familiar white fibro house, and in the yard there was a German Shepherd, much like Khan, who was also chewing on a bone, but the bone was much larger, big enough to be a human leg or arm. Suddenly, the dog began running around the yard as though someone was chasing it. Now the scene disappeared, and I found myself back in my own yard. 'Shit, that was friggin' weird!' I thought to myself.

After I'd recovered my composure, my first instinct was to check on Ashleigh's safety, but she was nowhere to be seen! Panicking, I jumped up and started searching. I looked everywhere. I was frantic! I'd lost my little girl! There was only one place left, her cubbyhouse, so I ran down to it and peered inside, but there was no sign of her. That was it! She was gone! Sue was going to kill me.

In my distress, I'd forgotten that the cubby was on raised brick piers, but eventually I thought to look underneath. Much to my relief, she was there. My heart started beating again as I gently pulled her out. 'How many times have I told you; never crawl under those piers!' I said with mock sternness tempered with a father's love as I folded her in my arms and began walking towards the house. Suddenly, I heard the phone ring, and the cold shivers returned.

'Pete,' Sue called from the kitchen.

'Yep?'

'It's work.'

'What do they want?'

'Dunno,' she said, the disappointment evident in her voice, 'but I reckon you'll be home late, because they want you to go in early.'

Sue hated me being called in early. If they called me in early, it meant a big job was on, and that *always* meant I'd be home late. She put up with it because she knew my job sometimes required it, but she was never happy about it. I'd first met Sue when I was still living with my parents and the alarm had gone off. Sue was living there with another lady whilst she studied at teachers' college. The cops hadn't come, despite Sue ringing them repeatedly, so Sue came over to tell Mum about the alarm and the non-appearance of the police. Mum had informed Sue that I was a cop and, always on the lookout for a hot girl for me, and deciding that Sue certainly fitted the bill, made a point of introducing me. I was immediately attracted to Sue, with her long dark hair and beautiful smile, and not more than half an hour after she'd left, I went next door and asked her out to the local club for a casual drink.

Sue was in a troubled relationship at the time, and was initially reluctant about going out with me, but I gradually wore her down. Despite her hesitancy, I just kept ringing. Whenever I saw her out the front, I'd made sure I spoke to her, and always asked her out. Eventually, she agreed, and things moved pretty quickly after that. I don't really remember, but Sue assures me that after about a week or so I told her that I was going to marry her!

I proposed to her on Australia Day in 1985, and we were married that same year. The wedding day itself, whilst amazing, was a bit of a blur. I was more nervous than I can ever remember being. Disarming potential bank robbers armed with sawn-off shotguns paled in comparison as I waited for the wedding to start, dancing around the place like a cat on a hot tin roof. I was so excited to be marrying the woman who I thought was the most magnificent creature in the world. As the big moment drew closer, I became very jittery. When I saw Sue walk into the church, I remember thinking to myself, 'This is just amazing! She's so beautiful! I'm the luckiest guy on Earth, and I'm going to make sure nothing in this world ever hurts her!'

It felt like there was no-one else in the church. When the priest asked her if she promised to love and care for me until death parted us and she said 'I do', I was happier than I'd ever been. When he said, 'You can kiss the bride,' I suddenly became painfully aware of everyone's eyes on us, but it was one of the happiest days of my life.

After the wedding and honeymoon, I went back to work with a new spring in my step. I'd grown up in a family that instilled a strong sense of morals, duty and justice, something that only intensified now that I was starting a family of my own. As the years passed, I came across every type of crook, murderers, rapists, thieves and conmen. I knew it was my job to deal with the scum of society and, for the most part, I did what I had to do. I went about my job, and tried not to let it get to me, but I found it increasingly hard.

My defining moment as a detective came when my wife became a victim. A bush-rock delivery guy took an inappropriate fancy, and started stalking her. He'd call the house when I was on late shift and do the whole heavy breathing thing. He'd tell her he was watching her, and was going to come around to the house and rape her. Sue, not being the most secure woman in the world, became increasingly nervous and agitated, and absolutely hated it when I was on night shift. Afternoons were okay, as long as I didn't work too much overtime, because she found it impossible to get to sleep until I got home. That's why I brought Khan: for Sue's protection.

The delivery guy really knocked Sue for six. To make matters worse, Sue was pregnant at the time, and miscarried due to the stress. The picture of that little baby on the screen at the doctor's surgery with no heartbeat is something I'll never forget. I was gutted, but my heart went out to Sue, because she was the one who had to endure the miscarriage. It was a difficult time for both of us and, needless to say, I held a deep hatred for this guy. Thankfully, my boss gave me permission to conduct the investigation, even allowing me to concentrate solely on it.

Eventually, I managed to trace one of the calls to a house in Blackett. I checked the address, and then checked the name against the school records at nearby Bidwill where Sue worked, thinking there may be a connection – nothing. I rang the home from where the call had been placed. A woman answered, and I told her I needed her to come into the station to answer some questions. She came in, and I interviewed her. I asked her who lived at her house, and she told me it was just her and her child. The only other person who sometimes came around was her boyfriend. Then I dropped it on her about the phone calls, but I didn't tell her it was *my* wife who was the victim.

I told her I wanted to know where he was. She said he was at his grandmother's, but pleaded with me not to go there and grab him, promising to bring him in herself. I said that would be okay, and gave her thirty minutes.

I was the second-in-charge of the four Ds stationed at St. Marys, and the other three were out on a job, so thirty minutes gave me time to get them back in time to do the interview.

The fellas returned and we were sitting in our office when the Uniform boys rang through to say that the bloke had arrived. They brought him down to our office, where I was sitting on the edge of my desk. He didn't see me as he walked past, but as soon as I saw him I realised who he was. I jumped up and was about to throttle him when my boss grabbed me by the shoulder and motioned with his head for me to come outside. He closed the door behind us and said, 'So who is this arsehole?' I told him, adding that I was going to kill the bastard.

'You're not going anywhere near him until we get him confessing it on paper!' the Boss said. The boys had a five-minute chat with the guy, and got the written confession. Fortunately, due to the boss keeping his head, the guy was kept away from me, and I didn't do anything silly, but it created a burning hatred inside me of guys who commit crimes against women.

Sue was, and still is, the most important thing in the world to me. We share a mutual trust and respect that strengthens our marriage. I never told Sue too much about the jobs I did, not wanting to worry her but, at the same time, she had the knack of knowing when I'd had a bad day, and would always make me a great dinner or breakfast and make easy conversation, which helped take my mind off things. Sometimes I'd confide in her about things, such as domestics I'd been to, and we would often talk about how and why relationships could deteriorate so badly from a time when these people must have loved each other dearly.

'I hate that I have to leave Sue alone yet again,' I thought to myself as I walked inside and she handed me the phone. I could see that she was really anxious because she knew it was something big and I wouldn't be home for hours. I checked my watch. It was just after one. 'There goes two hours of family time,' I thought to myself as I put the phone to my ear.

'Hello,' I said, somewhat apprehensively.

'G'day, Pete,' said one of the blokes from the office. 'Sorry to ring, mate, but the Boss wants you to come in right away. They've got a body in a burnt-out house in Tregear.'

'Male or female, mate?'

'Female. Mick Lyons is already at the scene, but I don't know much more than that.'

'Okay. Give me a few minutes to jump in the shower and tell him I'll get there as soon as I can. What's the address?'

'Wilkes Crescent. Mick's already organised Forensics.'

'Thanks.' I put the phone down and made for my bedroom. Burying my head in my wardrobe, I started to gather my clothes together. I sensed Sue was behind me, so I grabbed a handful of ties and turned around to ask her opinion. 'Susie, which one of these…' I started to say, but there was no-one there. 'Susie?' I called.

'I'm down in the kitchen with Ashleigh,' she yelled back.

I lay my trousers, shirt and a selection of ties on the bed and went out into the hallway. I looked up and down its length, but couldn't see anybody. 'This day's getting a little weird,' I thought to myself.

I started to think about the information I'd been given, wanting to have things squared away in my head before arriving at the scene. I knew I'd heard the name Wilkes Crescent before, but I couldn't remember what it was in connection with.

I was trying my ties against my shirt when suddenly I felt a woman's presence again. I spun around and nearly had a heart attack when I saw Sue standing there.

'Are you okay?' she asked.

'Yeah, yeah,' I said, regaining my composure. 'Which tie do you think?'

'That one.' I put the other ties back in the wardrobe, and Sue sat down on the bed. 'Pete?'

'Yep?'

'What's wrong?'

'Nothing. I'm fine.'

'No you're not. Honey, you know I can read you like a book. What's wrong?'

'Nothing. It's just that a few weird things have happened today. They've found a woman's body in a burnt-out house in Tregear. I'm sorry Susie, but I'll probably end up being home late tonight.'

'I already figured that. Just try to get home as early as you can.'

'I will, I promise,' I said as I walked into the ensuite. Half talking to myself and half talking to Sue, I said. 'I feel like I know that address for some reason, but I'm buggered if I can put my finger on why.'

Standing under the shower, I closed my eyes and let the water wash over me, enjoying the feeling of cleanliness. It was going to be a long night, and so I tried to put work out of my mind for a few seconds, but as soon as I stopped thinking, it came to me. 'Shit, that's it!' I said to myself. 'That's the address of that missing woman.'

I leapt out of the shower, quickly towelled myself dry, raced out into the bedroom and, in my haste to get dressed, got tangled up in my trouser legs and fell over.

'What are you doing?' Sue laughed, walking back into the bedroom right on cue to see me sprawled on the floor. I pulled myself up, managed to put my trousers on, and sat down on the bed while I started to put my shirt on. Apparently concerned with my ability to dress myself, Sue stood in front of me and buttoned up my shirt.

'Hey, I remembered why I knew that address,' I said.

'Yeah?'

'I did a Missing Persons file on the woman who lived at that address a couple of years ago. I wonder if she's come back, and that's who they've found.'

'What was her name?'

'Jean Angela Keir. If I had a dollar for every time I went around to that house with that Missing Persons file and no-one was home we'd be bloody rich by now.'

SEVEN BONES

CHAPTER 3

Flames of
Concern

Here I was driving down Wilkes Crescent once again. The street was in complete contrast to the last time, no longer quiet, but choked with emergency vehicles. As I inched my way along the road, it was like gridlock during peak hour. On either side, I could see small groups of neighbours, some wildly waved their hands as they talked while others covered their mouths and shook their heads. I parked a short distance away and then ducked and weaved my way through the onlookers to the front gate. As I stepped into the premises my eyes were immediately drawn to Thomas Keir sitting on his veranda with his head in his hands. As I looked at him, I clicked straight into investigation mode, weighing up facts, questions and possibilities as I thought back to the Missing Persons file.

Fact 1: Jean Angela Keir left her husband, and three-year-old son for another bloke.

Fact 2: She called Keir a few months later, but made no contact with any other family member. Surely she would have called them.

Possibility 1: Things haven't worked out with the other bloke, and she's come home to try and patch up the marriage. If that's the case, she would have been better off staying away.

Possibility 2: If that's why she's come home, the bloke she ran off with might have decided that if he can't have her, then no-one will.

CHAPTER 3

I started to make my way towards the door, but it was hard going because of all the people, and I prayed that not too many of them had been inside. It was essential that I view the crime scene while it was still fresh, and before some well-meaning person unintentionally contaminated it. It doesn't take much – something moved or brushed aside and the focus is completely altered. I just hoped *everything* had been left *exactly* as it was.

'Peter,' I heard a woman's voice say. I scanned the area to my right, but couldn't see anyone.

'Peter,' the voice called again. This time I turned to the left, and saw a female constable motioning to me. 'Peter,' she repeated, 'Mick Lyons is over there. He told me to tell you he wanted to speak to you as soon as you got here.'

'Thanks,' I said, my eyes moving to where she was pointing, halfway along the path between the house and the front gate. Mick, was a gentle giant, over six foot two inches tall and well built. We'd been mates since 1984 and had worked together since 1986, when we'd both been transferred to Penrith then subsequently to Mt Druitt. He had short black hair and, like our boss Mick O'Connell, loved a laugh, except there was one thing different about Mick Lyons; he loved telling jokes. The only problem was, sometimes they were absolutely terrible, and he'd be the only one laughing. I don't remember seeing him without a tie too often, except in summer, and he always wore short-sleeved shirts. Mick took a lot of pride in his appearance, and was always immaculately presented, even when wearing something a bit more casual. He knew we were the public face of the police force, and he knew the importance of first impressions.

Mick hated criminals as much as I did, and was just as relentless in his pursuit of the truth. He rarely got angry, but boy, when he went, he *went*. One time we'd locked up this young bloke from Cranebrook. We knew he was guilty as hell, but we didn't have enough evidence to charge him. The bloke wasn't going to make any admissions, despite the fact that we knew he was lying through his teeth, so Mick went absolutely ballistic playing 'bad cop', while I just sat back and played 'good' cop. Sure enough, the bloke caved in under Mick's verbal barrage and told us everything.

'G'day, Mick. What have we got?' I said as I joined him.

'We've got a female body on the bed in the main bedroom. She was badly burnt in the fire, pretty much unrecognisable. It looks like she's been strangled with the cord from the bedside lamp.'

'Have we got any idea who she is, and what happened?' I knew it was Jean Keir, but I still had to ask.

'Yeah, mate. Looks like it's the wife of that bloke over there.'

'Horrible end to a Missing Persons file,' I thought. It was sad, but not really that surprising. Ninety per cent of Missing Persons cases are resolved in the first forty-eight hours. If they drag on for months and years, we always fear the worst.

Mick nodded towards Keir on the veranda. I looked over to see him now sitting with his arms around a small boy. 'Poor little fella,' I thought to myself. I really did hate seeing kids in pain.

'So, the body belongs to Jean Keir?' I said to Mick.

Mick shot me a 'What the hell are you talking about?' look. 'No, mate, I was told the body belongs to his wife; *Rosalina* Keir, not Jean Keir. Anyway, he was the last person seen leaving the house before it went up in flames. We've got some neighbours who saw him leave with his son, and within about ten minutes there was smoke billowing from under the eaves at the front of the house.'

'Mick,' I said, now confused, 'I did a Missing Persons file on this bloke's wife. She disappeared in 1988, and her name was *Jean* Keir, not *Rosalina*. You're not going to believe this, but he was the star witness in that assault on me and Dave by those two footballer idiots.'

'Mate,' Mick said, in a tone that suggested his confusion matched mine, 'My information is that his wife's name is Rosalina, and they haven't been married very long.'

Nothing made sense. 'Mick,' I said in utter disbelief, 'we now have a dead second wife and a 'missing' first wife. We've got a huge problem here!'

'Looks that way. If we can find the body of the first wife, assuming she's dead, we might be able to get him for two murders. That's his van over there if you want to take a look,' Mick said as he motioned towards a red Mazda van parked in the street outside the house. I glanced towards the vehicle. I knew Forensics would go over it with a fine-tooth comb, but I still wanted to check it out. I was intrigued, and wondered if it contained the key to solving the puzzle, something to indicate Keir's last movements, something to make this an open-and-shut case. I walked over to the van and peered through the passenger-side window.

Clue 1: Two brand-new T-shirts.

Clue 2: Wrapping paper and birthday cards.

Clue 3: A bottle of Black Douglas with a few swigs missing.

Clue 4: A packet of smokes and a black lighter on the passenger's seat.

I went back into the front yard to ask Mick if there were any witnesses. He was standing on his own in front of the Colorbond fence reading through his notebook. 'Mick,' I said, as I pulled up beside him.

'Yeah, mate?' Mick replied as he looked up at me.

'Have we got any witnesses?'

'Yeah, the next-door neighbour. His name is Max Wormleaton,' Mick said as he flipped through his notebook. Finding the page he wanted he continued. 'He said he's been out the front all morning paving his driveway. He saw Keir and his son drive off earlier, heading towards the Tregear shops. When they came back, he said something seemed a little odd. He reckons Keir parked across the road and left his son in the car while he went into the house. A short time later, he came back out and drove off. At first Wormleaton said he wasn't worried when he saw smoke, because Keir apparently burnt rubbish in his backyard all the time, but he reckons that within ten minutes he could see smoke billowing out from under the eaves. He said he tried to put the fire out with a hose, but it was too well alight by that stage. Then the firies arrived and took over, and he went back to his front yard. Keir turned up after we'd all arrived, but I haven't had much of a chance to speak to him yet.'

A witness was better than nothing but, however helpful, it was still circumstantial. We needed something more concrete; one bloke's word wasn't enough to put a potential murderer away. 'Did he see anyone else go into the house or anyone else hanging around?'

'Nope.'

'Did he hear anyone scream?'

'Nope, he said he didn't hear anything.' As if reading my mind, Mick pointed over to Wormleaton. 'Mate, that's him there if you wanna have a chat.'

I didn't really, not yet, anyway. I needed more information. He looked like a decent sort of bloke, a typical knockabout Aussie, and he'd probably already told Mick everything he knew.

Mick and I made our way back towards the house, and saw that Keir was talking to an ambulance officer. My immediate reaction was to have a good look at him and check for any visible injuries, perhaps burns or any sign of a struggle with his wife as she'd tried to defend herself, but Mick continued to fill me in on the details. 'The neighbours who live on the other side of the street saw the same thing; Keir driving towards the Tregear shops with his son, and then returning shortly afterwards. They all saw him go into the house, and then come back out and leave.'

'Don't tell me!' I said in mock shock. 'They didn't see anyone else leave or go into the house either!'

'You're not just a pretty face, are you?' Mick replied with a wry smile. Multiple witnesses with identical stories; the circumstantial nature of the evidence was rapidly disappearing. 'They all saw smoke coming from under the eaves,' Mick continued. 'The neighbours across the road were the ones who called the Fire Brigade.'

My guts started to churn. The closer I came to the house, the more nauseated I became. The same sensations I'd had the first time I'd visited Wilkes Crescent had now returned, but this time with far more conviction.

'Are you alright, mate?' Mick said, seeing the pained expression on my face.

'Yeah, I just feel a little crook thinking about all this. Did any of the other witnesses hear screams from the house?'

'No, mate.'

'This bloke's got some serious questions to answer. Where *exactly* did he go the last time he left the house?'

'He says he drove down to Market Town, Mt Druitt, with his son, bought a couple of things and then came home. When he arrived, we were all here.'

I looked past Mick at Keir and watched him intently for a few moments. He appeared to be genuinely grieving as he hugged various relatives, but I didn't buy it. I'd seen it all before. The best way to try to put the cops off the scent was to overplay your emotions.

Mick saw that I was checking Keir out. 'I reckon I've got enough to arrest him,' he said. 'I'll go and have another chat, and then I'll take him back to the station to do a Record of Interview. You right to do it with me?'

'Actually, mate, I'd prefer to have a look around here. You've got Clarkey, and he's a bloody good typist. Would it be sweet if he did the interview with you? If there's any dramas, just suspend it and give me a call. There are a few things that just aren't sitting right.'

'Yeah, no worries,' Mick said. 'Forensics are here too, and they'll probably need a bit of a hand. Can you organise the witnesses and get them back to the station?'

'Yeah, of course, mate.' Mick went to talk to Keir, who was out on the lawn now hugging a middle-aged woman, while his son stood beside him. Keir eventually walked off, back towards the house, and Mick went to talk to the woman. Even though I was standing a few feet away, I could still hear what was being said. Mick started by asking her who she was.

'My name is Irene Page. I'm Jean's aunty,' she replied.

'We're terribly sorry for your loss,' Mick said.

'Thank you,' she replied, as she dabbed away her tears with a handkerchief.

'Can you tell me what Tom just said to you?' Mick continued.

'Um, Tom just came over to me with his son and put his arms around me and started crying. After a while I asked him what had happened, and Tom told me they wouldn't let him into the house. I asked him where Rosalie was and he said she was still in there, and that he hated the house and didn't want to live here anymore.'

'Thank you. Mrs Page. If you need anything else, Detective Seymour will be here to answer your questions,' Mick said, pointing at me, before walking over to where I was standing. 'Pete, I want to chat to the ambulance officer about any injuries Keir may have sustained.'

'You read my mind, mate.'

We walked over to the ambulance officer, who told us that Keir had a few cuts on him and some mild symptoms of shock, but nothing too serious. Mick then walked over to Keir, who was now sitting on the veranda again. Meanwhile, I examined the front of the house and tried to collect my thoughts, but I wanted to hear what Mick was saying to Keir.

'I'm Detective Lyons and this is Detective Clarke,' he began. 'Can we speak to you in private please?'

'Yes, over here,' Keir replied, motioning to the gate of the Colorbond fence. They came back over to where I was standing and Mick began to question Keir.

'Is your name Thomas Keir?'

'Yes.'

'Is this your house?'

'Yes.'

'Unfortunately, there is a woman deceased in the main bedroom.'

'It's my wife. What happened?'

'We are investigating the cause of her death, and we want you to come with us to Mount Druitt Police Station to assist us with our inquiries. Do you understand that?'

'Yes. What about my son?'

'Can he stay with your wife's Aunty Irene?'

'Yes, I think so. I'll speak to her first.' With that, Keir went straight over to Irene Page and hugged her, and then began to sob. She was very comforting, assuring him his son would be safe.

Mick then escorted Keir to the car. He could have gone through the whole drama of arresting him and putting the cuffs on, but he thought it best that, with so many people around, we remove him from the scene with a minimum of fuss. Some of the bystanders noticed Keir being taken away, but most of them just kept on talking among themselves. I watched until the car disappeared from view, and then made my way inside.

The first person I came across was Dave Hurst, the Forensic Officer, dressed in his customary blue overalls. He gave me a quick run-down on the scene.

'We've got the body of a female lying face down on the bed in what appears to be the main bedroom. The body, and the bed, are both severely damaged from the fire, and the woman has the cord from the bedside lamp wrapped around her neck. Come in, mate, and I'll show you around. The detached garage has been damaged by fire as well. There are a couple of containers that appear to have petrol in them; could be our fuel source. Oh and by the way, the firies had to force entry through the front door.'

Dave led me inside, first into the lounge room and then down the hallway. The further we went, the more apparent the severity of the fire damage became. On the walls, the plasterboard had been completely burnt away, exposing the timber framework and roof beams. Most of them were blackened with the kind of charring you find on the trunks of trees after a bushfire, and some of the beams were almost burnt right through. It looked like a fireball had ripped through the bedrooms and exploded out into the hallway. I examined along the length of the blackened beams, and felt complete disgust; nobody deserved to die like this. In among the burnt skeleton of the framework, the firies were sifting through the debris searching for the main seat of the fire. Stepping carefully as I made my way further inside the house, I maintained a watchful eye, just in case they unearthed anything unusual, but seeing nothing of note, I made my way to the main bedroom.

The upper half of the door was completely destroyed, and the bottom part had a flash fire scorch. The carpet had also been severely damaged. I took a closer look at the scorch marks, and could see from the patterns that the door must have been open when the fire started.

I stepped into the room, and scanned the scene. I never got used to murder scenes. Each one had a distinct smell and look, and there was always an eerie silence. The sensation that a life had ended was inescapable. I'd been to suicides, stabbings, etc., and always found it hard to push the thoughts of the physical and mental suffering the person must have endured before their untimely end from my mind. What were Rosalina Keir's last thoughts before her final moment? What were her last words? Who was the last person she thought of?

Yesterday, she'd been a young woman brimming with life, and now she was just a charred corpse lying face down on the bed in front of me.

I walked around to the side of the bed and began to wonder; what were her hopes, her dreams? Love? Family? Friends? What had gone through her mind as her killer pulled the cord tighter and tighter. Was the last thing she saw her husband's furious face?

I moved from one side of the bed to the other, examining Rosalina's body carefully. All her distinguishing features were gone, vaporised. The fire had stolen any semblance of femininity, and she looked like a dark mannequin that, unable to serve any further purpose, had been callously discarded. She was face down, and her arms were crossed at the elbows beneath her chest.

Her hands were up near her neck, and it was obvious from the tension in her fingers that she'd tried in vain to save herself. The bedside lamp was still lying on its side, to the right of her body. It was slightly burnt, and the cord around her neck was clearly visible.

The bed was a little over six feet long, and her feet were a good foot short of the end. Being so tiny, she'd never had a chance. Keir, if he was the killer, was a big fella. He could have easily pinned her down and there would have been nothing she could have done about it. Bile started rising into my throat. The thought sickened me. If Keir had done this, he'd defiled the bedroom, the sacred place for a man and his wife. He'd defiled a place of love, compassion and caring. He'd defiled the place belonging solely to him and the woman he'd chosen to spend his life with; well, the second one, anyway. Sacredness had given way to anger, shame and horror.

I took a deep breath. The smell of petrol and death hung unmistakeably in the air, like a thick morning fog. 'Smells like you were right about the petrol,' I said to Dave.

'Yep. I took a couple of samples from the bedding and carpet too,' he replied.

I continued to examine the body. It always paid to take a second, third and fourth look, because even the tiniest detail can often secure a conviction. Engrossed as I was in my grisly task, it was a little while before I took a good look around the room.

Only the upper part of the bed had succumbed to the fire. The bedding and the top of the mattress had been burnt away, revealing the wire springs underneath. They had retained their tension, which told me the fire had been fast, because slow fires build up heat and cause the springs to distort. Some of the carpet had been burnt away, but the polished timber flooring remained intact. There was a burnt purse lying on the bed, with coins scattered on the bed and the floor. There were two bedside drawers, one on either side, two wardrobes and an ironing board towards the front of the room. 'Hey, Dave,' I said. 'There's an iron on the floor. Do you reckon that could have started the fire?'

'Nah, mate. I looked at that. When I picked it up the carpet underneath wasn't burnt. If the iron was the seat of the fire, it would have burnt the carpet. Instead, it acted as a barrier against the heat. There's no way that iron was turned on.'

I'd just started a closer inspection of the floor when, suddenly, the strange sensations returned, even more powerful than before. I was absolutely certain there was someone else in the room, and it totally freaked me out. My friend had once told me that ghosts stuck in purgatory are souls taken before their time, such as murder victims, and I wondered if it was Rosalina's ghost I could feel in the room. Maybe she was compelling me to find some important piece of missing evidence.

My spine tingled, and I shivered. Every part of me screamed to get out of the room. 'Dave, I've got to drop back to the station and get some gear, but I won't be too long,' I said anxiously.

Dave didn't seem to notice my uneasiness. 'What's happened with the husband?' he said very matter-of-factly, obviously not feeling the same sensation and pressing need to vacate the room that I was.

'Mick's taken him down to the station to interview him,' I said as I edged towards the door. 'Once I've been to the station I'll come back here and start taking statements from witnesses. You got everything under control here?'

'Yeah, mate, she's sweet. The government contractors are on strike today, so either the ambos or our people will have to take the body to the mortuary. Once the post-mortem is done, we'll know whether the fire killed her or whether she was dead before it started.'

'Righto, mate. I'll be back soon.'

Despite my intense desire to get out of the house, I had to tiptoe and shuffle, taking care not to brush up against the blackened walls or to tread on some as yet unseen but vital piece of evidence.

Once I was back outside, I took several deep breaths. The crisp, clean air cleared my mind, and thousands of thoughts began to run through my head.

Two mysteries: one murder, one missing person. I wasn't sure where to start, but then I noticed Max Wormleaton standing on his semi-paved driveway. He was the prime witness, so I figured he was the best place to begin. I walked out the gate and along the footpath.

'Mr Wormleaton?'

'Yes?'

'I'm Detective Peter Seymour. Would it be alright if we spoke?'

'Sure.'

'Can you start by telling me about yourself, and then about what you saw?'

'Yep, no dramas. Um, I'm forty-two. I've got a wife and four kids. I've lived here for the past six years.'

I took a close look at him. He was dressed in an old pair of jeans and a grey top, and was wearing battered old work boots. His neat, slightly wavy, slicked-back brown hair suggested a man who took some pride in his appearance, and when he spoke, his voice was quiet but deliberate.

'And can you tell me what you saw?' I asked, as I tried to ascertain the location of the driveway in relation to Keir's house. It was right on the boundary of the two properties. Wormleaton would have had an uninterrupted view.

'I've been out here all day, working on my driveway, putting these pavers down,' he said with a sweep of his hand. 'As you can see, I've got a pretty good view of the house. I was working away when I saw Tom walk up the path and into his house. About five minutes later he came back out. He was wearing grey trousers and a blue T-shirt, if that helps. It would've been ten minutes after he left that I saw black smoke. I thought he was burning off rubbish or something, so I yelled out to my wife to shut the front door and I went down the side of the house to shut the windows. When I came back out the front, I saw smoke coming from the bedroom. My first thought was that his young son was still inside, so I grabbed a pick, jumped the fence and started yelling to see if anyone was inside. I got no answer, so I smashed one of the front windows. There was still no answer, so I went to the front door, but the screen door was locked and the main door was closed. By that time the fire had well and truly taken hold, so there was no way I was going inside. Another bloke, John, came over to help. We were standing out the front when the bedroom window exploded and showered glass all over the lawn. The missus chucked the hose over the fence, and John and I started pumping water in through the bedroom window. Didn't do much good, though; the flames, heat and smoke were too bloody intense. Not long after we started hosing, the Fire Brigade showed up.'

I leaned over the fence and took another look at the glass on the lawn. 'So do you get along well with Mr Keir?'

'Yeah, he's alright. Bit of a weird bloke, though.'

'Weird? How so?'

'Dunno. Like, he's always burning stuff. He's always out in his backyard, you know, doing God knows what.'

'Did you know Rosalina?'

'Not really. Seen her a couple of times and said "hello", you know. He hasn't been married to her long.'

'You said you've been here for six years. Did you know his first wife very well?'

'Oh yeah, Jeannie was a lovely girl. We had a lot to do with her; she was friends with my daughter and that. Shame about her running off, though. Maybe it was for the best.'

'What do you mean "for the best"?'

'I dunno. Over the last couple of months before she ran off, she seemed, like, not herself. Maybe she just needed to get away and get her head together. I used to hear them arguing a lot.'

'Is there anything else you can tell me?'

'Nope. That's pretty much it.'

'Thank you, you've been very helpful Mr Wormleaton. I just have to go back to the station, but I'll be back to speak to you again and get a statement of pretty much what you just told me.'

Wormleaton nodded, and then turned and headed inside. I made my way back to my car and sat in the driver's seat for a few moments, wondering what type of man Thomas Keir really was. Several of my suspicions had just been confirmed by Wormleaton, and I knew I needed to gain a clearer picture of Keir's relationship with his wives. I started the car and pulled away from the kerb. As I drove slowly down the street, which was still choked with traffic, I ran all the facts through my head.

Point 1: If the bedroom had exploded, there must have been an accelerant, probably the petrol. How long would it have taken after Rosalina was murdered for the killer to exit the house, grab the petrol, presumably from the garage, and return? Did any other neighbours see that happen?

Point 2: If Keir went out, came back, set the house on fire and then left again, when did he kill Rosalina? Had he been walking around the shops thinking about what he'd done and decided, whoops, I'd better go home and destroy the evidence? Or was he being more calculating? He would have known it would look better if he had shopping receipts as an alibi; then he could turn up with the police here and say 'Oh my God! What terrible thing has happened to my wife?'

Point 3: Where was the son? Did he see anything? Did Keir take him away so he wouldn't be a witness? Surely, if he'd been around, he must have seen his dad go out the back and get the petrol from the garage?

I arrived at the station, parked the car and rushed inside, eager to get started on the investigation. I really wanted to have another look at Jean Keir's file. Perhaps, by looking at it with fresh eyes, I'd find something I'd missed. If I could work out how to find her, then perhaps it would give us more information about Rosalina. If Jean was still alive, and we could get her to tell us what kind of man Keir was, she'd make a very useful witness. However, this was not really something I considered. Deep down in my heart, I knew it was too coincidental for Jean to disappear from the same house where Rosalina had been found murdered. It was almost inconceivable that Jean hadn't met with foul play.

I sat down at my desk, one of many located on the open plan floor of the Detectives' office. The whole station was one big rectangle, with a hallway running down the middle and separating the two sides. The Detectives' office was at the eastern end of the building, facing out onto Luxford Road. Mick O'Connell's office sat at one end, and there was an interview room at the other end. The second interview room, where Mick was currently interviewing Keir, was across the hallway outside the Detectives' office.

For a bunch of blokes, we were generally pretty tidy, and my desk had a neatly stacked 'In Tray' that was constantly filled with papers and big yellow A4 envelopes from various cases. In the middle of the desk there was a typewriter, and below it there was a grey steel two-drawer filing cabinet. As I reached out to open it, another shiver ran down my spine. What was going on?

'I'm losing my marbles,' I thought to myself. Pulling the drawer open, I rued my lack of attention to detailed filing, and wondered if I even still had the file. I reached in and pulled out the first file. Much to my surprise, it was the 'tick and flick' form. Even odder was that I'd photocopied it, not standard police practice. It was lucky, otherwise I would have had to contact Missing Persons, which would have taken time, time we didn't have. I re-read the form.

Missing Person – Jean Angela Keir.

Recorded as a missing person on 1 May 1988.

Reported missing by her sister and father, Heather and Clifford Strachan.

Report closed 30 October 1988.

Leaning back in my chair, I rubbed the back of my neck and stared at the roof. Something was missing. Something just wasn't right. Then it came to me! Why hadn't Keir reported it himself?

Leaning back over my desk, I read on and found that a witness had reportedly seen Jean at Emerton shops. The file also confirmed what Keir had said about him being the only person Jean had contacted. I was suddenly aware of someone standing in front of me, and raised my eyes to be greeted by Mick Lyons' big frame.

'Keir's in the interview room,' he said, gesturing with his thumb. 'He hasn't said much. I'm gonna ask him a few questions about his movements, and take his clothes for analysis. Can you go back to the scene to get witness statements? Take Macca with you.'

I stood up from my desk and looked for Macca, which wasn't hard. Macca wasn't a big fella, but had an athletic build, and also played for the police footy team. He had a longish face and sandy brown hair. A young, knockabout bloke, he was always keen to learn and always very excited about getting as involved as he could. I was happy to take him along, because I felt a sense of responsibility about showing the young blokes the ropes. The older guys had done so much for me when I was making my way up the ranks, and I felt duty-bound to do the same. 'Macca!' I called across the office. 'You're with me. Grab a set of car keys and I'll meet you down in the car park.'

Macca nodded and set off like a greyhound towards the boss's office.

I reached into my desk drawer and grabbed my gun and holster. Detectives' were required to have these on them at all times when on duty, but I hadn't had them with me earlier because I'd gone straight from home to the murder scene. Now I strapped the holster to my leg, and felt a sense of purpose wash over me as I rolled my trouser leg back down over my gun.

I made my way to the car park, where I found Macca standing beside a red Ford Falcon 'POS'; piece of shit. We'd got these brand new, and some had already started blowing smoke from the engines. I hoped this particular vehicle would actually get us to the scene, but I wasn't filled with confidence. Macca started the car, and it began to splutter and cough. 'Great, that's all we need!' I said.

Fortunately, the Falcon didn't let us down. Macca drove towards the scene, while I sat back and watched the world rush by. We were barely a few streets away from the station when I suddenly turned to Macca. 'Bloody hell! What have we stumbled across?' The full extent of what was transpiring had finally dawned on me. 'Where the hell are you, Jean?' I asked out loud.

'Is that the dead girl in the house?' said Macca.

'No, mate, Jean's the missing wife. Rosalina is the name of the wife at the crime scene.'

'So what's the go with all this then, Pete?'

I told him.

'Shit!' was all he had to say. 'So, we reckon he's killed his second wife, and the first wife is missing. Do you reckon he killed her too?'

'I've got a bad feeling about this whole thing, mate. There's going to be a helluva lot of work in this one.'

I couldn't get it out of my mind. What *had* happened to Jean Keir? Maybe I was jumping to conclusions. Whilst all the evidence pointed to Keir killing Rosalina, he hadn't even been charged, and someone else *could* have killed her. Also, we had no proof that he'd killed his first wife, or even that she was dead for that matter. Maybe Jean *had* run off with another man.

Macca eventually pulled back into Wilkes Crescent, and I suddenly remembered the drunken footballers incident, and began to think about how one thing in life affects another. If it hadn't been for those two clowns, we might have been able to have a good chat with Keir. Maybe we would have uncovered the truth about Jean and, in so doing, saved Rosalina.

Macca, had to drive at snail's pace along the street, inching forward while people moved to the side, like Moses parting the Red Sea. Once we got through the crowd, however, the remainder of the street was cordoned off, and we managed to park right out the front.

Macca and I made our way to the house, and as we walked inside we could see the Fire Investigation Unit still sifting through the debris. The cause of the fire might have seemed pretty obvious, in that you could still smell the petrol, but we had to be absolutely certain how much time had passed between ignition and flames. Accidental fires rarely had accelerants; killers used accelerants. Different ignition sources take different amounts of time to burst into flame. Knowing this, we could work out how long the killer had spent in the house. Whilst I had my suspicions as to the killer's identity, I still had to keep an open mind.

When we reached the doorway we saw one of the Forensic Ds videoing the scene. 'You all done here?' I asked.

'Yeah, boys, it's all yours.'

I checked my watch. Three o'clock; the time I was supposed to start work.

As I stepped back into the bedroom, I was a little apprehensive. The odd sensations had returned, but not like before. Now it was more of a nagging feeling. I felt like I should be looking somewhere else, and for something else. Hunches, sensations and intuition were important tools in a detectives' arsenal, but I decided to keep my feelings to myself. We needed to focus on what we did have, not on things that I *felt* could be there.

Dr Dianne Little, the Forensic Pathologist, walked into the room. She had long, slightly unkempt brown hair, and wore glasses. I was glad she was there; her opinion would be gold in trying to gain a conviction.

'Hello, Detective Seymour,' she said, as she noticed me standing to one side of the bed.

'Hi, Dr Little,' I replied. 'Not a pretty sight, is it? I reckon she was dead before the fire started, but it will be interesting to see what the post-mortem tells us.'

'Yes,' she said. 'Fire certainly does a lot of damage to bodies, but it should be easy enough to tell if she was breathing or not when the fire started.'

What Dr Little was referring to was the fact that if someone is alive when a fire begins, there are telltale signs. Smoke is actually hot, and smoke inhalation scalds the lungs. Fires release hot gases, and fire victims usually die from inhaling poisonous gases, particularly carbon dioxide, not burning to death.

Scanning the room, I quickly checked to see if I'd missed anything the first time, but seeing nothing new, I concentrated on watching Dr Little examining the body. As I did so, I realised that there was one thing that was bothering me; the position of the body.

A friend of mine in the Firies had once told me that, whether they liked to admit it or not, all firemen wanted to be heroes. Why wouldn't they? How good a feeling would it be to pull a person from a raging inferno? He also told me they were instructed, if they found a body in the house, to leave it *in situ*, a Latin term meaning 'in the situation it is in', but only when it was blatantly obvious that something suspicious had occurred. Therefore, the firies had left Rosalina's body *in situ*, because it seemed fairly obvious that this had been a murder. If she'd been alive when they arrived to extinguish the blaze, they would have tried to save her.

I continued to watch Dr Little as she moved around the right-hand side of the bed and donned her white latex gloves. The first thing she did was to roll Rosalina's body over, which produced a horrible sound as her burnt skin began to crack. This also flicked particles of skin into the air, and I soon had the smell of charred human flesh clinging to my nostrils.

Dr Little kept turning her until Rosalina was face up. There wasn't much of the front part of her that was not affected by the fire, only the lower chest and pubic area which had been slightly protected by the mattress. The rest of her was burnt beyond recognition. No hair, no facial features. Dr Little moved in for a closer look, paying particular attention to the cord around Rosalina's neck.

She paused to fill out the certificate pronouncing 'life extinct', and handed it to me. I put it in my folder, and then watched as she took swabs for possible traces of semen. She also collected some fingernail clippings for DNA evidence, in case Rosalina had scratched the murderer during her desperate, futile struggle for survival.

Dr Little's final report would be vital, particularly pertaining to the cause of death. Her report (prepared later) read:

The body was extensively burnt with sparing of the central part of the lower chest and abdomen down to the level of the pubis with extension onto the anterior aspect of the upper two-thirds of the right thigh...the total area of burnt skin was approximately 85% of the body surface area. In some areas of the body, there was extensive tissue loss...the legs were flexed at the hips and knees. The feet were plantar flexed. The arms were flexed beneath the body. The head was extended at the neck. The head hair, eyebrows and eyelashes had been burnt off...

Eyes: brown. The oral cavity was normal. No petechial haemorrhages or injuries were seen. The tongue protruded through the teeth and the tip of the tongue was burnt...

Around the neck at a distance 8.5cm above the sternoclavicular joint there was a piece of electrical cord present. The cord was tied once at the back of the neck and extended approximately horizontally around the neck...

In the fingers of the right hand, were two long black straight hairs. Two long black hairs were also present in the fingers of the left hand...

The trachea and main bronchi were normal. There was no soot within these structures.

I checked my watch, again. It was just after three-thirty.

'Okay, Doc, I'll leave you to it.'

'Bye, Peter. I shouldn't be here too much longer; this seems pretty clear-cut.'

Macca and I headed back outside. We'd made it as far as the front gate when Mick Lyons and Clarkey turned up.

'Hey, Pete,' Mick said as he came through the gate.

'Hey, Mick,' I replied. 'How did you go with Keir?'

'He didn't say much. I'll run you through it later. Did you sort all the witnesses out?'

'Yeah, I spoke to one of the senior Uniform guys and told him to arrange it all. Dr Little is still inside examining the body.'

'Good,' Mick said. 'Think I'll have a chat to her. You coming in?'

'Actually mate, I've just got this feeling that I need to have a poke around the garage and the yard. I can't shake the feeling that there's something here we're missing.'

Mick and Clarkey continued on into the house, while Macca and I went around the back. The instant I set foot in the yard, I knew that this was the house from my previous vision. I checked the back door, which was closed but not locked. Then I looked at the windows, which all had security grills fitted from the inside. I looked to my left, and saw that there was a fibro garage, and the roller door was open. Fire had damaged the structural beams, and there were several fire-damaged lounge suites sitting out in the yard. Between the garage and the house there was an empty five-litre plastic container.

I walked across to the other side of the yard. There was an orange tree towards the front of house, just inside one of the Colorbond fencing panels, but nothing much else. I looked at the brick piers of the house and realised how similar they were to the ones supporting Ashleigh's cubby house. I had a quick look under the house, but there didn't seem to be anything untoward.

'Peter,' someone called from the front yard.

'Yep?' I called back.

'We're taking the body to the mortuary.'

With the contractors who would normally have moved the body on strike, it looked like the task had fallen on us. I walked around to the front of the house and suddenly realised that there were dozens of media people crowding the street. I distinctly remember hearing the clicking of cameras as Rosalina's body, wrapped in a white plastic bag, was carried out of the house and placed into the back of the waiting van.

The other guys and I started to make our way back to our cars, but we had to push through a large number of journos who were crowding around the front gate. As we passed through, they kept asking for interviews, or at least a comment, but in accordance with our training, none of us said a word. Well, that's not entirely true. Some of us did speak, but the only words we uttered were 'No comment.'

CHAPTER 4

A Hidden Secret

The witnesses arrived at the station in dribs and drabs, and we ushered them into separate offices because we wanted to take their statements in relative anonymity. We certainly didn't want to let them see the accused. Experience dictated that, if a witness saw the accused, they'd close their mouths tighter than a clam. We needed their own recollection, not what they thought the others were saying. When I was done with all the interviews, I was exhausted and slumped down at my desk. Rubbing my face with the palms of my hands, I ran the massive amount of information I'd accumulated through my head. We felt pretty certain we could build a watertight case against Keir for Rosalina's murder, but we were still no closer to finding Jean.

I'd just started to go over the Missing Persons file again when I saw Mick Lyons weaving in and out of the desks. We truly got along like a house on fire, pardon the pun, and we always bounced ideas of each other. As the saying goes, two heads are better than one:

'Hey, Mick,' I said as he pulled up in front of my desk. 'Why would a woman who'd left her husband only contact him and no-one else? You'd think she'd contact family or friends, wouldn't you? And, by the way, he can't have been too heartbroken, 'coz it didn't take him long to remarry.'

'Doesn't look good, does it?' Mick replied wearily. I could see that the Rosalina investigation was already taking its toll on him, but I still had to throw in a quick jibe.

'Thanks mate! Load of help you are!'

'Tom's brother has just turned up downstairs,' Mick continued. 'Do ya reckon you could come with me? We'll tell him we're going to interview Tom, and that he needs to get a change of clothes for him.'

I slowly pulled myself up out of my chair. Mick's fatigue was becoming somewhat infectious. 'Are you going to tell him we're going to take Tom's clothes?' I asked.

'Yeah, and I'll tell him we're taking them for analysis. I'm curious to see if there are any traces of accelerant. Oh yeah, I forgot to tell you, Tom has a Band Aid on his finger. Whaddya reckon we get that analysed as well?'

'My oath we do! You never know, we might get lucky.'

We went downstairs to see the brother, and then back up to the charge room. Keir was sitting on a bench inside the dock, completely wrapped in a grey blanket except for his left wrist, which was cuffed to a metal rail. His head was bowed as if deep in thought, but when we walked into the room, he looked up. I examined his face closely. I was expecting some sign of dismay, but there was nothing; just that same statue-like expression. Mick and I stood directly in front of him whilst Mick informed him that we were going to remove the bandaid to have it analysed. It was only a small thing, but we wanted to make him stew, piece by piece; we wanted him to know we were closing in. Perhaps, with the net tightening, he'd save us the trouble and confess.

We paused at the door. Keir looked up and we shot him a deep stare, just to let him know we *would* do anything to get him. We then went back to the Detectives' room, and had barely sat down before Clarkey came rushing in, highly excited. 'Hey, guess what? I finished getting Max Wormleaton's statement and, after he signed it, he told me Keir was a queer kinda bloke who used to bury stuff in his backyard! Here's his statement, Mick.'

I leant forward as Mick started to read. 'What sort of things? I asked Clarkey.

'All sorts of shit; a car engine, car panels, gates, lumps of concrete and, get this, a forty-four-gallon drum.'

I suddenly had an epiphany, and looked straight at Mick, who was sitting opposite me. 'Mate! Jean's not missing, and I reckon I know where she is; in that drum!'

Mick's worried face mirrored mine. 'I'd hate to think so. You'd better go speak to Max Wormleaton. Maybe we can get enough out of him to get a search warrant to dig up the backyard. Clarkey, you come with me and we'll do a Record of Interview with Tom about Rosalina, and try to quiz him about Jean.'

Mick and Clarkey went to interview Keir in one interview room, while I went to the other, my mind swirling with possibilities.

'Hi again, Max,' I said as I entered the interview room and sat down opposite him. 'You mentioned in your statement that you saw Tom burying things in his backyard.'

'Yeah, like I said, he's a bit of a strange bloke. I guess he just didn't like going to the tip or something.'

I made sure I looked extremely interested in what he was saying. I'd learnt the importance of body language and non-verbal communication in my early days at Blacktown. The older cops had taught me to talk to victims and witnesses with sensitivity, and to not get in their faces, but it was the complete opposite with a crook. Rather than pander to them, you talked 'at' them, often using emotionless stares and getting right in their faces.

'You reckon he buried a forty-four-gallon drum?' I asked, leaning towards him.

'I saw him digging all the time and, yeah, I saw him bury a drum, but I couldn't tell you exactly where.'

'That's perfectly okay. Anything you tell me will be a big help. Do you remember when he did all of this? Was it before or after Jean disappeared?'

Wormleaton leant back on his chair, put his hands behind his head, looked at the ceiling, and then back at me. 'Yeah, he buried stuff all the time, both before and after Jeannie disappeared.'

After noting everything down, I thanked him and told him he could go. After he left, I went back to my desk and started re-reading all the witness statements. I also checked if there were any records of domestic disputes involving Tom and Jean Keir.

As I worked through file after file, I couldn't shake the visions of Jean's body stuffed into a drum. I was desperate for Mick to finish the interview, because I wanted to know if we'd be able to get a warrant. My epiphany had filled me with hope. I knew I could find Jean, and finally let her rest in peace.

Suddenly, the phone rang. It was the fellas downstairs letting me know that the rest of Keir's family had arrived. The brother had returned, and was waiting in the front foyer. There was also an elderly couple who introduced themselves as Tom's parents. They were both short and a little round, and I couldn't be sure, but they looked to be in their late sixties. They both had grey hair, and the mother wore glasses. The father's face carried a worried look, but the mother had more of an angry appearance. She fervently protested Tom's innocence, and insisted on knowing what was going on. I wasn't about to be bullied, so I only told them what I had to; Tom was upstairs being questioned. She wasn't happy, and left in a bit of a huff. The brother gave me the plastic bag containing the change of clothes and followed her. I watched them leave, and then went back upstairs to continue searching the database while waiting for Mick to finish. Not long after, he came out and handed me the Record of Interview. I quickly read through it.

'What is your full name and date of birth?'

'Thomas Andrew Keir, 1, 1, 58.'

'What is your wife's full name and date of birth?'

'Rosalina Cecilia Keir, 26, 8, 66.'

'Will you tell me your movements from when you got out of bed today?'

'I got up around 8 to 8.30. Had coffee, watched TV with my son. Went to the garage, did some work and then my son helped wash the van.'

'Where was your wife?'

'Inside. I went in and spoke to her about the party and we decided on shirts as a present.'

'What party?'

'Her uncle's at Kelvin Road, Bringelly.'

'Where was your son when you spoke to your wife about the party?'

'Out the front playing.'

'What happened after you spoke about the party?'

'I got my son and drove up to the Tregear shops and bought these Winfield Reds.'

'What time did you drive to the Tregear shops?'

'Around 12.30.'

'What happened then?'

'Drove home, parked out the front and went inside and spoke to Rosalie about birthday cards.'

'How long were you in the house?'

'Two or three minutes, and then I came out and went to the Great Western Shopping Centre and did some shopping with my son.'

'What did you buy at the shops?'

'Shirts, cards; the shopping is in the van.'

'Do you have any receipts?'

'Yes.'

[Mick later told me that at this point Keir pulled four receipts from his pocket and put them on the table.]

'What happened after the shopping?'

'I drove home and saw the fire brigade and police.'

'The fire was reported to the fire brigade at 12.56 pm. Do you know anything about the fire?'

'No.'

'I want you to understand that you do not have to say anything about this matter unless you wish, but whatever you say may later be used in evidence. Do you understand that?'

'Yes.'

'What is your occupation?'

'Upholsterer.'

'What is the name and address of your employer?'

'I'm self-employed. I work from home in the garage.'

'Do you own the house at Wilkes Crescent, Tregear?'

'Yes, I have paid it out in full.'

'Is the house insured?'

'Yes, with the NRMA for about fifty-two thousand, I think. I'm not sure.'

'Were the contents of the house insured?'

'Yeah, with Avco for about twenty-nine or thirty thousand.'

'Can you tell me whose bank account with the State Bank did you operate to withdraw the one hundred dollars today?'

'It's Rosalie's account.'

'Did you have your wife's permission to operate that account?'

'Yes. We use it as a spending account for both of us.'

'I've been told that your van was seen parked in Wilkes Crescent about 12.40 pm to 12.45 pm today. What have you got to say about that?'

'I know it was about 12.30 when I was there.'

'I've also been told that smoke was seen coming from your house about five minutes later. What have you got to say about that?'

'I don't know nothing about the smoke.'

'I've also been told by another witness that black smoke was seen coming from your house no more than ten minutes after you had left the premises. What have you got to say about that?'

'I know nothing about it, I have already told you.'

'Do you own a German Shepherd dog?'

'Yes.'

'Is it a good watchdog?'

'He seems to be.'

'Does he bark if people try to enter the rear yard?'

'Sometimes he does, sometimes he doesn't.'

'Was the dog in the backyard when you left shortly after 12.30 pm?'

'Yes.'

'Did you close the back door when you left shortly after 12.30 pm?'

'Yes.'

'Did you lock the back door shortly after 12.30 pm?'

'Yes.'

'Was the front door locked about 12.30 pm?'

'Yes.'

'Would you describe your red van fully please.'

'It's a red 1983 Mazda long-wheelbase van.'

'I've been told that you were seen to purchase an ice-cream from an ice-cream van near your premises about 11.45 am today. What have you got to say about that?'

'That's right.'

'I've also been told that you appeared to have blood smeared on your cheeks. What have you got to say about that?'

'No.'

'I've also been told by the same witness that when you parked your van in Wilkes Crescent with your son in the front passenger seat, you were seen to enter your house through the front gate and the front door. What have you got to say about that?'

'No, I went through the back door.'

'The same witness has told police that you left the house about five minutes later via the front door and the front gate. What have you got to say about that?'

'No, I went out the back door then through the side gate and then through the front gate.'

'It would appear that two separate fires were lit at your premises today. One of the fires originated in the main bedroom of the house. Can you tell me how the fire started?'

'I know nothing about the fire.'

'Did you light the fire in the house?'

'No.'

'Did you light the fire in the garage?'

'No.'

'Do you know who lit either of those two fires?'

'No.'

'It would appear that your wife was strangled prior to the house being set alight. The electric cord of a bedside lamp was located wrapped around your wife's neck whilst she was lying face down on the double bed. Can you tell me anything about this matter?'

'No.'

'Did you strangle your wife?'

'No.'

'Do you know who did strangle your wife?'

'No.'

'Did your wife have any enemies?'

'None that I know of.'

'Did you have any enemies?'

'There are several people who don't like me. I was assaulted and robbed by this guy and his mates a couple of years ago.'

'Do you know anyone who would want to kill your wife or burn your house down?'

'No.'

'One witness told police that smoke was seen coming from your premises about five minutes after your van was seen parked in Wilkes Crescent. Another witness has told police that smoke was seen coming from your house no more than ten minutes after you had left your premises. Are you suggesting that someone entered your house, strangled your wife and lit the two fires with flammable liquid within those five to ten minutes?'

'Yes. I had nothing to do with anything.'

'I understand that you sometimes burn rubbish off in your backyard. Would you *agree with me that it can take some minutes before a fire is well alight?'*

'Yes.'

'Did you see or smell anything unusual when you returned home at approximately 12.30 pm as you have stated to me earlier?'

'No.'

'Will you tell me the date of birth of your son?'

'31st of the 12th, '84.'

'Had you been drinking prior to 12.30 pm today?'

[It is relevant to note here that we would later speak to a cousin of Rosalina's who told us they'd been at the hospital the night before, and the cousin had asked Keir if wanted to go out for a smoke. Keir had responded by saying he couldn't because Rosalina had asked him to give up the smokes and the drink, and he'd agreed to do so.]

'No, but I had a mouthful of Black Douglas to gargle because I had a sore throat.'

'Did you have any arguments with your wife today?'

'No.'

'Did you have any domestic problems with your wife as of recent times?'

'No.'

Mick had sat down opposite me while I was reading the statement, and when I'd finished reading, he said, 'As you can see, he wouldn't make any admissions. He wants a coffee. Reckon I'll have a tea myself. You want something?'

I put my hands on the back of my neck and stretched my head from side to side. I'd been sitting in the same position for a bit, and my neck and back were pretty stiff. 'Yeah, I might join you.' I got up and we made our way along the corridor to the meal room. 'He must know we've got him,' I said. 'It'd be a lot easier if he'd just confess, but I reckon we've got enough to get a warrant to dig up the yard. Mick, we might be able to charge him with two murders.'

'Mate,' Mick said as we reached the meal room, 'I noticed a semicircular cut just below Keir's ear, on the right-hand side of his neck. I'll give him his coffee and you give him his clothes and, while you do, have a squiz at it and see what you think. Rosalina might have scratched him if there was a struggle.'

After quickly making the cuppas, we retrieved the plastic bag full of clothes and made our way back into the interview room. 'Your brother brought some clothes for you,' I said as I leant down to put the bag on the table. As I did so, I had a quick look at the scratch. The cut was shaped like a crescent moon, and looked like a perfect match for a fingernail. Mick then questioned Keir regarding the origin of the scratch.

'I notice you have a small cut on the right side of your neck, just below your earlobe. Can you tell me how that happened?'

'It happened yesterday or this morning, when I was pulling the staples out of a lounge suite, or something like that. I don't know exactly.'

I nodded for Mick to join me outside. When we were out of earshot I said, 'Mate, that looks pretty fresh. I wouldn't mind grabbing a photo just in case she did manage to scratch him. The exhibit room will be shut, so I'll have to shoot home and get my camera. I'll get back as quick as I can.'

'Righto, mate,' said Mick. 'I'll get the interview adopted [or 'legitimised', adopted basically means that another copper verifies we've done the interview properly] by Graham Lower. He's the Supervising Sergeant. I'll finish it off while you're gone.'

Mick resumed the interview, while I drove home with all I'd seen, read and heard throughout the day replaying over and over in my head. When I pulled into my driveway and walked through the front door, I felt like I was returning from the Twilight Zone and stepping back into the real world.

People often asked me how I could go from seeing what I'd seen to being back at home with a lovely wife, how I could push away all thoughts of a charred body and put on a happy face for my wife. The answer was, I couldn't. All I could do was try to put it to the back of my mind.

I knew my wife was asleep, but try as I might to tiptoe around, she woke up, and was more than a little annoyed to discover that I wasn't home for good. I told her I was sorry I couldn't stay, but I'd be back soon. I kissed her, grabbed the camera and rushed back out the front door.

I ran into Mick as soon as I got back to the station. He'd just finished the interview, and was waiting for Sergeant Lower to come down and do the mandatory adoption questions. Before Lower arrived, we went back into the interview room. 'Detective Seymour is going to take some photographs of the cut below your ear,' Mick said.

I took three photos, and had barely snapped the last one when Lower arrived and Mick and I had to leave the room. We waited anxiously outside, pacing up and down like blokes waiting for their wives to give birth. Eventually, Lower emerged. 'Yep, all good, boys.'

The words had barely left Lower's lips before Mick went back into the interview room and sat down opposite Keir. 'Thomas Andrew Keir, you are going to be charged with the murder of your wife, and setting fire to the house to endanger life. Do you understand that?'

It might seem pretty obvious that lighting a fire is endangering someone's life, but it always paid to have a backup charge, just in case the more serious charge didn't stick. Blokes can exhibit any one of a range of emotions when they've just been told they're being charged with murder, such as anger or frustration, but Keir simply maintained that same blank expression. All he said was, 'I never did it, and I'm getting the blame for it.'

'That's what they all say,' I thought to myself. 'Every bloke in jail is innocent.'

Despite Keir's declaration of innocence, Clarkey and Mick took him to the charge room, where he was placed in the dock and formally charged with the murder of his wife.

It was close to midnight, and after all the paperwork was done, he was placed in a holding cell. You gotta wonder what goes through a bloke's mind at a time like that. It's like that Cold Chisel song, 'Four walls…Wash basin… Prison bed…'

Left to your own devices, you have nothing to do but sit there and contemplate what you've done or, should you truly be innocent, to pray to the Big Fella upstairs that the truth will come out, and there won't be a miscarriage of justice. However, if you know you're guilty, you'd have to be thinking about whether you've done your best to make sure you get away with the crime. Has your subterfuge been successful? Did you leave any piece of evidence lying around? Will you be a free man, or is what you're experiencing now a taste of what you'll know for the remainder of your days? We left Keir to muse over his fate.

All the boys sat down in the office for the debriefing while we all enjoyed a well-earned cuppa. Mick went over the lines of inquiry and plan of attack for the next few days. Time had seemed to somehow stand still at the start of my shift as I'd tried to come to terms with what we were dealing with, but as I'd got into the investigative swing, and because we'd been working our guts out for the last few hours, the second part had seemed to fly. That's one thing I loved about the job; you were never bored. I couldn't have stood being a clock-watcher in an office; it would have driven me insane.

As for the next few days, Mick and the Homicide Squad were to concentrate on gathering as much evidence as they could in relation to Rosalina's murder, whilst I was to concentrate on Jean's disappearance.

I felt numb with fatigue as I walked to the car to *finally* go home. Part of me wished I had an 'off' switch and could completely forget about work, but I didn't, and images of both girls danced through my head like a couple of phantoms as I drove home. At this stage, I didn't know what Jean looked like, but I'd created a picture in my head, and I couldn't shake the vision of her body crumpled up inside a drum. I also couldn't shake the picture of Rosalina's charred corpse, and the sheer cruelty of burning her. Firm in our suspicions that Keir was the culprit, it dawned on me that this was his final insult to her. Yes, he'd burned her, but it wasn't just to cover his tracks; he'd taken away her looks to make sure no-one else ever gazed upon her beauty.

CHAPTER 4

When I got home, I was overjoyed to be home to be with *my* girls. I'd been running on adrenaline all day, and now that I'd finally stopped, the sheer extent of my exhaustion became apparent. Sue was barely asleep, and heard the car pull in. By the time I got up to the bedroom, she was wide awake. I kissed her softly on the cheek. 'Honey, I'm home for good this time.'

She cuddled into me and fell asleep almost immediately. I tried to sleep, but to no avail; the two dead girls wouldn't let me. Tomorrow would be the start of a hectic investigation. Tomorrow, I'd begin searching for the truth.

SEVEN BONES

CHAPTER 5
Two Wives — Two Investigations

I'd barely fallen asleep, or so it seemed, before I was back in the car and on my way to work. When I arrived, it was like a bloody beehive. Aside from the rostered-on blokes, there were a helluva lot of others who'd been roped in to help even though they weren't due to work today, or were due to start a lot later. Most of them had been called in for Rosalina's murder, but I was concentrating on Jean's disappearance, and my mind was firmly fixed on discovering her whereabouts.

The briefing started at 8.30 am. Mick O'Connell went over everyone's jobs, and told them where to start. 'The first forty-eight hours are the most crucial in a murder investigation,' he began. 'People forget things, get confused, evidence gets damaged and the list goes on. Everything has to be done there and then; the longer you take with something, the more chance the case has of going cold.'

Mick Lyons and I began by meeting Jean's family, the Strachans. It didn't take us long to get there, as the family only lived five minutes away from Wilkes Crescent, in the neighbouring suburb of Blackett. One of the key people we needed to speak to was Keir's son. Christine Strachan confirmed that he'd been staying with them, and had agreed to talk to us that morning.

With the briefing done, Mick, Rod Dayment, who was a Homicide Detective, and I went down to make a cuppa. Rod was a very experienced Homicide officer who stood just over six feet tall. He was a well-dressed bloke with an athletic build, even though he was in his forties. He also had greying hair with a whitish moustache. As we walked he talked. 'Well, it looks like you boys have got this one under control. The missing first missus is a bit of a concern, though. What's the go there?'

'She went missing in Feb '88. Pete did a follow-up, but nothin' ever came of it,' Mick said.

I put in my two cents worth. 'Keir was the last person to see her alive. He reckons he's been in contact with her a couple of times, but she hasn't contacted her family, which I find a bit strange.'

'Boys, the first wife disappears, and the second wife turns up dead,' said Rod. 'You don't have to be a rocket scientist. The whole thing stinks to high heaven, but there isn't enough evidence to warrant Homicide's intervention. She's still a missing person, so we'll leave it to you local boys. If you need a hand with anything though, just let us know.'

Rod left, and I returned to my desk to begin sifting through the Keir interview from the night before, just to make sure I hadn't missed something. Finding nothing new, Mick and I decided we needed to have another look at the crime scene before we went and spoke with Jean's family. We also had a photo of Rosalina, and had to take it to the Strachans for a positive I.D.

Pulling up outside the Wilkes Crescent property, Mick and I surveyed the scene, and were both immediately struck by the contrast. Yesterday, the house had been a hive of activity. Today, it was completely still and silent, apart from the chequered blue-and-white police tape swaying and flapping in the breeze. Something in the silence stirred the strange sensations in me again. It was almost like I could hear Jean's voice telling me that I was on the right track, and not to stop now. It almost felt like she was willing me on, guiding me to find her.

'Fair bit of damage, ay?' Mick said.

'Reckon they'll have to knock it down?' I replied.

'Mate, there seems to be bad karma attached to this house. Perhaps it'd be best if they did.'

We walked towards the house, and as soon as we approached the fence the dog started to bark.

'Wonder who's gonna take care of the dog?' I said.

'We'll tell the Strachans. They can sort it out,' Mick said.

We only took a cursory look around before going on to the Strachans' house. Their small, neat and tidy brick home had a carport on the left-hand side, and the block sloped gently up from the road to the house. There were steps leading up to a small veranda and a wire screen door with a timber door behind. We walked up to the front door and knocked. Death knocks were the hardest part of the job, because they were so personal; there was nowhere to hide. When someone opens the door and sees a couple of cops standing there with ashen faces, they know there can be nothing good coming from the visit.

I came from a very close-knit family, and initially struggled with these jobs, because I always imagined what it would be like if it was someone in my family who had passed away. In my first couple of years in uniform, I did about three or four death knocks, and they never got any easier, even though I came to know what to say, and the typical reaction to expect. All I could say was, 'I'm sorry,' and then allow the family to let out their emotions. Then I'd sit there with them, trying to answer the inevitable 'When?' 'Where?' and 'How?' questions, typically followed by, 'What happens now?'

Usually, the incident had occurred in another police patrol, such as out in the country, and we'd get a message with very little information apart from the contact details for the investigating police. We could only ever give the family the bare details, and urge them to contact the police in charge of the matter. The thing was, you never wanted to say too much in case you give them the wrong information, which could then cause problems, especially as people were upset and emotional, and sometimes didn't hear exactly what you were saying and could easily get things mixed up. If they asked about what happened next, I would tell them that normally a body was taken to the local mortuary. I had to tell them that they'd need to view the body and formally identify it for the local police, after which the post-mortem would be carried out. I'd tell them that everything would be explained in more detail once they spoke to the police in charge of the matter. Finally, I'd ask if there was anything I could do, such as contacting other relatives, and then I'd leave my name and number in case they needed to speak to me.

As I stood at the Strachans' door, I felt like I was back on one of those first death knocks, only this time I wasn't referring the family onto someone else; I was the officer who would be providing the information. It made me a little uncomfortable, a feeling which was only intensified when Christine Strachan answered the door. She was short, with cropped brown hair, a Filipino woman, but not what you'd call 'typical', in fact she looked more European than Asian. She had a kind, welcoming face, and spoke with a slight accent as she politely invited us inside.

Entering the house, we went straight into the lounge room. There was a hallway off to the right, and then the kitchen to the left. The humbleness of the house seemed quite reflective of the family. What struck me most were the dozens of family photos scattered around the room, including many photographs of Jean.

Christine sat down on the sofa and motioned for us to do the same. She was obviously apprehensive and pensive as she sat there fidgeting and squeezing her hands together. I scanned the room, and when I looked more closely at the photos, my gaze fixed on a wedding photo of Keir and Jean. I thought about my wife, and how I'd made a promise to love, protect and cherish her, and about how Keir had made those same promises, and had broken them. I couldn't understand it. No matter how bad things ever became with me and Sue, there was no way I'd ever contemplate killing her. I looked at a few more pictures. There were some of Jean in her basketball gear, and others of her in school uniform. I started thinking about Ashleigh, and what she would look like when she grew up, and then it hit me like a sledgehammer: Jean had grown up in this house.

I became even more apprehensive. Jean had been missing for three years now. Her mother had endured three years of anguish and torment, and I knew that she'd ask me a thousand questions, questions to which I knew I had no answers.

I looked at her kind face. It was warm and inviting, but etched with wrinkles that spoke of the burden of years of not knowing.

Just as Mick and I sat down, her husband, Clifford, came into the room. We rose to our feet again and shook his hand, and when he said 'hello' it was plainly apparent that he was a Scot. His shimmering silver hair stood out against his close-cropped beard, moustache and large, oval-shaped rimmed glasses. He was tall, and you could instantly tell that he'd been an athletic man in his younger days.

Christine leant forward, her hands clenched together on her knees, while Clifford sat in a chair beside her and reached over and took hold of her hand in an effort to stop her trembling. Mick looked at Christine. 'We're terribly sorry about yesterday's events, and what happened to Rosalina, but we have a photo here we want to show you.'

Christine took the photo from Mick, examined it, and then handed it to Clifford.

'Is that Rosalina?' Mick asked.

'Yes. Yes…it…is,' Christine said shakily, her voice slightly broken and unsure. 'We introduced her to Tom after Jean disappeared. I can't believe Tom would do something like this.'

Clifford was still looking at Rosalina's photo, and I tried to read his body language. He hadn't said anything, but his face bore a heavy frown, and v-shaped worry lines. I could tell that something was troubling him deeply, something more than Rosalina's death. Whatever it was, I hoped he was in a talkative mood.

'Tom was so upset when Jeannie left,' Christine continued. 'It wasn't like Jeannie at all not to contact anyone. We all felt so sorry for him, the poor bugger. Imagine, losing your wife to another man. So, we introduced him to Rosalina at a wedding when she came out from the Philippines in 1988. They hit it off straightaway, and began seeing each other.'

'Did Rosalina and Jean know each other at all?' I asked.

'Why, of course. They're distant cousins.'

'How surreal is this?' I thought to myself, shooting Mick a look of sheer disbelief. It was like a big bloody spider web. Two women, related to one another, marry the same man; one vanishes, and the other one is murdered. I wondered if Keir was into poetry and literature, and if he'd ever heard the line from Sir Walter Scott's *Marmion*: 'Oh, what a tangled web we weave when first we practise to deceive.' Only, this was a case of: 'Oh, what a tangled web we weave when both my wives end up deceased.'

'It was a really happy marriage between them,' Christine continued. 'Rosalina's aunt and uncle were having a housewarming out in Bringelly yesterday. It was a BBQ lunch, and Rosie was really excited. I can't believe this has happened.'

'How did a day start full of excitement and anticipation for the family end up in tragedy and despair?' I wondered. 'Was he the obsessively jealous type, or a guy who just flies off the handle at the slightest thing?'

Christine obviously had more to say, but her voice started to waver, her bottom lip started to quiver, and she was clearly on the verge of breaking into tears, whereupon Clifford instantly took over. Sensing I'd seen something in his face, he looked straight at me. The whole time Christine had been speaking, I'd noticed him stealing looks at me more so than at Mick, almost as if he were trying to catch my eye. Now his eyes met mine. It wasn't a penetrating or piercing stare, but a look of shared knowledge, father to father.

'Detective Seymour, you know our daughter Jeannie went missing three years ago, but I never liked Tom from the moment I met him.'

'Can you elaborate?' I asked.

'Yeah, when Jeannie first met him, he still lived with his parents, not far from us. Whenever I'd walk past their place on my way back from the pub, he'd have his cattle dog with him, and he'd encourage it to have a crack at my border collie. One day, I said to him, "If your dog ever gets out and attacks my dog, I'll kill it!" He just thought it was funny to stir me up. I always referred to him as "That bastard English boy from down the road."'

The expression on his face suddenly became dark and melancholic, as though a shroud had descended over his thoughts and hopes. That 'bastard English boy' had married his daughter, and I knew he was certain Jeannie had suffered the same fate as Rosalina. 'So you haven't heard from Jeannie since her disappearance?' I continued.

'No,' Clifford said. 'She hasn't contacted us, or any of her friends.'

'Can you give us the details of her closest friends, so that maybe they can shed some light on her relationship with Tom?' I asked.

'Yes, of course,' Christine said, having recovered her composure. 'There were the twins, Fiona and Shona Chalmers, and there was also Maria Mateo. Jeannie had so many friends but those girls were the closest. Fiona lives in Sydney, I think, and Shona got married and moved out to the country. I think she's Fiona McDonald now. They became best friends around the age of thirteen. The girls had been together since kindergarten, and they all lived in the same street, but it wasn't until they went to Plumpton High that they became friends. Jean also became friends with Maria Mateo at Plumpton.'

'Can you tell me the circumstances under which Jean and Tom met?'

'A friend of mine, Barbara, told me that a company called Freeport Furniture was looking for a machinist. I was doing it tough, and I needed the work. I think it was early in 1979. Anyway, they gave me a trial. Tom was the boss. One day he brought over some cushions for me to sew. Jean was getting ready to go to school, and answered the door. Tom asked if he could speak to me. Jean said 'yes', but that I was in the shower. She came into the bathroom and said, "Mum, there's a man at the door, and he's the ugliest man I've ever seen. He looks like Frankenstein. He has one big long eyebrow."'

'And can you tell us how they came to form an intimate relationship?' I asked.

'Um, the girls would often come to the factory after basketball practice on a Friday afternoon, and wait for me to finish. One afternoon, the guys decided to have a game of cricket in the car park, and Tom asked me if the girls could join in. To be honest with you Detective Seymour, I was becoming a little bit concerned.'

'Concerned about what?'

'He was a little *too* keen, if you get what I mean. She was only fourteen, for God's sake, and he was in his twenties.'

The longer I listened, the harder I found it to maintain a calm demeanour. Every new revelation only served to intensify my dislike of Thomas Keir. I also began to imagine what I would do if a twenty-something-year-old guy took an inappropriate fancy to Ashleigh when she turned fourteen.

'So did you act on these concerns?' Mick asked.

'Well, during the game, he said, "If you bring Jean in on Saturdays, I'll pay her to put the buttons on the cushions." I still had my concerns, but I figured I'd always be around, and it was a good chance for her to earn some pocket money. She was getting twenty dollars a week, and she loved working with me. A year or so later, in 1981 I think, he came up and asked me if he could take Jean out on a date. I said no way, she's only fifteen, she's not going on any dates!'

'Yeah, he kept turning up all the time after that,' Clifford said. 'He'd get all dressed up and come around to chat to us. I didn't like him, so I'd go off to the pub. I used to always tell Christine that there was something about him I didn't like.'

'He was always such a gentleman, though,' Christine added.

'Even so, I said to him that the only way he could possibly see my daughter was if he brought me a case of beer every Saturday and, bugger me, he did.' Clifford shook his head.

'We eventually said he could take her out, but Jeannie's sisters had to go too,' Christine continued. 'I don't know if he was happy about it, but he agreed. When Jeannie turned sixteen, he came to the house with sixteen red roses and a bottle of champagne for me. I told him I didn't drink champagne, but he was so insistent. They kept seeing each other and he brought her a ring when she was seventeen. They went out for a dance one night, and she came home all upset because he wouldn't let her dance with anyone. She got angry and chucked the ring at him and ran out of the house.'

'Is there anything else you can tell us that might shed light on the nature of their relationship after that?' I asked.

'Yeah,' said Clifford, 'he asked to take her out for her eighteenth birthday. I wasn't too happy about it, but she was an adult, so what could we do? Then a bit later, we found out that Jean was pregnant. Chris was so pissed off she smacked him in the side of the head. She hit him that hard she knocked him straight on his arse.'

We looked at Christine's tiny frame as she nodded her affirmation. I looked at the wedding photo again. Tom towered over Jean, and I wondered how someone Christine's size could have put him on his arse, and how he'd felt about it. Even Jean and Rosalina were bigger than Christine, and I couldn't even begin to imagine his sheer psychopathic fury when he'd overpowered them and *allegedly* killed them.

'They told us they were going to get engaged,' Christine said, 'and they were married on 11 August 1984 at the Holy Family Church in Emerton. The reception was held at Rooty Hill RSL. It seemed okay at first, but before long, things started to go bad. Jeannie began to tell me what her marriage was like. I knew something wasn't right, and she just seemed to get sadder and sadder, but then her son was born and she came to life again.'

Mick and I were having trouble believing most of what we were hearing. It wasn't that we didn't think it was true; it was just that everything seemed rather bizarre.

'It was really weird though,' Christine continued. 'Jean loved her son like you wouldn't believe, but Tom didn't like it. He would even pull his son's hand away from Jean's breast if he tried to touch it, if you can believe that? Tom would say it wasn't right for him to touch her *there*, and not to let him do it again. I only have one photo of Jean and her son together; Tom cut the rest of them up because he reckoned she was showing her bum. There were photos of her in her swimmers, and he used to make me change her costume because he said her nipples were showing. He often left work early so he could go home and check on her. She rang me one day and said, "Mum, he gets angry with me if I ever muck around with my cousins, especially when I hug them. He even gets jealous of me hugging my son, and he won't speak to me for days. It's as if he gets depressed or something." I went over there, and she was listening to that song, you know the one about the girl who's getting bashed. It starts, "My name is Luka." Jeannie started to cry, and I asked her what was wrong. She told me that they were just having a few problems, but everything would be alright. I had a chat to Tom, and it all seemed alright.'

Both Mick and I were extremely interested to find out more, but we were suddenly distracted by a child's voice, and swung our heads around to see the son and Irene Page.

'This must be your grandson,' Mick said with that exaggerated voice you use when you first meet a child and want them to be comfortable with you.

'Yes, this is my grandson,' said Christine, as he ran to her. She swept him up in her arms and embraced him in the way only a grandmother can. She sat him on her lap and wrapped her arms tightly around him, as if trying to protect him from all the bad things in the world.

I examined him closely. He had a slight build, with fair skin, like his mother. From his father, he'd inherited short dark hair and similar facial features, with the exception of the monobrow.

'He's six years old, aren't you?' Christine said, bouncing him on her knee.

'Yeah,' he replied, not too sure about what he should or shouldn't say. It's funny how kids instinctively know when someone is there to ask questions, and instantly become guarded.

'Would it be possible to ask your grandson some questions about what happened yesterday?' Mick said.

Christine leant in to talk into her grandson's ear. 'Will you tell these nice men about what happened yesterday?' Despite bowing his head and drawing it back between his shoulders, he nodded affirmatively.

'Young man,' Mick said softly, 'We're going to go out to our police car and get a typewriter so that we can write down what you tell us. Is that okay?'

The boy nodded.

I ran out to the car, returned with the typewriter, and set it up. Once the carbon paper was in place, I nodded to Mick.

'Young man, do you know the difference between right and wrong?'

'Yeah.'

'And you know the difference between telling the truth and telling lies?'

'Yeah.'

'Will you tell us *everything* that you did, in order, from when you got up out of bed yesterday; who you saw and who you spoke to?'

The young fella fiddled with his hands and looked down at his lap as he began to speak. 'I woke up in the morning and put the telly on and then I watched it.'

As kids do, he interpreted things literally, and meant to tell us *everything*. This was why it was always good, as a detective, to talk to kids because they *did* tell you *everything*, while adults had a more refined sense of themselves, and of what they would say to suit the circumstances, and sometimes it was hard to separate the smoke from the fire (again, pardon the pun).

'And when me mum and dad woke up, me mum and dad watched telly too. I made myself some breakfast, and then I went into the lounge room and sat on the chair and put my breakfast on the table. Then I ate my breakfast and then when I'd finished I helped me dad wash the van. Mum was still watching telly and Dad told me to go and play with my friends.'

'What happened then?' Mick interjected, interested that the boy's dad had 'told' him to go and play with his friends.

'Then I went inside and got me car out and then I was playing with it. Then I went outside and me friends came over and I let them play with it, and when I let them play with it I decided they could make some jumps in the dirt and we made some big ones. Then I tried my one out.'

'What happened after you played with your car?' I asked.

'I played another game outside. In the middle of the game me dad told me we had to go to the shops, and then we went to the first shop, then we went to the Great Western shops at Mount Druitt. Then first we went to buy some T-shirts for a birthday and then we went to the bank and then we went to get me a pair of shoes and then we went to get a plant and then we went home.'

'What happened when you got home with your dad?' I continued.

'There was a fire at the house. I saw broken things and broken windows and the Fire Brigade man said "I had to do that". I saw heaps of police cars and I saw two fire engines. Then, a bit later, I saw an ambulance come.'

'Which was the first shop you went to with your dad?'

'The Tregear shops.'

'What did you buy at the Tregear shops?'

'Me dad bought some smokes and a new lighter, just in case the black one runs out. Sometimes he takes the black one too when we go fishin'. He bought me some lollies.'

The boy was more confident now, his voice becoming louder.

'Where did you go after the Tregear shops?' I pushed.

'Home, just in case, because me dad asked me mum if we needed to buy some birthday cards. She said two of them and then we went to the Great Western shops.'

'What did you do when you got home after being at the Tregear shops with your dad?'

'I waited in the van for me dad. Dad went inside and then me dad asked me mum if we needed two birthday cards and me mum said "yes" and then he came out the back gate and then he came over the front gate. Then he got in the van and then we went to the Great Western shops.'

Now the apparent inconsistencies became more obvious and, more alarmingly, he was repeating things as though he'd memorised the answers.

'Hang on, how do you know your dad asked your mum about the birthday cards?' I asked.

'Because he told me,' he replied, rather annoyed I'd questioned him.

Not wanting him to clam up I changed my tone. 'Sorry, when did he tell you?'

'No, he didn't tell me,' the young fella corrected himself. 'He told me he was going to ask Mum about the cards. When we went to the Great Western shops I knew he was going to get them when he went into the shop and there was one "Uncle" one.'

'Did you see your mum when you got back from the shops at Tregear?'

'Me dad saw her but I didn't because she was still inside watching telly. I don't know what she was doing because I think she was cleaning up the house.'

Tapping away at the typewriter, I knew he hadn't seen his mother. He'd been 'told' to go outside and play and he'd been 'told' to stay in the van. However, I needed clarification. 'Did you see your mum after you were playing with your friends and before you went to the shops?'

'No, because when me dad first told me to go and play with me friends I changed me T-shirt. I saw me Mum at breakfast.'

I shook my head at Mick. 'I don't think he's seen anything.'

'No,' Mick agreed. 'I think we'll leave it there for the moment.' Mick grabbed the piece of paper from the typewriter and handed it to Christine. He asked her if she could read the answers back to Keir's son to confirm that they were correct. Mick then asked the boy to sign it, which he happily did. Irene and Christine were also asked to sign. Irene then took the boy from the room.

'So you've had no contact from Jean since she disappeared?' I asked Christine.

'No, nothing at all.'

'Has she contacted anyone else, any friends or relatives, apart from Tom?'

'No, and this is the strange thing, Jeannie would never have left her son. He was everything to her. No matter how bad things may have been between her and Tom, she would never have left her son. I just don't understand it.'

I started to feel particularly bad for the little boy who'd just left the room. How do you cope at such a young age when you lose *both* your mothers?

'She would never have left her son and never have taken off without contacting us,' Clifford reaffirmed, his voice sounding desolate. One father to another, I could tell he was shattered, and I wondered how I would, or if I could, cope if I was in his shoes. Mick, sensing I was elsewhere, took over the questioning.

'We've been told that Tom would sometimes bury items in his backyard. Were you aware of him doing that?'

Christine's eyes opened wide. 'Oh, yes,' she said. 'The neighbour's daughter knew our kids, and she'd tell them that Tom was burying things in the backyard. He also used to burn things in a big drum, which annoyed them. I asked him about it once, and he said he did it because he couldn't be bothered taking it to the tip. He'd go the tip sometimes, but then other times, he'd bury things.'

'What was the name of the neighbour?' I asked; my mind back on the job now.

'Max Wormleaton's daughter, Lisa,' Christine said.

Clifford's face became even more wrinkled and even more pained. 'Why... why...do you ask?'

'It's just a line of inquiry we're required to follow up,' I said, realising that I needed to alleviate his concerns quickly. 'Do you know when he last buried something?'

'Wouldn't have a clue,' Clifford replied, seemingly satisfied. 'He's probably done it for years. He was always a bit odd, you know. Not too many of Jeannie's friends liked him either.'

'Mr Strachan, can I ask you *exactly* why you didn't like him?' I continued.

'A lot of things,' he said. 'I just didn't trust him. He was very possessive of Jean, and would make her change her clothes if he thought what she was wearing was too revealing. I remember I was doing some tiling at their place during the summer. It was very hot, and Jean had a pair of shorts on; just normal shorts, for God's sake. He came home and had a huge row with her and made her change. Now, what sort of bloke does that?'

'Like I said,' Christine interrupted, 'Tom would even alter Jean's clothes, like swimmers and shorts, if he thought they were too revealing. He'd always give her the filthiest looks if she hugged another man, even her own relatives.'

Keir's *modus operandi* had now become as clear as a bright blue sky. Needing to know the extent of his jealously, I pushed further. 'So would you say Tom was insanely jealous?'

'Oh, yes! Jeannie could never go anywhere without Tom wanting to know where she was going and who she was with,' Christine said ardently.

'Do you know if Tom was doing any digging around the time of Jean's disappearance?'

'He might have done. Why do you ask?' Christine said, her voice quivering. She must have known that the question was largely rhetorical, but I could tell that she didn't want to know the answer.

'I know why they want to know,' Clifford interjected. 'You think he might have done something to Jeannie at the house,' he said, looking me squarely in the eye.

'There is that possibility, and it's something we have to consider,' I said, as gently and as reassuringly as I could, but both of their heads dropped. My reassurances were as hollow as a drum. Christine clenched her hands tightly together and her body quivered. Sheer pity was all I could feel for them. In the deepest recesses of their souls they must have known that their daughter was gone, but I knew, as a parent myself, that they clung to even the slightest sliver of hope. It was understandable that, considering Keir's apparent personality, a girl would run away. The Strachans had pushed the worst-case scenario out of their mind and allowed themselves to believe that their daughter had run off, but now reality started to dawn. Christine now recovered and suddenly became quite animated. 'And to think we introduced him to Rosie! We actually felt *sorry* for him when he said that Jeannie had left him! I just can't believe this is happening!'

'Can you tell us what happened when he met Rosalina?' I asked.

'Well, Rosie had to go back to the Philippines at the end of 1988, and Tom went with her to meet her family. He came back early in 1989, then went back to the Philippines and married her. He brought her back here, and they lived with Tom's parents while they rented the house out to a lady and her son for a few months. Her name was Denise Wilkes. Then he told her that she'd have to leave, because he wanted to move back in. I helped Tom to clean up the house before they moved back in. There were lots of mice running around the place, and there was a God-awful stench. I remember picking up a large bone in the backyard, and asking Tom what he was feeding his dogs.'

I suddenly knew that my first priority after we left the Strachan household was to talk to the tenant. 'Do you know where we can find Denise Wilkes?' I inquired.

'Yes, she still lives around here. I see her at the shops sometimes,' Christine replied.

'I think that's all we need for the time being,' Mick said. We could have sat there all day and pressed further, but there was an ongoing murder investigation.

'We'll have to speak to you again, and probably other family members as well,' I said, 'if that's okay?'

'Yes, that's fine,' Christine said.

Mick and I stood and shook hands with both of them. When I took Christine's hand in mine, an emotional bolt of lightning shot between us. I hated her having to go through this. No mother deserved to suffer what she had.

Christine smiled at me as she stood at her front door seeing us off. Her smile melted my heart, and I made a silent vow: I'd discover what had happened to their daughter. No matter how many hours, no matter what it took, I'd find the answer. The family deserved to know the truth.

CHAPTER 6
The Dig Begins

Despite my vow, at this point we had very few leads to go on.

We waved goodbye to Christine, and hopped into the car. Mick turned the key in the ignition, but then paused and turned it back off again. He bowed his head, and I could sense that he was feeling the same weight of expectation as I was. He looked at me. 'Well, at least they confirmed that Keir buried things in the backyard.'

'Yeah, true. I thought the young bloke's statement was interesting. I wasn't happy with how he spoke at all; it was almost like he'd been coached. You gotta feel sorry for the kid though.'

Mick sighed heavily, his voice tinged with resignation as he restarted the car. 'Well, I don't reckon we'll get much more out of him at this stage. It'll be good to get the stuff like the hair samples back from Forensics, but in the meantime we'll speak to Homicide about Jean. I reckon we should interview Keir about her later today and see what he has to say, see how he reacts.'

'It'll be bloody interesting to see what he says about burying stuff in the backyard too,' I said.

Mick and I drove back to the station, whereupon I went straight to the meals room and was making yet another cup of coffee when Clarkey walked in. 'Hey, Clarkey,' I said. 'How do you feel about doing another Record of Interview with Mick this arvo?'

'What's this one for? Does Mick want to go over some things from the first one?'

'No, mate, he's going to interview Keir about his first wife. The Strachans confirmed that Keir buried shit in his backyard.'

'Bloody hell,' said Clarkey, genuinely surprised. 'So ya' reckon he's buried his first wife in the backyard?'

'Dunno, mate, dunno. I'd rather find her alive and safe and well, but I reckon it's a pretty sure bet that's where she is. We'll find out soon enough.'

Visions of Tom digging up his yard with Jean's body lying prostrate next to him filled my mind, and I wondered if we had enough for a warrant; surely we did. However, we were working on a hunch, and warrants are funny things; they don't always get granted. We went and found Mick.

'D'ya reckon it'd be alright if Clarkey does the second interview with Keir?' I said.

'Yeah, mate, that's fine,' said Mick. 'I don't think it'll be a long interview anyway. I'll just go over things around the time of her disappearance and see what he says about their marriage. I won't push too hard. I don't want him shutting up shop because he thinks we know too much. You happy to type the interview, Clarkey? Just don't make so many bloody spelling mistakes this time!' Mick said with a hearty laugh.

'Yeah, mate, I'm happy to do it,' Clarkey replied, ignoring Mick's dig.

'Righto then,' I said. 'While you blokes are doing that I'll chase up Denise Wilkes and see if I can find Jean's schoolfriends.'

I made my way back to my desk, reached into the side drawer and pulled out the White Pages. Denise Wilkes wasn't hard to find, and I phoned her and made arrangements for her to come down the station later that night. Finding the other people of interest wasn't as easy. I scoured scores of phone books and databases, and eventually located Fiona Chalmers in Redfern and made another call.

'Fiona Chalmers?'

'Yes.'

'My name is Detective Peter Seymour from Mt Druitt police. I'm ringing because I'm making inquiries into a missing person named Jean Keir. Was she a friend of yours?'

There was silence for a moment before Fiona responded to my question. 'Yes, she's my friend. What's happened?'

'Her husband, Tom, has been charged with murdering his second wife, and we're now investigating Jean's disappearance. I was hoping you could give me some information about their relationship that may assist us in our investigation.'

'I never liked that man,' she replied. 'He was just plain evil. I know he did something to Jean. He dragged her away from the caravan park the day she disappeared, and no-one has seen her since. My sister and I told the police that we thought Tom had something to do with Jean's disappearance ages ago, but we had no evidence to prove it.'

'Why did you think that?' I asked.

'He was very jealous and very possessive. She used to have to put make-up on after she left the house because he would go crazy if he saw her with it on. She would lie about going for job interviews so she could come and have lunch with us. She had to hide her contraceptive pills in the cupboard because he was trying to force her to have another baby. She once told me she wanted to leave him, but she was scared because she thought he would track her and her son down and kill her.'

'Would you be able to provide us with a statement?' I asked.

'Of course, I'd be more than happy to. Do you want my sister's number as well?'

'Yes, that would be very helpful. Some of my colleagues will be in touch with you to arrange a time to take a statement. Thank you so much for your assistance.' I hung up the phone, feeling somewhat cold, and then rang Shona McDonald, who told me the same thing her sister had. She agreed to give her statement to her local police, and she also gave me the contact details for Maria Meteo, who lived in Hebersham, not too far away from Mt Druitt.

My mind was churning like a sea in a cyclone. Fiona had given me definitive proof of Jean's concerns about Keir killing her. Lost in my thoughts, I didn't notice that Mick had appeared in front of my desk. 'Here, mate, have a read of this,' Mick said as he passed me the Record of Interview. I took it from him and began to read.

'As you know, Detective Clark and I are making inquiries in relation to your first wife, named Jean Angela Keir, formerly known by her maiden name of Strachan, who was reported missing to the Mr Druitt Police Station on 1 May 1988. I want you to understand that you do not have to say anything about this matter unless you wish to, but whatever you say will be recorded and may later be used in evidence. Do you understand that?'

'Yes.'

'For the purpose of this Record of Interview, what is your full name, date of birth and address?'

'Thomas Andrew Keir, 1st of the 1st, '58, Wilkes Crescent, Tregear.'

'Will you tell me the date and place where you married your ex-wife, Jean Keir?'

'August 11 '84. It was at the Holy Family Church on Luxford Road.'

'Will you tell me the last time you saw your ex-wife prior to her being reported missing?'

'I think it was 10 February '88.'

'Will you tell me the location where you last saw your ex-wife?'

'At home.'

'Will you tell me what your domestic situation was with your ex-wife at that time?'

'It was just starting to get better.'

'Can you give me a reason why your ex-wife would leave you?'

'Because she was in love with another man.'

'Will you tell me when and what your ex-wife told you about this other man?'

'It was in December that she told me she'd been having an affair for a couple of months. Then she said she was going to stop, but then in January I found out it was still going. So after a lot of discussion she said she needed time away. Jean's mother and father came around and they suggested she go down to their caravan at Culburra and stay there for a week. Her sister, Heather, and Heather's boyfriend went down with her and stayed down there. A couple of days later she phoned me up and thanked me for the flowers I'd sent her for her birthday, but she seemed a bit distressed, so I decided to go down and pick her up.'

'Will you tell me what happened when you went to pick her up?'

'At first she didn't want to come home, then she did want to come home, and then she didn't want to come home, so I ended up picking her up and putting her in the car. Then she jumped out of the car, but then she got back in the car again, and we drove off. On the way home, we talked about getting the marriage settled down so we could get the marriage to work out right. Then we got to a place just before Liverpool - I can't remember the name of the place, but it started with 'L' - and stopped at a service station. It was on the Hume Highway. She went to the Ladies toilets while I went to the Gents. When I came out, I went and waited in the car, but after a few minutes had gone by, I thought she seemed to be taking too long in the toilet, so I went and asked the lady behind the desk if she could go and see if there was any problem. When the lady came back from the toilet she told me there was no-one in there.'

'When did you next have contact with Jean?'

'It was about seven o'clock that night. She rang me…no, actually I rang Carl's house to ask him if she was there. He said she'd been there, but was already on her way home. Then he told me that he'd just looked out the window and could see that she was still standing on the beach in front of his house. He then said he would go and pick her up and drive her home. He rang me at eight o'clock and said they were at Auburn, and that Jean was in a distressed state and didn't want to come home. Then I spoke to Jean and she agreed to come home. She eventually arrived home at about midnight.'

'Was she with anyone when she arrived home?'

'Yes, she was with a bloke named Carl Nidi…I think you spell it N-e-i-d-i-n-g.'

'What happened when she returned home?'

'We sat on the lounge and talked for a while. She said she was sorry for everything that had gone wrong, and that we were getting the marriage back on the rails.'

'Was Carl at your house when you were having this conversation with your ex-wife?'

'No.'

'Did you speak to Carl that night when your ex-wife returned?'

'Yes.'

'What was the context of the conversation you had with Carl that night?'

'I said hello to him and thanked him for bringing Jean home and then invited him into the house for a cup of coffee. He said it was too late and that he had to work in the morning and he wanted to go home. Then he left.'

'How long did your ex-wife remain at home prior to leaving you?'

'She left the following day.'

'Did Jean tell you she was going to leave you?'

'No.'

'Do you know where she went?'

'At that stage I had an idea she'd gone back to Carl.'

'Had you met Carl prior to 9 February 1988?'

'Yes.'

'Will you tell me the circumstances under which you met him?'

'I went down to find him, to find out if he was definitely having an affair with my wife. That was in December, and he told me that there was nothing going on, and that they were just friends.'

'Do you recall Carl's address and telephone number?'

'No, I can't remember the name of the street. I only went there once. It was in Bondi.'

'When did you next hear from your ex-wife?'

'It was a couple of weeks later when she phoned home. She told me that she was pregnant, but she told me not to worry because it wasn't mine. I think she asked me how her son was, too. I told her he was doing fine, but that he needed his mum back. She got upset and hung up the phone.'

'When did you next hear from her?'

'It was two or three months later. She asked me how things were, and how her son was again. We started talking, and she hung up again.'

'Did you report your ex-wife as missing to the police?'

'In April I came to the desk at the police station and told one of the young blokes on the desk about her being missing, and he told me that I couldn't report her, and that I would have to get someone from her immediate family, her mother or father, sister or brother to report her missing. I rang Christine Strachan that night and asked her to do it, and she said she would.'

'When, after coming to the police station in April 1988, did you next hear from your ex-wife?'

'She rang up at the end of May, and then the next time would have been either November or December.'

'Can you tell me what the context of those conversations was?'

'In May she rang up to find out how her son was - it was only a short conversation - and in November she rang to tell me she'd had the baby. She said it was a little girl, and she was doing fine, and so was the baby. She told me she had a good job, and that she'd split up with Carl. I asked her to come back home, but she said she wouldn't, and hung up.'

'Were these telephone calls made locally or STD?'

'They were local.'

'Do you know if they were made from public telephones?'

'No. A couple of times you could hear background noises.'

'Did she ever tell you where she was residing?'

'She never said.'

'When was the next time you heard from her after November?'

'It was in April '89, or maybe May. She rang me at home and asked me who the Vietnamese girl was that I was going out with. I told her that she wasn't Vietnamese, and that it was her cousin, and that we were getting divorced. She started screaming and shouting down the phone, so I hung up. That was the last time I spoke to her.'

'Did your ex-wife take her clothing with her when she left on 10 February 1988?'

'She took a couple of bagfuls, and then she came back the following day and took some more.'

'Did she take other personal effects, such as jewellery and make up?'

'Yes.'

'Have you seen your ex-wife since she left on 10 February 1988?'

'No.'

'Has your ex-wife, to your knowledge, returned to your house since 10 February 1988?'

'She's been back on a couple of occasions.'

'On what occasions did your ex-wife return to your house?'

'One was in May of '88, and she left her wedding ring and engagement ring behind on the table next to an ashtray in the lounge room. Stuff in the cupboards had been moved, but I didn't notice anything missing. The next time would have been the end of June '89. There were Alpine cigarette butts in the ashtray. She's the only one I know who smokes them, and she still had the key to get in. She must have only had the back door key because the time before, she left the front door key with the rings.'

'Was anything missing from the house on the occasion in June '89?'

'No, nothing.'

'Had any personal effects been disturbed?'

'No.'

'Do you know if anyone else has heard from or seen your ex-wife since she left you on 10 February 1988?'

'She has been in contact with Christine, her mum, at least once. They arranged a meeting, but she never kept the appointment. And one of her friends, Jenny Solo. She works in a fruit and veg shop in Emerton. She said she'd seen her in the shopping centre. My mum seen her down in the shopping centre. Dad seen her in the laneway near the school. She rang up Mum when I was in Manila. I can't think of anybody else.'

'Do you hold any fears for your ex-wife's safety?'

'No.'

'Is there anything further you can tell us relating to your missing ex-wife?'

'No.'

'Did you ever threaten your ex-wife because of her affair with Carl?'

'No.'

'Did you assault your ex-wife because of her affair with Carl?'

'No.'

'I have been told you dug a number of large holes in your backyard. Can you tell me if this is true?'

'Yes.'

'Will you tell me when you dug the holes, and for what purposes?'

'The last one was when I changed the motor of the van, four or five months ago. I dug a hole in the corner of the front fence and side fence at the back. Threw the old motor in it. There's another one down near the back gate. There's a sink, part of a gate, some metal items and lumps of concrete in that. There's one behind the garage where I used to mix compost and stuff, up near the goose pen. I dug a trench for the telephone cable, too. That went from the side of the house to the garage.'

'Is there anything further you wish to tell us about this matter?'

'No.'

I finished reading the Record of Interview and put it down on my desk. 'What do you think?' I asked Mick.

'Well, at least he confirmed he buried stuff in his backyard,' Mick replied. 'Should be enough for us to get a warrant. Anyway, I'll take him back to the cells.'

Leaning back in my chair, I knotted my hands at the back of my head and closed my eyes. Everything we'd discovered played over and over in my head. Something wasn't sitting right. 'Come on,' I thought to myself. What's wrong here? What are we missing? Re-reading the Record of Interview, several points stood out.

Point 1: I wasn't comfortable with Jean returning to the house. If Fiona and Shona had told the truth, then why would she risk going back to the house? Not only that, Keir had stated that Jean had come back more than once. If she felt her life was in danger, she'd be mad to return to the house once, let alone multiple times.

Point 2: If she was starting a new life, why come back and leave the rings, the only things of value she possessed?

Point 3: Keir told Mick that Jean had rung Christine, but Christine had never mentioned the phone call.

Point 4: The Chalmers girls said Jean was using contraceptive pills. Keir may not have known about the pills, but there was only a slim chance she could've gotten pregnant to some other bloke.

Mick and Clarkey returned from taking Keir back to the cells. 'Boys,' I said as I tapped the Record of Interview on my desk. 'He reckons Jean was pregnant, but one of her friends just told me she was on the Pill.'

There was something else in the statement I'd missed at first but then realised afterwards Keir had mentioned all the things he'd buried in his yard, except for one thing. Now my epiphany refined itself. 'Oi, fellas. He confirmed he buried everything that Wormleaton told us; all except for the forty-four-gallon drum! And I'll tell you why: Jean's body is in it!' At that moment, the phone rang, rudely interrupting my vision. I picked it up.

'Yep, yep. No worries,' I said, and put the phone back down.

'What is it?' Mick asked.

'Denise Wilkes is downstairs.'

'I've got this one,' said Clarkey, already moving towards the door.

'So what else did you find out?' Mick asked as he sat down next to my desk.

'I got a hold of Fiona Chalmers and Shona McDonald, and listen to this…they both told me they reckon Keir had something to do with Jean's disappearance, and that it was totally out of character for her not to contact them. They both independently confirmed that Jean had said Tom would kill her if she ever tried to leave him. I'll arrange for the local Ds to take statements.'

'Well,' Mick said with more excitement in his voice than he'd had in days. 'With what we've got from the neighbours, and now this, I'll have a chat with the Boss and see what he reckons about getting a search warrant. I don't know about you, but I'm stuffed. When Clarkey's done with Mrs Wilkes, I reckon we call it a night.'

Clarkey returned about half an hour later, sprinting across the Ds office waving Denise Wilkes' statement back and forth in his right hand. He grinned broadly as he reached my desk and slammed her statement down between Mick and myself. 'Have a read of this, guys!'

I picked it up and started to read. Clarkey couldn't control his excitement, shifting his weight from foot to foot like a little kid needing to go to the toilet. It was more than a little distracting, and to make matters even worse, I'd barely begun reading before he started asking me questions.

'What do you make of it?' he said.

I shot him a look, the one that says, 'I'll let you know when you shut up and let me read,' but I couldn't leave Clarkey standing there like a kid who's drunk several gallons of red cordial, so I commented as I read, my visions of a backyard now making perfect sense.

'So she moved into Keir's house in February 1990 and says there was a "rotten meat" and a "real dead" smell coming from her son's bedroom. Hmmm. Tell you what concerns me most is the brown stains on the bedroom wall. If they were dots or smear marks, they could be blood splatter. What the hell is this! Her dog would bring clumps of hair from under the house! It had bones that she hadn't given to it! Christine mentioned bones being in the backyard too! Shit! You don't think the dog found the body?'

'Dunno,' Mick said. 'Doesn't look very good.'

Our weariness now gave way to a new wave of excitement and hope. We packed up our gear for the night, and looked forward to tomorrow with a renewed sense of purpose; our biggest lead had just presented itself. Tomorrow was also Keir's first appearance at Westmead Coroner's Court, and we hoped like hell he'd be refused bail on Rosalina's murder charge. The bastard must have known we were onto him about Jean and, if he was granted bail, we were sure he was going to do a runner.

The next day, we took him from the holding cells and down to the court. When we arrived, we found out that the usual Coroner, John Hiatt, was away, and another magistrate was filling in.

'Fuck ol' Daisy,' we thought to ourselves, this being one of Mick's favourite sayings, knowing that this would increase his chance of getting bail.

Keir had originally had no legal representation, which would have worked in our favour, but there was a local Penrith solicitor who'd agreed to represent him. Mick was a little late getting into the courtroom because he'd been down to talk to Dr Little beforehand, as she was yet to do the autopsy on Rosalina's body.

The Coroner went through all the formalities. We felt more and more confident. We were sure he wasn't going to get bail, and then…

'Conditional bail will be granted. Set at $75,000.'

Our jaws dropped in unison. We were horrified; the difficultly of our task had just increased a thousandfold.

'How the bloody hell did they grant him bail?' I thought to myself. Stacked and weighed, all the evidence pointed to him being guilty. Cursing the outcome, we all shook our heads in disbelief but, just as we thought the whole thing had fallen apart, we caught a break. Keir had to raise the money, and would be taken to the Metropolitan Remand Centre at Long Bay Gaol until he could.

Time now became a luxury we didn't have, and the next day the Ds office was going bananas. Blokes raced to and fro like they were on fast forward collecting files, briefs, statements, evidence, everything we needed to snag Keir before he made bail. Mick and I were called into Mick O'Connell's office to brief him on everything.

'G'day, boys,' O'Connell said as we walked in. 'I've just received a faxed copy of Shona McDonald's statement,' he said, handing it to Mick. 'It makes bloody interesting reading, fellas.'

Whilst Mick was reading, I told the boss about Keir's burying habits.

'Well, get a friggin' warrant and dig the place up! Mick, get on to Homicide and get them out there to help out. We don't want any stuff-ups, or anyone giving us any bloody dramas. Probably best to get the Rescue Squad out there too, to make sure the dig's conducted properly. There are more than enough blokes in here today to give you a hand. Tee up Forensics to be there too. Pete, give Dave Hurst a buzz.'

Like I said, the Boss was a no-nonsense guy! 'Yeah, no worries. I'll call them now and put them on standby. What's in Shona's statement?'

'Pretty much everything you told us about Tom threatening to kill Jean if she left,' Mick said, still reading the statement. When he was done, he handed it to me. It painted a chilling picture of a tormented relationship, of a woman trapped in a living hell. Keir had tried to take total control of every aspect of Jean's life, to the point where she felt like she was going crazy. I finished reading the statement and looked across the desk toward O'Connell, who was staring out the window.

'This prick's done 'em both!' he exclaimed with an unfamiliar ferociousness in his voice. 'We just have to find Jean's body to prove it! Get that warrant, boys!

We called the Clerk of the Court, who put us through to Sean McCosker, the Chamber Magistrate who ran the court office, and who was the authority to authorise all search warrants for the police. McCosker told us there was sufficient evidence for the granting of a warrant to *search the grounds of the Keir house, Wilkes Crescent, Tregear, for the body of Jean Angela Keir.*

It disturbed me she was referred to as such. She should've been referred to as Jean Angela *Strachan*. Why should a woman who had, seemingly, been murdered by her husband still have to carry his name? Aside from that, she'd received nothing but grief and a cutting short of her life. The only good thing she'd ever gained from Thomas Keir was a son, but now that son would have to go through life knowing he'd lost *two* mothers.

With the warrant granted, Mick and I went back to the Ds' Office, where the Rescue Squad was already giving a briefing on how they would go about things. There was a bloke there, Col Kelson, who'd worked with me when I'd first joined the cops down at Blacktown. Col was an ex-sailor, and in the navy the guys at the bottom, like the apprentices, were called 'pursers'. Col had worked his way right to the top, but 'Pussa', the bastardised version of 'purser', had stuck. Now, Pussa was a top bloke who called a spade a spade, and a quality Rescue operator. He had rugged facial features, with slightly wavy dark hair. He was your typical seaman, with tattooed arms and, whilst he was only of medium build, he was very fit from his Rescue training. Standing at five foot nine, he was a real 'man's man', encapsulated by his raspy voice that rarely minced words. I reckoned there must have been a lot of people around Sydney who owed their lives to Pussa and his rescue efforts, and therefore his opinion on how to conduct the dig would be vital.

'Pussa, what's the best way of doing this?' I asked him after the briefing.

'Pete, I reckon it's best if we use long crowbars to dig into the ground. We'll make holes all over the place and, if there's a body buried, the smell will come straight to the surface. Mate, it's pretty unmistakeable. If we find something, we'll know it quick smart.'

The dig started at 3.30 pm on 16 April 1991, and Wilkes Crescent became a hive of activity once more, the sight of the large Police Rescue truck causing the neighbourhood children to gather around for a closer look. It was bloody funny watching Pussa trying to work with a thousand kids swarming around him like flies.

'What's this?' 'What's that?' they asked as they trailed along behind and beside him. To his credit, Pussa was a patient bloke, and answered all their questions with good humour. Along with the kids, the media had flocked to the scene, and now took up every vantage point as they leant over Max Wormleaton's fence filming every move.

As I watched on, I began to empathise with Jean's father, Clifford. I felt removed from everything, and it was *me* watching the TV. It was *my* house, and they were looking for *my* daughter. I shook and trembled. I became filled with a sense of utter hatred, angry that something so precious to me had been snatched away. I pictured Ashleigh as a grown woman who'd married a monster, my little girl's hopes, dreams, and aspirations all snuffed out in an instant because of one psychopath's insane jealousy. I recovered my composure, and wondered how I would cope if it *was* me.

The Rescue Squad started making their preliminary examinations. Pussa began by driving huge crowbars into any uneven parts of the grass. The rest of us stood on the perimeter of the yard and tried to keep out of the way. Hours later, we'd still found nothing.

'We're gonna have to get a backhoe in,' the Boss said. 'Otherwise we'll be here all friggin' night!'

Mick queried the Boss as to the likelihood of organising a backhoe, whereupon the Boss responded by telling him to look in the phone book and ring around. My opinion was that a local bloke would jump at the chance to help the cops. Sure enough, we found a bloke, and he arrived not long after, his large yellow backhoe lumbering loudly down the street. The neighbourhood kids went nuts again, whilst their parents and the other residents hung from their front porches trying to get a better view of proceedings.

I opened the Colorbond gates and watched as the driver drove the backhoe in from Wilkes Crescent up the double lines of concrete that made up the driveway. I was a little worried he might bash into the fence but the bloke managed to squeeze the backhoe through the gates with only a few centimetres to spare on either side. He manoeuvred his way to the back of the yard and began digging, quickly excavating to a depth of about five to six feet. Technology soon started to tell the tale.

We found the car engine, and my eyes lit up with anticipation. I could feel the excitement, but I couldn't shake the sickly sensations, which only intensified now I'd seen photographs of Jean. I envisaged her as a young girl brimming with life, and then imagined what she'd look like now after three years stuffed inside a drum. I could almost smell the body.

I knew from experience that for the first day or so, there wasn't an overly distinctive smell but any longer, especially in hot weather, and a body really started to get ripe. It's a rotten smell that stays up your nose, just like cigarette smells stay on your clothes. I started to think about other bodies I'd seen, and how they'd started to bloat, and how, when gravity took effect, the blood pooled at the lowest point of the body.

I watched as the backhoe continued moving slowly backwards, digging up the yard in a sweeping motion as it went. I was right; the driver was having a ball working for the cops. Dressed in a blue-and-pink-striped shirt, he had a huge grin on his face. He'd dig up a section, and then carefully replace the dirt before moving on to the next section. Pussa, who was around six feet tall, could have stood in the holes he was digging and only his head and shoulders would have been visible.

Blocks of concrete, car panels, wire gates; we'd found everything else that had been mentioned, but there was still no sign of the drum. We were just starting to feel a little dejected when one of the Homicide Ds noticed that there was a disturbed section of grass between the garage and Wormleaton's property. When they dug it up, they found a yellow rag with what appeared to be a bloodstain on it.

Night came, and the driver continued working under several generator lights, as well as the lights on his backhoe. He only had a small area to go now, and our faces lit up; surely we were about to find the drum. We didn't.

'Bugger it,' I thought. I'd been certain of what we were going to find, and it was a truly empty feeling to have watched them search for so long, only to find nothing.

However, there was still one section, down the side of the house, adjacent to Max Wormleaton's property, that was too tight for the backhoe. It was a long, thin strip of grass that stood out in stark contrast to the rest of the yard. It was flanked by the fence on one side and the house on the other, and there was an orange tree at the far end. Wandering down there, Mick began to look around. He lay down on his stomach and took a good look under the house. He had a little scratch around, but couldn't find anything so, picking himself up, he headed back towards the main part of the yard and joined the rest of the boys.

'No sign of the drum,' said Mick dejectedly.

I had another epiphany. 'No, mate, but I bet my balls that the drum *was* here and the bastard's moved it. No prizes for guessing why.'

'Well, we can't have you losing your balls, Pete, can we? The backhoe can't get into that section I looked at, so we'll let him finish what he's doing and then we'll call it a night.'

Despite my disappointment, and desire to close the case, I was glad to hear those words. I just wanted to get home and hold my daughter. 'Is the boss okay about how things went?' I asked, because if he wasn't, it was going to be another long night.

'Yeah, mate, he's fine. He just wishes we'd found that bloody drum.'

We told the driver he was done for the night, so he manoeuvred his machine back out onto the street and into the waiting crowd. The media, seeing that the backhoe was leaving, decided to pack it in too. As for the rest of us, we all headed back to the station to have a chat about what needed doing over the next few days.

When the briefing began, I knew I shouldn't have been annoyed with what I was hearing, but I was fuming. Not finding the drum meant Jean's disappearance would be put on the backburner. It was no longer our main priority. Our best chance of gaining a conviction was with Rosalina's death. Our focus was to establish the true context of their relationship, and Keir's motives. I consoled myself with the knowledge that we could get him on Jean's murder once he was safely squared away in jail for killing Rosalina. Something in my soul told me that Rosalina's death would help us solve Jean's disappearance. She couldn't speak to us in life, but she would speak to us in death.

The briefing came to an end. I could sense that some of the others' enthusiasm, buoyed by expectations of finding the drum, was now draining away like sap from a tree, but for me the fires of desire burned more brightly than ever. I made myself yet another coffee and walked back to my desk. Ever since I'd stepped into Clifford's shoes, I'd wanted to ring home and make sure Ashleigh was safe. I phoned Sue, and she reassured me that my little girl was fine.

Comforted, I sat and stared blankly around the office. I couldn't help but think of Keir's son. The poor little fella had been embroiled in all of this through no fault of his own. Keir had dragged his son into his sick world, and it made me despise him all the more. What kind of man kills his wife with his son still in the house? What kind of a man raises a child in the same house where he killed the kid's mum and then buried her in the backyard? What kind of man marries again and brings his second wife to live in the same house in which he'd murdered his first wife? I felt sick to the stomach, and then I heard one of the boys yell out, 'Pete, pizza's here!'

I wasn't sure I wanted any, but I dragged myself up from my chair and made my way over to the meals room. I could hear the boys tossing jokes around about how Keir should be grateful: he'd had his lawn aerated for free, and it was going to be a lot better than before. One bloke even said that we should close the station and become landscapers. It sounded callous to make light of what was a very serious situation, but we needed to let off steam. The frustration of the case was boring into us like termites into a length of timber.

The boys tucked into the pizzas, and I allowed myself a wry smile at their jokes, but I couldn't shake the thoughts of Jean from my mind. I forced myself to have a slice or two and, as I ate, I worked through what I needed to do over the next couple of days. Tomorrow, I'd talk to the Strachans again in an effort to get more contact details for Jean's closest friends. The ones I'd spoken to so far had proved invaluable. By building a profile of Jean and Tom's marriage, I knew I'd discover how he'd killed her.

SEVEN BONES

CHAPTER 7
The True Motive Uncovered?

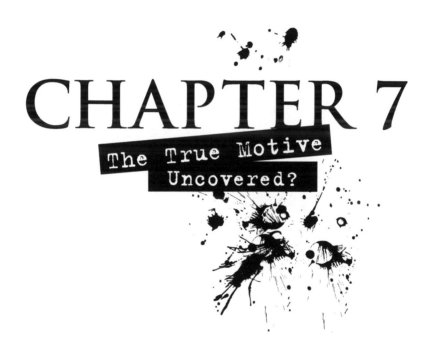

Driving home from the station, I couldn't fathom what Keir had done; if he'd truly loved Jean, and Rosalina for that matter, how could he kill them? Till death do us part, they say; Keir had taken that a little too literally.

How was I going to find her? It seemed impossible. Negativity had begun to creep in as the magnitude of what I was up against became clear. I was searching for the proverbial needle in a haystack. I was almost home when I let out a deep sigh. In reality, we had Buckley's chance of finding Jean.

Suddenly, those familiar sensations washed over me like water over the banks of a flooded river: I wasn't alone. I looked at the passenger seat. No-one. I looked in the rear seats. No-one. I pulled into my driveway, and the sensations instantly evaporated. I made my way inside, and headed straight for Ashleigh's room. Silently, I opened her door and peered in. She looked like a little angel, sound asleep. Tiptoeing over to her bed so as not to wake her, I bent down and kissed her on the forehead, then made my way out of my daughter's room and headed for our bedroom. Sue stirred as I bent down and kissed her.

'Is everything OK?' she said, sensing something amiss in my demeanour.

'Yeah, I'm just tired that's all.'

I lay flat on my back and knotted my hands behind my head. Sue cuddled up to me and rested her head on my chest. Considering my advanced state of fatigue, I thought I would fall asleep straight away, but I didn't. I lay there for ages, thoughts racing through my mind. Everything, every shred of evidence, played on the whiteness of the ceiling like a movie projector. Again and again, I replayed everything I'd seen and thought I knew. Eventually, I drifted off, but my sleep was fitful, the type when you know you've slept but you feel like you haven't.

I was up and out the door pretty quickly the next morning, and as I drove to work, I felt a little apprehensive, but the trip passed without incident. I walked into the office at about eight and made straight for the meals room to make my umpteenth cup of coffee in the last few days. Just then, Mick Lyons walked into the room. 'Mate, we might just get Christine Strachan in here to make a statement about Jean and Tom. Whaddya reckon?' he said.

Mick had read my mind. 'Sounds good to me,' I said, happy in the knowledge that whilst the other officers were otherwise occupied on Rosalina's murder, I could count on Mick to keep pushing with Jean's. I'd seen a tear in his eye when Christine and Clifford had realised that the most likely possibility was that their daughter was dead, and I knew that, like me, he'd never rest until we put Keir behind bars. 'I was going to go around and have a chat with her today anyway,' I continued. 'I'll give her a call and ask her to come in. It'll be interesting to see what she says about the marriage, considering what Fiona and Shona said. From what they told us, Keir was a real bastard to Jean. I wouldn't have blamed her for taking off, but I'm bloody sure that's not what happened.'

Later that morning, Christine Strachan arrived at the station, and Mick took her to the interview room so that they wouldn't be disturbed. When Mick was done, we walked her to the foyer and thanked her for coming down. She smiled that smile of hers, and we watched her walk to her car. When she was gone, we went back inside and made our way back to our desks. Just before we sat down, Mick said, 'I think you'd better have a read of this, mate.'

I took Christine's statement from him and thumbed through it, eight pages all up. We couldn't speak to Jean about what had happened so, thinking that she surely must have confided in her mother, I began to read with interest. The affair had come about after Jean had decided she needed a day away. She'd told Tom she was going for a job interview. Instead, she went to the foreshore near the Opera House and sat down on Mrs Macquarie's Chair, staring out across the harbour, watching the ferries ply their way from the Heads towards Circular Quay as she contemplated how her life had gotten to this point. Just then, Carl Neiding had happened to walk past and, upon seeing her sitting by herself looking so sad and lonely, had asked her if she was okay. He sat down beside her and they began to talk. They walked into the Botanic Gardens, took some tea, and talked some more. Eventually, they drove to Carl's flat in Bondi and had sex.

When she returned home, Jean went straight around to her mum's house and told her everything. 'Tom doesn't need to know,' Christine said. 'You mustn't do anything that will wreck your marriage.'

Jean went home, but as soon as Tom came home from work, she promptly spilled her heart out. 'I went to Sydney today, and met a man named Carl. I feel really guilty, and I have to tell you; we had sex in his flat at Bondi.'

Tom flew into an uncontrollable rage and grabbed her arms and demanded to know where Carl's flat was. Jean struggled to get free, screaming at Tom to let her go, but his grip tightened, and he told her that she'd better tell him or he would kill her there and then. She told him the general area in order to get him to stop, and he let her go.

The next day, he went to work and went straight up to Christine. She said he looked pale and expressionless. 'Jeannie told me about that fella, and where he lives,' he said. 'Don't try and stop me. I'm going to find him tonight and break his neck.'

'How can you find him?' Christine replied. 'He lives in a block of flats in Bondi.'

Christine's stomach churned with the thought that Jean had told Tom what had happened, and she feared what he'd do.

'If necessary, I'll burn down the blocks of flats. I'll get the bastard.'

Christine left work and went straight to Jean's to try to convince her to tell Tom that what she'd said about the affair was just a lie. She found Jean at home, and said, 'Tom was furious today. He's going to do something really bad, I can feel it. You have to tell him that the whole thing was just a lie.'

Christine's pleading convinced Jean. 'Okay, Mum,' she agreed. 'I'll tell him I made it all up just because I wanted to make him jealous.'

'Give me a call and let me know how it goes,' Christine said before kissing her daughter and leaving the house.

That night, Christine's phone rang. Eagerly anticipating news of how her daughter had fared, she was surprised to hear Tom's voice on the other end. 'What are you ringing me for?' Christine asked. 'Is everything alright?'

'I'm in Bondi looking for Carl,' he replied.

Scared out of her wits, Christine tried to convince him not to do anything silly. 'How do you know where he lives? You'll never find him.'

'I'll ask around, knock on doors.'

'Tom, you must come home. Jean told me this afternoon that she made the whole thing up.'

'Why would she do that?'

'I don't know; she's confused about your marriage, and maybe she just wanted to make you jealous or something. She's just said something dumb; come home and talk to her about it.'

The lie was complete, and Tom calmed down, but Jean repeatedly confided in her mum that she couldn't stop thinking about Carl. Over the next two weeks, she called Carl four times, begging him to see her again. He was understandably hesitant, and told her he didn't want to get involved with a married woman, but Jean was insistent and he eventually consented. They met again, but Carl became more and more uneasy about the situation and told Jean he was going to drive her home. She made him drop her at Granville Station, and then made her own way home from there. The lie, despite its initial success, hadn't worked, and Tom was still furious. He drove her to Bondi, and forced her to tell him where Carl lived. She did, but said she didn't know the number of the flat, so Tom began knocking on doors until he found someone who knew which flat was Carl's. Tom then went back to the car, where Jean was waiting nervously, and drove home. The next night, he drove to Carl's flat with the intention of 'punching his head in'.

Later, when we spoke to Carl, we found out that he'd come home from work to find a man sitting on the front fence outside his block of flats. Tom came over to him and said, 'Are you Carl?'

'Yes,' he replied.

Confronted by a far larger man than he, Keir completely backed down and tamely said, 'Well, I'm Tom. Jean's husband. Can we talk?'

Carl agreed, and he and Tom went inside. As they sat and talked, Tom relayed his marriage problems to Carl, and told him that he knew about the affair. 'Jean said she wants to leave me. I can't let that happen. Seeing as how she confided in you, I thought you might be able to talk to her and convince her not to leave me.'

Carl felt sorry for Tom, and agreed to talk to Jean. He handed the phone to Tom and told him to call her. When she answered, he said, 'It's Tom. I'm at Carl's flat.'

Jean was horrified. 'Is...everything...okay?' she stuttered.

'Yes, everything's fine. Carl said he wants to talk to you. I'll put him on.' With that, he handed the phone to Carl.

'You know, you really should try and sort things out with your husband. Tom really wants to make your marriage work.'

'I'll try,' was all Jean said before hanging up the phone. She was alone in her house, terrified about what Tom might do to Carl and, even worse, what he would do to her when he got home. Tom stayed at Carl's for another three hours, telling him that he wasn't brave enough to do anything physical about it, but he was talking to Carl to try and make him stay away from Jean.

Christine found out about the visit when Tom talked to her at work the next day.

'I went to Carl's place last night,' he told her. 'I went there to punch his head in, but we ended up talking for three hours, in between cups of tea.'

'What did you talk to him about?' Christine asked nervously.

'It was mostly about Jean and our marriage. Carl told me Jeannie was a very depressed and confused young lady.'

'I'll talk to her myself, and see if I can make her see sense and to not have anything to do with Carl,' Christine said, hoping to placate the stony-faced Tom. She called her daughter later that day. 'You mustn't speak to this Carl again for the sake of your marriage.'

'Mum!' Jean replied sternly. 'Stay out of this! I can't stand being married to Tom, and Carl is special. I can talk to him, which is more than I can do with Tom.'

'I don't care, Jeannie. You're married to Tom, and that's what matters. Think of your son.'

Jean became upset now. 'Why do you always take Tom's side? Why can't you ever see things from my point of view?' she said, before hanging up on her mother.

Over the next few months, the situation between Tom and Jean deteriorated even further. Carl, thinking that it was better if he wasn't around, and somewhat spooked by Tom's visit, decided to take a trip to Malaysia, as he'd often done before. Back in Tregear, there were more and more arguments about Carl, wherein Jean would scream at Tom and tell him she was leaving. The arguments increased in intensity, and Tom became more and more violent towards his wife.

It was January 1988 when she phoned her mum one night. 'Mum, Tom and I had another argument and he punched me in the face. He hit me so hard it knocked me down the hallway and I wet myself.'

'What?' Christine cried down the phone. 'What were you arguing about? Are you alright?'

'Yeah, I'm okay now. I got back up and punched him back. He's gone to bed. Mum, I can't take much more of this.'

'Do you want me to come over?'

'No, it's okay. I'll talk to you tomorrow.'

'Don't worry, Jeannie. I'll speak to Tom tomorrow and sort him out.'

The next day, Christine confronted Tom at work, giving him the tongue-lashing of an angry mother. 'Jean told me you punched her last night. How dare you!'

'I only pushed her and she got up and hit me,' Tom argued.

'I don't care! You told me you would always take care of her! You told me you'd never do anything to hurt her, and you lied! You should never hit a woman; don't ever do it again!'

Whilst Christine was berating Tom, Jean finally decided to talk to Clifford about things, and went around to her parents' house. As she sat on the lounge, she looked up at her father with desperation in her eyes. 'Dad, I need to get away and spend some time alone.'

Clifford looked at his nervous, emaciated wreck of a daughter and, he would later tell me, his heart shattered. 'Go down to the caravan at Culburra and stay with your sister. Get your head together and decide what you want to do. You know I will always look after you, no matter what you decide.' He put his arms around her and hugged her ever so gently, scared that he'd break her in two.

Christine said that Jean had agreed to the idea of going to the caravan, and made plans with Heather for both of them to spend a week down the coast. Jean confronted Tom and told him she needed some time alone to get her head together. Tom consented, but told Jean there was no way their son was going with her.

I put Christine's statement down. It had got me thinking. 'This is what blokes like Tom Keir don't get. They become so possessive they don't realise that all they're doing, ultimately, is driving their woman into the arms of another man. They invest so much time and energy into making sure their wife doesn't leave them that eventually the one thing they are trying to prevent becomes inevitable.'

I re-read Fiona Chalmers' statement to see what matched with Christine's. Both women had said the sparkle in Jean's eyes had gone. Both had said she'd begun to listen to her favourite song, *The Rose*, by Bette Midler, more and more.

I wondered which of the lyrics she thought best summed up her life.

Some say love, it is a river that drowns the tender reed.

Was she the tender reed and Keir's jealously the river?

Some say love, it is a razor that leaves your soul to bleed.

Was her soul bleeding from his psychopathic razor?

Both her mum and her best friend had said her stunning smile had evaporated and her body had become gaunt and withdrawn. Fiona had also stated that she'd visited Jean at home one day and noticed bruises on her arm. Jean spent so much time trying to protect everyone else by not telling them the truth but she eventually broke down and told Fiona everything, which Fiona then told me. Tom would become enraged when Jean had friends over. She would argue back that if he let her go out with her friends then they wouldn't have to come over all the time. Tom would fly into fits of rage, slap her around, grab her by the arms and shake her.

Fiona's statement revealed more and more horrors.

Revelation number one: Tom was trying to drive Jean crazy by tying her up and forcing her to have sex with him.

Revelation number two: He'd hide in the hallway and jump out to frighten Jean. She'd sit in the lounge room and he'd go outside and peer at her through the window. He'd come back inside and she'd confront him. Tom would deny everything and accuse her of making up stories.

Fiona said that she'd passed on her concerns to Shona and Maria, and the three girls had later noticed that the bruises on Jean's arms had become more frequent and more pronounced. As time went by, Jean finally opened up and told her friends how truly depressed she was, and how Tom was gambling away all their money. Christine confirmed this, and told me Jean was embarrassed that her mum had to pay some of the household bills, something that became a major bone of contention between Jean and Tom.

Her friends told her she had to leave. She'd agree, but then say she couldn't leave her son, because Tom would never let him go. She said that he'd told her, 'If you leave me, I'll cut you up and feed you to the dogs.'

Exacerbated, I put the statements down, leant back in my chair and let out a deep sigh. I just couldn't believe what I was reading. I'd dealt with dozens of domestic violence cases before, but nothing as bizarre as this. I picked Fiona's statement up again and was flicking through it when suddenly I found something I'd missed, something that sickened me to the core. Fiona was the only one who'd been brave enough to still go to the house knowing that she had to keep up her presence to show Tom there were people who cared for Jean's welfare. On the final night she went there, Keir's son was crying, and Tom slapped his face as hard as he could. Fiona was appalled. The child's crying increased, and Tom merely laughed. Then he started to mimic his son by screaming with him. Fiona said this was the moment that confirmed this man was a monster. She promised herself she'd do everything she could to get Jean and her son away from him.

There were several things I wanted to clarify, so I rang Fiona and asked her to confirm that she'd actually heard Tom threaten Jean.

'Sure he did,' Fiona said. 'He'd say things like, "If Jean ever left me, I'd cut her up and feed her to the dogs."'

'Did he say this more than once?' I asked.

'Oh, yes, he said it all the time! I even heard him say, "It's easy to dispose of a body. You cut the flesh off, feed it to the dogs, grind the bones down and use them as fertiliser and then you burn the hair. You know, cops are idiots. They only solve crimes if people are stupid enough to open their mouths."'

I thanked Fiona for her assistance, put the phone down and shook my head in astonishment. I knew I had to put this man behind bars.

CHAPTER 8

Loose Lips
Sink Ships

I read over the reports and statements again and again and again. There was one other thing in Keir's statement that just didn't sit. 'Some time' in May, Jean must have come home, he'd said, because he'd found her wedding and engagement rings left on the coffee table in the lounge room. It seemed entirely implausible. She feared, with every justification, that her husband would kill her. Why would she return with the distinct possibility of him being there? Why return the only valuables she possessed?

Fitting the pieces of the puzzle together was like trying to shove a square block into a circular hole. There were dozens of inconsistencies, but I didn't have enough evidence to make a charge stick. I needed a break. I needed something to blow the whole thing wide open. Meanwhile, I consoled myself with the fact we'd get him for Rosalina.

Unable to make bail for the time being, Keir was transferred from the Coroner's Court to Long Bay Gaol whilst his family and solicitor set about trying to find the $75,000 required. We prayed that they wouldn't.

Keir was now thirty-three, and had never been in gaol before. It must have been a daunting prospect, and I wondered what went through his mind as he walked through the processing area and was given his green inmate's uniform and taken to his cell.

The first inmate he came into contact with was a guy called Joseph Perkins, although it would take us some time to discover his identity. According to Perkins, he wasn't in the cell when Keir arrived, and it wasn't until Keir was taken out into the exercise yard of Wing 5 that he met his new cell mate. Perkins was still a young man, but had a lengthy history of convictions. Perkins said it was he who initiated contact with Keir, because he wanted to meet the new guy to 'check him out, to see what his "go" was.'

It was midmorning when he spotted Keir standing conspicuously on his own off to one side of the yard. He sidled up to him and asked the first question any prisoner asks another:

'What are you in for, mate?'

'Murder,' Keir replied quietly.

'Shit, ay. Do you want a cuppa?'

Keir nodded.

'We'll go to the cell and make one then, ay?' The two men walked back to the cell, and while Perkins made coffee, he continued to quiz Keir. 'So what's going to happen to your missus now you're in here?'

'That's why I'm here. They charged me with murdering my second missus.'

'Your second missus?' Perkins said suspiciously. 'What happened to the first one?' Keir moved towards Perkins, gesturing for him to come closer. 'What I'm about to say is never to be repeated, you understand?'

Perkins nodded.

'I got rid of me missus.'

Perkins looked at him dubiously. 'Sure, mate. Every bloke has gotten rid of a missus at some stage in their lives.'

'No, mate, you don't get it. She's gone. I got rid of her. She's dead. I bashed her, then I choked her, and then I buried her standing up under the back corner of the house. Yeah, the cops are trying to pin that one on me too, but they won't be able to.'

Perkins was aghast at Keir's openness, but tried to keep a blank face. He told us later that he wasn't sure what to make of things. Perhaps Keir was trying to establish a name as a bit of a hard-arse. 'So, she's just there lying under your house?' Perkins pushed.

'No, I told you. She's not lying there, I buried her upright.'

Keir then left the cell, while Perkins stayed and finished his cuppa, wondering whether Keir was a bullshit artist or not. Then he went back out into the yard to find his mate, Brian Riley, who was in for a rape charge, which he strenuously denied. He eventually spotted Riley in the middle of the yard. Both men, athletic in build from their time in the prison gym, Perkins with sandy brown shoulder-length hair and Riley with the same length hair but darker, stood in the centre of the yard and looked around them like two schoolboys keeping watch for the teacher while they snuck a smoke. Perkins scanned the area for Keir and then, certain he wasn't nearby, began to speak. 'Riles, I've got a bit of a story for you here. This new bloke just came in, he reckons he murdered his missus and then got rid of her body.'

'You're bullshittin' me,' Riley said quietly.

'Nah, mate, I fuckin' swear. He just told me. I dunno if I believe him, but that's what he said. He reckons he bashed and choked her and then buried her under the house, but the cops ain't got enough to charge him for it.'

Riley's mind began to work overtime. His bail hearing was on 9 May, and because he'd already breached his bail once it was unlikely this new application would be approved. Here was his chance to do a deal.

The next day, Riley saw Keir standing alone in the yard, holding a cup of tea in his hand. Riley walked up to Keir, looked around to make sure there was no-one in earshot, and went straight into it. 'Where's your wife? What's going on?'

'I dunno. I haven't seen her. I only spoke to her on the phone a couple of years ago,' Keir fumbled.

'You're bullshittin'. You knocked her. Mate, it's okay. Perko told me what you told him. If I can tell you where the body is, will you tell us what's going on?'

'I don't know what you're talking about,' Keir protested.

'You put her underneath the house,' Riley pushed.

Keir began to shake, and he spilt his tea. Riley continued to push. 'See, see. I know. See.'

'I don't know what you're talking about.'

'Don't treat me like a git; tell us what's going on. Did you have a blue or something? Was she fucking around on you?'

The anger now swelled in Keir, and the words tumbled out before he could stop them. 'Yeah, I found out she was cheating on me. I had a blue with her and I strangled her and buried her under the house.'

Riley now had his piece of gold, but the only question was, what to do with it? On the one hand, it would certainly help his bail application, but on the other hand, if it was refused and the other inmates found out he'd dobbed, he'd be branded a 'dog', and his life on the inside would be made a living hell. Nah, the opportunity was too good to pass up, he decided, so he went down to the screws and asked to make a phone call.

Whilst this was going on, I'd been down to see Keir myself. Part of the investigation involved me serving an Occupier's Notice to the lawful occupier, Keir, for the search warrant from 16 April. I met him in the interview area, and as I sat down at the table I couldn't help but wonder how he'd been getting on here in Long Bay. I knew that there was a pecking order amongst prisoners, a pyramid of sorts, which ran as follows:

At the bottom were the paedophiles and/or child murderers. Many inmates had kids of their own, and to even the hardest of hard cases, doing anything to a child was simply unacceptable. I'd heard stories of what prisoners did to these guys, one of them involving placing barbed wire inside a length of PVC pipe, shoving it up the sex offender's backside and then pulling the pipe out, leaving the bloke to get the barbed wire out himself. This was why these guys had to be isolated, and very rarely found themselves in the general prison population.

Next up you had rapists. Whilst they hadn't done anything to a child, in the minds of prisoners who also had wives and girlfriends, harming a woman wasn't on, either.

It continued upwards, with the armed robbers and murderers usually occupying the top spots, especially lifers who had nothing to lose because they would never be free men again. I hoped that Keir, as an alleged two-time wife murderer, was near the bottom, and the other prisoners were giving him one heck of a hard time.

When he walked into the room dressed in the green prison uniform, I thought to myself, 'You look good in prison green, Keir. It really suits you. I hope you get used to it.'

He sat down, statue-like as usual. I handed him the notice and outlined why I had to give it to him. He had a quick glance at the document, and then stared blankly at me. I could tell he was trying to suss me out, to see what I really knew. I gave him a wry smile as I left. I knew enough.

I returned on 30 April to interview Riley. He'd originally phoned the Randwick Ds, and two of their blokes had gone to Long Bay to speak to him.

'So, what have you got for us?' they said, sceptical. All cops are somewhat cynical about informants. Sometimes their information is good, but more often than not it's complete bull.

'It's about that new bloke, Keir, who's in here for killing his second wife. Well, guess what? He told me he did in his first wife as well. He whacked her and put her under his house. I only want to speak with the cops that charged him but.'

'We'll find out who those officers are and pass your information on,' they told him. When they got back to their office they looked up the records and found that it was Mick who'd charged Keir.

I arrived at work early the next morning to find Mick more animated than usual, positively bouncing around the place. 'You alright, mate?' I laughed.

'Mate, I'm better than alright. Yesterday I got a call from the Ds at Randwick. They told me they've got info about a prisoner who reckons he knows where to find Jean's body. Apparently, Keir spilled his guts to this bloke, and he wants to pass it on to us.'

'What? You've got to be joking! After all that's gone down, he's stupid enough to open his trap?' I said in disbelief.

Mick raised his right hand, palm outwards. 'I swear to you Pete, Keir has opened his big mouth and fessed up.'

For hours after hour, day after day, I'd tried to work out how to get a conviction. I just couldn't believe he'd be stupid enough to confess. For a moment, I became almost as animated as Mick, but then I tempered my emotions; one thing I'd learnt was that a lot of crooks are full of shit. 'What's the prisoner's name, Mick?' I asked, wanting to know if the bloke was a habitual bullshitter.

'Brian Riley.'

It didn't ring a bell.

'Can you speak to him sometime today?' Mick asked.

'Bloody oath, mate! I'll have to go and pick up the Boss from the airport, but I'll swing by before then. Who else is on today?'

'George Radmore. Take him with you; it'll be good experience for him.'

'No dramas. I'll give the gaol a bell, and when George gets here we'll head off.' While I was waiting for George, I thought I'd better ring Long Bay to make sure there actually *was* a Brian Riley there. They confirmed that there was. 'Is there a place I can talk to him in private?' I asked. 'I don't want the other prisoners to know that he's talking to us.' I knew he ran the risk of being labelled a 'dog', and if he felt uncomfortable, he wouldn't open up.

'Hang on a tick and I'll check,' came the reply.

'Gees!' I thought. This informant is the key to me nailing Keir, and they have to 'check'?

The prison officer returned to the phone a few moments later. 'You can speak to him in the Superintendent's room. You'll have total privacy there. What time d'ya reckon you'll be here?'

'About quarter past ten, is that okay?' I replied.

'Yeah, no dramas. I'll have him ready to go when you get here.'

'By the way, what's he in for?'

'Sexual assault.'

'Yeah, no worries, we'll be down there soon.'

I'd just put the phone down when big George arrived. George was a bloody top bloke, a more-than-handy league player and well-liked by everyone in the office, one of those gentle giants. I had to laugh at seeing this big, burly bloke with thinning blond hair jumping around like a kid at Christmas when I told him what we were doing and where we were going.

'We have to pick the Boss up from the airport at midday, but we've got plenty of time.'

'Yeah, no worries, Pete,' George said, his enthusiasm plain to see. I always liked to see young fellas this keen about the job; it meant they would listen and learn.

We arrived at Long Bay at about a quarter past ten, and were ushered into the Super's room. It was a bit weird, with a long rectangular table in the centre and a couple of old wooden chairs, and we'd barely sat down when there was a knock at the door. Two prison officers walked into the room with Riley sandwiched between them. They escorted him to the table, and told him to sit down. 'Do you want us to stay or wait outside?' one of the officers asked.

'Outside would be good. Cheers, mate,' I said, knowing Riley wouldn't want the screws around. As soon as they'd left, I began.

'So, you're Brian Riley, is that right?'

'Yeah.'

'I'm Detective Seymour and this is Detective Radmore. We're from Mt Druitt Detectives. The boys from Randwick told us you had some information relating to Thomas Keir. Is that correct?'

'Yeah, but before I open me mouth I wanna know what kind of deal I'm gonna get?'

'What are you in for?' I knew full well, but I thought it prudent to play dumb; his explanation about the charges would give me an idea of what kind of bloke he was.

'Sexual assault,' Riley said. 'But it was a fair root, mate. She was a good girl, and I was from the wrong side of the tracks, if you get what I mean. She got caught with me when she shouldn't have, so she cried "rape". Look, I shouldn't be in here. Are you gonna get me bail, or are we just wastin' our time?'

'Mate, I'm not gonna promise you anything until I know what you've got for us. I don't know you from a bar of soap, and forgive me, but I don't trust you. You could tell me a whole load of shit, so until I hear what you've got to say, there'll be no deals."

Riley's head dropped and he rubbed the bridge of his nose with the thumb and forefinger of his right hand, pondering his immediate future.

'Mate,' I continued, 'It's your call. You're the one that came forward. I don't really care if I leave here empty-handed. You're the one trying to get a deal. If you tell me something that turns out to be good, then we'll look at doing something for you. When's your bail hearing?'

'A coupla weeks.'

'Mate, still your call. You give me something that helps me, then we can arrange a letter of comfort to the court for your bail hearing. The court will look kindly on you helping a murder investigation. It might be the only way you get bail.'

'Look,' Riley said, leaning forward and placing his elbows on the table. 'I'm taking a big chance by being here. If anyone finds out I've spoken to you, then I'm a dog, and you know what happens to dogs in here; I'll be dead.'

I leant forward as well, placed my palms flat on the table and spoke clearly and calmly. 'Mate, we've taken all precautions to ensure that no-one knows you're here. If you want, you can tell them we were talking to you about your case. There'll be no suspicion, but there are no deals, mate. You tell us what you know, and we provide the letter. You don't, we walk out and you get nothing.'

Riley put his head in his hands. 'I'll tell you,' came his muffled response, 'but you swear to get me that letter?'

'Yes, it won't be a problem, but first I need all your personal details.' Riley gave them to me, and then told me about his previous breach of bail. I studied his face intently; the face was usually the key to deciding whether someone was full of shit. Riley looked genuinely worried, but I could see that he wanted to open up, so I pushed him. 'So, tell me about Keir. Do it slowly, so I can write it all down.'

Riley stared at the floor and began to speak. 'A coupla days after Keir came in, his cellmate came up and told me Keir had told him he'd topped his wife and knew where the body was. He told me Keir had buried her in an upright position under the house. I didn't wanna ask too much, but I fronted him the next day in the yard. I said: "Where's your wife? What's going on?"

'He said, "I dunno. I haven't seen her. I spoke to her a couple of years ago when she called me."'

I'd wondered whether Riley was yanking my chain, but now I knew he wasn't. His body language and the way he spoke convinced me he was on the level. The mention of the phone call sealed the deal. I knew he was genuine. No-one except me and the two Micks knew about the alleged call. There was no way Riley could have known that without Keir telling him. I repeated Riley's words to make sure I hadn't misheard him. 'So Keir told you the last time he spoke to his wife was two years ago when she phoned him?'

'Yeah, that's what he told me.'

'Okay, what happened then?' I said, now very keen to see what else he had to say.

'I said, "You're bullshittin'. You knocked her," and Keir said, "I don't know what you're talkin' about." I said, "If I can tell you where the body is, will you tell us what's going on?" and he said, "I don't know what you're talkin' about" again, so I said, "You put her underneath the house." He had a cup of tea or coffee in his hand, and a smoke. When I told him where the body was, he started shakin' like a leaf and almost spilt his cup. I said, "See, see. I know. See." He looked at me and said, "I don't know what you're talking about" again, and I said, 'Don't treat me like a git, tell us what's going on. Did you have a blue or something? Was she fucking around on you?'

"He shrugged his shoulders.

"I said: 'What happened? Was she sleeping around on ya' and you had an argument or somethin'?'

"'Mate,' I said. 'Don't treat me like a fuckin' git just tell me what went down.'

"'I was pissed off and we had an argument,' he said. 'So I strangled and buried her.'

"I told him to get away from me and then he went off with some other mates."

I looked expectantly, at Riley but his eyes told me he was done. 'I want you to read what I've written down so that you're happy with it,' I said. 'I need you to be satisfied that what's in this notebook is correct, okay?'

'Yeah.'

I passed him the notebook, and he read it and then handed it back to me. 'Are you happy to sign this? Is it correctly recorded?'

'Nah,' he said. 'I'm not signin' nuffin' till I get legal advice.'

'Yeah, no dramas. That's fine. In the meantime, we'll check out what you told us and get in touch with your solicitor. I'll do my best, okay?'

'Yeah, well, you'd better,' said Riley. 'And no-one betta find out about today, or I'm a dead man.'

'No worries, mate. You can go with the screws in a minute and, if you're telling me the truth, you may just get lucky.'

George and I got up and walked to the door. George opened it, and the two officers walked in. 'Give it a coupla minutes before you take him out,' I said. 'If anyone asks why he was here, just say we were talking about something in his past, or talking about his case, but there was nothing to it. That's all you know.'

'Fair enough,' said one of the officers.

George and I walked to the car, and I could see that he was antsy to know my thoughts. As soon as we were in the car he said, 'So, whaddya reckon, Pete?'

'He's got to be on the up and up,' I said, talking to myself as much as to George.

'Why's that?' said George.

'The only people that knew he'd said that his missus had phoned him were me, Mick and the boss. Keir must have told Riley that his wife had rung him. How else could Riley have known that? Keir must have opened his trap; there's no other explanation. So, that being the case, we must assume that everything else is true. We'd better have a look under the house. We'd better go and collect the Boss from the airport. We can fill him in then. That'll be enough to get us another warrant.'

CHAPTER 9

The Second Dig

Thankfully, the Boss's plane arrived on time. With our new information, I don't think I could have handled a delay. He spotted us as soon as he came through the gates. I felt a bit sorry for him, because he'd been out in the country sitting on a job interview panel, which was never that much fun, but fortunately for him, he had two weeks holiday coming up.

'G'day, Boss,' I said, shaking his hand warmly. 'How was the trip?'

'Good, fellas. I hear there's been some developments in the Jean Keir investigation?'

'We've just come from Long Bay, Boss. It looks like he's opened his mouth to some fellow prisoners. One of them wants a deal. He reckons Keir told him he buried her under the house.'

'Yeah, that's all well and good, but how much can we trust him?'

'I wasn't sure at first,' I said, 'but then he told us that Keir told him that Jean rang him about two years ago. He could only have got that info from Keir. Plus, he said the body was buried upright under the house. The bloke's from the eastern suburbs, so he wouldn't have a clue whether the houses in Tregear are on concrete slabs or up on piers. I guess he's a fifty-fifty chance of getting it right, but I reckon he's telling us the truth.'

We jumped in the car and headed back out to western Sydney. George was driving, the Boss was in the front passenger seat and I was in the back. I leant forward between the two front seats and passed my notebook to the Boss. 'Here's what he gave us. I've added some personal notes for our reference. He has a Supreme Court bail hearing on the 10th, so we haven't got much time if we're going to provide his solicitor with a letter of comfort, which is what I told him we'd do if his info was legit.'

The Boss studied my notebook with the same intensity as he normally would a form guide. When he'd finished, he handed it back to me. 'Right then, as soon as we get back, type up a search warrant and get it down to Blacktown pronto so we can get it sworn out. How many troops are on today?'

'Bugger-all,' I replied ruefully.

'No dramas. We'll call a few boys in on this, and just hope that this bloke is telling the truth and we find the body. You'll have to inform the Coroner, and get Forensics in. Grab a coupla Uniform boys to help with the digging. If you find anything, you'll have to let Homicide know, but there's no way they're taking it over. Just keep 'em in the loop so they don't get the shits.'

That was one of Mick O'Connell's most endearing qualities. He knew we'd do the job properly, and had felt entirely comfortable leaving things in our hands while he was away. It was important as a D that you felt like your boss had complete faith in you, a total trust. It meant you could get on and do your job without having to second-guess everything.

We arrived back to the station to find Mick Lyons waiting downstairs for us, busting to know how we'd gone.

'G'day, Boss. How was the trip?' he asked politely.

'Yeah good thanks, mate. Looks like you're going to be a busy boy very soon. Pete got some good info from the informant. It's enough to get another search warrant.'

I was standing behind the Boss, and reached around him to pass my notebook to Mick Lyons. 'Have a read, Mick, and tell me what you reckon.'

'What did you think of him?' he asked me when he'd finished reading.

'I wasn't sure at first, but he knew things, things that only we knew. I'm sure he's telling the truth.'

'Well, let's get the warrant typed up and down to Blacktown,' said the Boss. 'You might as well do it, Pete. After all, you got the info.'

I rang Blacktown and got Sean McCosker again. He was more than interested in the new developments.

'So you're looking for a body under the house now?'

'Yeah, that's the new info we have. We looked in the wrong place last time.'

McCosker made arrangements for me to be there at 2 pm. When I arrived I was ushered into his office. I'd been there numerous times before for drugs and firearms warrants, but this time felt different. I felt the same as I had in the car, like someone was there with me. This time, I knew for certain that it was Jean Keir.

I gave McCosker the warrant application, and he studied it intently. 'So, this informant. You think he's telling the truth?'

I put on the broken record and repeated what I'd said to Mick earlier.

'That's good enough for me,' McCosker said, and grabbed his pen and signed off on the warrant.

Knowing that I couldn't keep Mick in suspense, I phoned the office and by the time I arrived, the briefing had already started. There was probably a dozen or so officers sitting in the briefing room, many of them having been called in on their day off. The Boss had taken off on his holidays, so it was left to Mick and me to organise everything. To make things more difficult, Mick was also due to have a few days off, and he wanted to make sure everything was just so before knocking off that afternoon. It was one of the things about being a copper: you had to take your holidays, no matter what. If you cancelled your holidays every time an important lead presented itself, you'd never take them. Besides, we had the utmost faith in our mates, and knew we could trust them to look after things while we were gone. We stood in front of the assembled officers, and I sensed a renewed hope flowing through them. You could feel their restlessness, and I just knew that everyone was keen to get this one solved.

I started by reading the terms of the warrant, because everyone needed to know what they could and couldn't do, but, more importantly, I also needed to make sure that no-one stuffed anything up. 'We're expecting to find the body of Jean Angela Keir. She's been missing since the evening of 9 February 1988. We don't know how long this will take, but we'll execute the warrant and stay there as long as is necessary. Guards will be posted at the scene overnight to make sure we comply with the provisions of the search warrant. If you find anything, let me, Detective Sergeant Lyons or Detective Murray know about it.'

The digging was to be conducted by Steve Wye, a uniformed officer I'd known since 1981, back when he was a highway patrol cop. He had a medium build and medium complexion with a moustache and thinning light-brown hair.

'G'day, Steve,' I said after the briefing had finished. 'Is there anything you reckon we need to do a job like this; shovels and shit?'

'Nah, I reckon she's sweet,' said Steve. 'If we need anything when we get down there, I'll let you know. I reckon we'll just send a couple of us under the house and see if we can find any disturbed areas or any soil that appears to be different. If so, we'll start there. I hope we can find what you're looking for, Pete.'

'Yeah, me too, mate. A part of me wants to believe she's still alive, for the family's sake, but the fact is, everything points to her being dead.'

We started just after three, and Wilkes Crescent soon became a hive of activity once again. The neighbours and the kids were back out in force, curious to see what the police were doing there for a third time, and I thought to myself, 'Third time's a charm.'

As I made my way into the backyard, the same old feelings returned, but I no longer feared them, in fact I felt flushed with hope. The grassy western section remained just as it had when I'd first taken a look under there. The Colorbond fence continued on and bordered this side of this property. On the western side where we were looking there was a gap of about a metre from the base of the house to the ground below. From here, the brick columns that formed the foundations were spaced about a metre and a half apart. The ground sloped down from the east, the Wilkes Crescent side, of the house. By the time you came to the Wilkes Crescent side of the house the separation between the house and the ground was no more than a few inches.

I watched the Rescue boys begin the dig. They paced up and down the grassy strip, carefully examining the sections in between each of the piers. Several times, they stopped, examined the dirt, discussed it amongst themselves, and then moved on to the next section. Eventually, they found a promising spot under the centre of the house and pointed to where they were going to begin. The chosen site was rather narrow, so they decided to cut holes in the floorboards directly above. It meant they could dig down instead of across, thereby minimising the risk of damaging anything. The Rescue boys grabbed a chainsaw, cut a triangular hole in the floor and then started digging.

Steve Wye was first in. Being another old-fashioned cop, he loved to get in and get dirty. With surgical precision, he carefully manipulated the shovel as he began expertly taking out small pieces of soil. After about half an hour, the ground became rock solid, and we quickly realised we weren't going to find anything. The afternoon settled over us like a heavy blanket, and as the crimson clouds started to form over the mountains to the west, we posted the overnight guards and began packing up. We'd just put the last bit of gear away when Mick came over.

'You right to look after things for the next few days while I'm off? It'll be just my luck that you'll find something while I'm not here, but give us a bell if you do.'

'Yeah, no worries, Mick,' I said.

CHAPTER 9

Mick gave me a smile, and I returned a tired one of my own. It had been a long day, and I wanted nothing more than to get home to my lovely wife. Our second child was due in a few days, and I felt far guiltier than I usually did for not being with Sue. The Boss had arranged for me to have time off, but a second chance had presented itself, and I wanted nothing more than to find Jean. It was odd, trying to find someone else's deceased child whilst my wife was about to bring my second child into the world, and I knew that was why I was pushing so hard; there was no way I could enjoy the birth of my child until I'd laid Christine and Clifford's child to rest.

It was well after eight before I got home and, once again, it took me a long time to get to sleep. Lying back in bed, the ceiling became a movie screen again, only this time it played a different feature. I replayed the Riley interview over and over in my head, the words tracing across the ceiling as if they were subtitles, or the words and bouncing balls from karaoke videos.

'Where the hell are you, Jean?' I said out loud. 'If only we could get a lucky break tomorrow, and at least put an end to your family's suffering.' I'd never had thoughts like this before, talking to a dead person whom I'd never even met, but I felt a strange connection to Jean. Fate had drawn me into this investigation, and I knew I was destined to be there when she was found. I eventually fell asleep, but my dreams were confused, muddled, and filled with visions of red.

When I woke the next morning, I was straight out the door. Today was the day. Today, we'd find her.

I arrived at the station at around 8 am, grabbed everything I needed from my desk, and waited in the briefing room. I could feel the pulse around the room, and was sure that everyone shared my confidence and excitement, but before we could start, I had to go through the daily tasks. Seeing as both Micks were off, and there was so much to do, I was bloody lucky I had Wayne Murray to help me. I knew him really well, as he'd joined the cops at the same time as me.

The briefing had just started when the worst possible news came through; Keir had somehow managed to post bail. 'Fuck it!' was the collective thought.

The occupier's notice still had to be served, but now, instead of making another trip to Long Bay, I had to go to his parent's house, where he was staying. I rang their number, and Keir answered. Much to my surprise, he told me he wanted to come in to the station to collect it.

'You cocky bastard,' I thought. 'You think you've got away with two murders, don't you? Now, you want to come in here and lord it over us.' My fires of desire now became a raging inferno. I hated criminals, yes, but I hated arrogant criminals even more.

Keir arrived at about 8.45 am. I was determined to make his decision to come in to the station a big mistake, so I shared my thoughts with Wayne Murray. 'Hey, Muzza, come downstairs with me while I talk to Keir and give him the occupier's notice. I might bring him upstairs to see if he has anything to say. You never know what might happen if we turn the screws a bit. He might decide to talk to us if he thinks we're close to finding the body, or we might just catch him off guard. Either way, it can't hurt.'

'Sounds like a good plan, Pete. Let's go.'

We went downstairs and walked up to Keir, who was standing in the foyer.

'I have some papers that I must serve upon you, Mr Keir,' I said. 'Will you accompany me to the Detectives' office?'

'Yes,' he replied coldly. In that instant, I could tell that my hatred was reciprocated. We went upstairs to the office, and into the interview room. Keir sat down, but Muzza and I remained standing so that we maintained the power, and Keir was in the submissive position.

'This is Detective Murray,' I said, indicating Muzza with an open palm. 'Yesterday, we executed a search warrant at your house after receiving information that your first wife could be buried in the grounds there. Here's the occupier's notice.' I handed Keir the notice, and Muzza and I both studied him intently to gauge his reaction. Nothing. Just that same stone-faced look.

'I want you to understand that you're not obliged to say anything unless you wish, but whatever you say will be recorded and may be used later in evidence. Do you understand that?'

'Yes.'

I thought that if I just came straight to the point, I might catch him off guard, a bit of a shock-and-awe tactic. 'Did you kill your first wife? Is Jean Keir buried in the backyard of your home?'

Keir dropped his gaze and looked at the notice.

'I take it then that you do not wish to make comment on this matter?'

'No,' came Keir's terse reply. At least I'd managed to get some sort of a response.

'You have the right to leave, but the police will continue to search your house. Do you understand that?'

'Alright,' Keir said as he stood. We led him back downstairs and watched him walk through the foyer and out the front door. It sickened me that we had to watch a man who we knew was guilty walk out the door a temporarily free man.

'Well, he's never going to tell us too much, is he?' Muzza said as we walked back to the D's office.

'Nah, he seemed pretty cool about the whole thing. It worries me a bit.'

'Why's that?' asked Muzza.

'Mate, we were deadset in his face. We pretty much told him we knew his wife was buried under the house. He must've known that his big mouth had given him away. Why was he so composed? Why did he seem so calm about the police searching his house again?'

'Maybe he thinks he's done a good enough job of hiding her that we won't find anything.'

'Yeah, I reckon you might be right. Mate, he's put her in the drum. That's why he's so cocky. I'm sure of it.'

I made my way to my office not long after Keir had left, knowing that I had to keep Jean's family informed of our progress, and phoned Christine Strachan. 'Christine, it's Detective Seymour here. I thought I'd better ring you and tell you that we're conducting another search at the house. We received some new information that may have given us a lead about what happened to Jean.'

I didn't have the heart to tell her exactly why we were going to the house again. How would a mother cope with that? What if we didn't find anything? I didn't want to get her hopes up. I didn't want her to suffer any more than she already had.

After I got off the phone, Muzza and I left the station and returned to the house. Steve Wye was already there, and came straight up to us as soon as he saw us. 'Boys, the ground is fairly hard, all clay and shit. It might be an idea to get a few more people down here, and probably a Kanga hammer as well. Otherwise, we'll be here for friggin' ever.'

'Muzza,' I said with conviction, 'we may only get one shot at this, so we'd better do it right. We'd better get Steve some more troops and a Kanga hammer.'

Muzza and I had to return to the station to get permission for the hammer, because it wasn't something that would be automatically granted. Ordinarily, I might have been a little worried, but on this occasion I wasn't, because Paul Clemson was the Superintendent. Not only did we have a good working relationship, but I'd worked with him at Blacktown, and I knew he'd give me what I needed. He respected me as an officer, so I had a lot of time for him.

When we got back to the station, I asked around, only to be told that Superintendent Clemson had the day off. 'Great,' I thought. 'Every bugger's off for the day, Keir's made bail…what else can go bloody wrong?'

I had to ring the Penrith Commander, Jim Cranna, to get more men and permission for the hammer. Fortunately, I got along famously with Jim, because he'd organised the first Penrith/Blacktown police rugby league team. I'd been a skinny runt, but quick and tough, so I always got picked, and the Commander was a big fan of my efforts at full-back and on the wing. That was one of the most important things as a copper; to be liked by your peers. If I'd been a knob, I doubt I could've got so many things to happen.

'Hi, Jim,' I said. 'It's Pete Seymour. How's things?'

'Yeah, good, mate.'

'Boss, we've got a search warrant down here at Mt Druitt looking for the body of a missing woman.'

'Yeah, mate. I know. What about it?'

'Jim, I've just spoken to the Rescue Squad boys, and they reckon we need a Kanga hammer. The ground under the house is as rough as. Boss, we need some more people on board. This is the second warrant, and we can't afford to stuff this one up.'

Jim went silent. 'Shit,' I thought, 'he's going to say "no",' but my fears were short-lived.

'I'll organise for some of the beat police to come down for the day. You'll have to hire the hammer locally. Get the admin squared away and get the invoice signed off. I heard you did a bit of damage down there yesterday.'

'Bugger me, gossipy bastards, word travels like lightning around here,' I thought to myself.

'Yeah,' I said. We had to cut through the floorboards to get to a spot we thought was promising. It makes it easier for us to work with the extra headroom. Anyway Boss, the house is all but stuffed from the fire, so it shouldn't be too much of a drama. Besides, we're covered by the search warrant.'

'Well, I hope you know what you're doing, Pete. This one's on your head. Let me know how things go, mate.'

'Yeah, no worries, Boss,' I said as I hung up the phone, now slightly concerned for the safety of my head. It'd been an absolute shit of a morning, and things were only going to go from bad to worse now I knew that the bosses at Penrith were having kittens. I couldn't see what the bloody problem was; the house was already buggered from the fire. What did a few floorboards matter? I was, to say the least, a little annoyed. I wasn't some bloody amateur; you'd think they'd have more confidence.

'How'd you go, Pete?' said Muzza.

'Mate, the bosses at Penrith are a little worried about us causing too much damage, but they're sending some beat police down, and we have permission for the Kanga. There's a place on the Great Western Highway down at Toongabbie where we can get one.'

We drove down to a place called GKN Rentals and spoke to the bloke, who ran us through how to use it. We carried the gear out to the caged truck we'd taken, but I hadn't had a good look at the truck before we'd borrowed it, and had failed to notice the blood splatters. I looked at the salesman with a grin on my face. 'The uniform boys must have had a hard time last night. You'd think they'd learn to clean their vehicles, wouldn't you?'

The salesman laughed. 'I've never been in one of these, and I hope I never am.'

'Ain't that the bloody truth!' I said.

We all had a good laugh, and then Muzza and I packed the gear into the truck and made our way back to the house. With not much else to do until he got the hammer, Steve Wye was waiting impatiently out the front.

'We haven't done anymore digging,' Steve said. 'We've just been having a squiz around the house, and there are a few places we want to try.'

'Alright,' I said, still thinking about the safety of my head. 'We've got a few blokes from Penrith coming in too.'

'Good,' said Steve. 'We're gonna need them.'

Thomas Keir and Jean on their wedding day on 11 August 1984.

Jean on her wedding day.

Jean with her parents, Clifford and Christine on her wedding day.

Thomas Keir and Jean early in their relationship.

Jean and baby son on the lounge at her home in 1985.

Aerial photo of Wilkes Crescent and Kemp Place cul-de-sac from a westerly direction. Arrow indicating Keir house.

View of front of premises showing fire damage as a result of Rosalina's murder in 1991.

View of the rear yard of the premises between the house and detached garage showing items removed from the house after Rosalina's murder in 1991.

View of front of premises showing fire damage as a result of Rosalina's murder in 1991.

Close up of Sergeant Steve Wye observing the final excavation of the western side of the house after the bones were found.

Close up of the hole where the bones were found. The bones were found directly under the edge of the house but digging continued out from the house.

General view of western side of the house showing backhoe excavation after the bones were found. Sergeant Steve Wye is observing the excavation.

View showing bones retrieved from alongside the brick piers at the side of the premises.

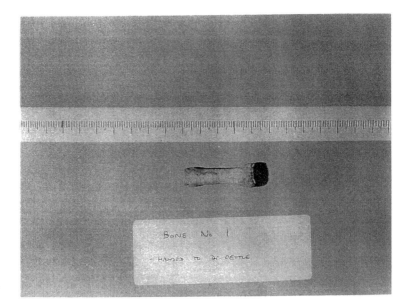

Bone number 1. Finger bone from the right hand.

Bone number 2. Proximal phalanx of the right big toe (base of the toe).

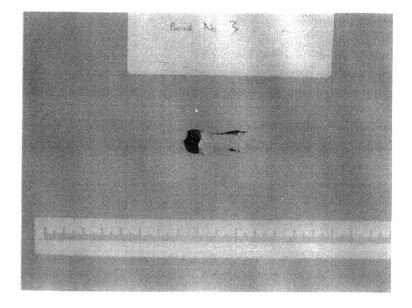

Bone number 3. Proximal phalanx of the right thumb (base of right thumb).

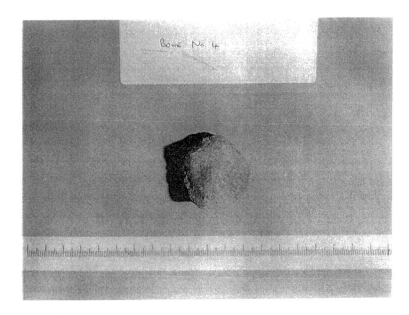

Bone number 4. Left patella knee cap.

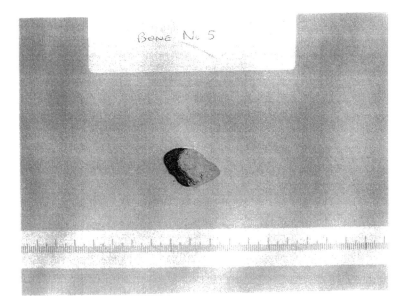

Bone number 5. Capitate bone which is one of the bones from the left wrist.

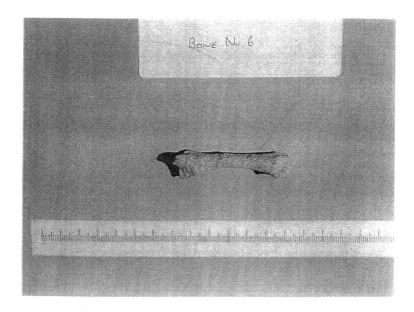

Bone number 6. 3rd metacarpal which is the bone at the base of the middle finger in the left hand.

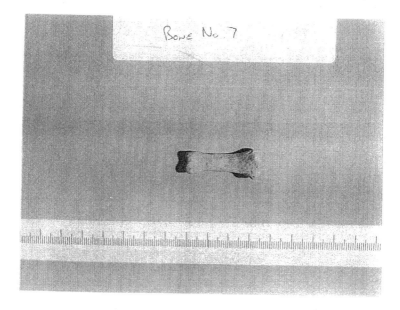

Bone number 7. Proximal phalanx which is at the base of one of the fingers from the right hand.

Close up of Jean in happier times, out with her friends.

Thomas Keir's second wife, Rosalina, who was Jean's cousin.
Thomas Keir married Rosalina in the Philippines in November 1989.

Detective Peter Seymour.

CHAPTER 10

Seven Bones

The dirt that was excavated was carried from underneath the house and placed near the western side fence. We all felt a bit like archaeologists looking for a lost tomb. I just hoped that we'd find what we were looking for, but it didn't seem like it was going to happen. The more we looked the less we found. We dug deeper, and the higher the pile of dirt grew, the more despondent I became. We didn't find the drum, and now Keir's brazenness and lack of response when I'd pressed him about Jean made sense. He'd hidden her too well. He knew we weren't going to find her.

After telling the fellas to take a break, Muzza and I stood there trying to figure out our next move. The safety of my head was now in serious doubt, but what really tore at me was that I wasn't going to deliver for the Strachans. I'd given them hope, and I was going to fail them. I felt sick to my stomach, and it felt like my intestines were contorting.

Suddenly, one of the uniform cops called out. 'Hey, Muzza, have a look at this!'

'What is it?' said Muzza as the officer came towards us.

'What do you think this is?' he said, standing in front of us and turning an object over and over in his fingers.

Muzza and I took a closer look. 'Where did you find it?' I asked.

'I was just standing over there taking a break and decided to have a little poke around near one of the piers. The dirt was a little easier to dig than that other hard stuff, so I kept going. I was about...I don't know...eighteen inches down when I found it.'

The officer handed the object to Muzza who also turned it over in his fingers. 'Looks like a chicken bone,' he said as he held it towards me.

'If you say so, mate,' I replied. 'I wouldn't have a clue how to tell the difference between a chicken bone and a human bone! Better bag it, Muzz, and send it down to Forensics to see what they have to say.'

I was feeling mixed emotions. I was enthusiastic, but tempered my excitement because Keir had had a goose pen down this side of the house, and we'd already found several other bone-like objects.

We continued to dig and sift for most of the day, but eventually the light began to fade so we packed up, posted the overnight guards and left. We returned to the station, where we put the bone and all the other evidence we'd found into the Miscellaneous Property Book. Pizzas were again the order of the day as Muzza and I debriefed the troops. When we'd finished, I realised that it had been two weeks since I'd spent an entire day with my wife. Every other bloke had had at least one day off, so I decided that, investigation or not, I was having tomorrow off. Susie needed me, with the birth of our second child imminent, and I was sure that, being a mother herself, Jean Keir wouldn't mind. I told Muzza I was having two rest days. Muzza, obviously aware of how tired and frustrated I'd become, agreed that it was a good idea, and told me that if they found anything worthwhile, he'd let me know.

I didn't get home until ten, whereupon I collapsed into bed. Sheer exhaustion had taken over, but I still had trouble getting my head down. I was just too tired to sleep. It didn't matter, though. At least I could have a sleep-in tomorrow.

Truth be told, I did feel incredibly bad for taking a couple of days off. I wanted to devote myself to my family, but was equally aware that I had to give everything I had to the Strachans. I just hoped Christine and Clifford would understand. Besides, the investigation had begun to wear me out, and I wasn't seeing things with clear eyes. A break was exactly what I needed. The amount of time I could have off was, however, dependent on when our second child decided to arrive.

Staring at the ceiling, I began to think about our second child. What would he or she be like? Would everything be OK? What would he or she grow up to be? The ceiling projector started to scroll through various slides, familiar Seymour family photographs. Suddenly, it changed entirely, and the slides became the evidence. Images of the 'chicken' bone, from various angles, appeared again and again, along with images of the house, the dirt, the garage, the drum; it all played over and over in my mind. Perhaps we *had* found a goose bone, and it occurred to me that we might actually be on a wild goose chase.

I'd just fallen asleep when the phone rang. Sue answered. 'It's your work,' she said handing me the phone. What the bloody hell were they doing ringing me at this hour? Despite my tiredness, however, I was excited; maybe one of the guards we'd posted had found something. I rubbed the sleep from my eyes and looked out the window; it was already morning! What had apparently been several hours of sleep had seemed like nothing more than a few minutes.

'Hello,' I said slowly, the exhaustion in my voice plain to hear as I picked up the phone.

'Pete, it's Superintendent Clemson. I've just had Bob Broad in here, and he's worried about the amount of damage being done to the house. From what he told me, I'm a bit worried about it myself.'

I sat bolt upright and ran my palms over my face. I couldn't believe what I was hearing. I was annoyed that they'd woken me up, and I was annoyed that they were calling me when I was supposed to be on leave, but I was absolutely infuriated that they were questioning what we were doing. Here we were on the verge of cracking the case wide open and doing one bloke for two murders and Bob Broad, who was in charge while Mick O'Connell was away, was worried about how much damage was being done to the friggin' house.

'*Boss*,' I said, not bothering to hide the irritation in my voice, 'we have a search warrant, which means we can take any steps we want in order to find the body. We're not doing anything illegal or wrong, so I fail to see the problem.'

'So what's the basis for the warrant?' Clemson asked.

By this stage, I was becoming *really* annoyed. 'I got info from a Long Bay informant and, on that basis, we got the warrant. It's all in my notebook.'

'I might just take a look at that notebook. Is it in your drawer at work?'

Whilst I liked Paul - he'd never questioned me in the past, and I knew he was just doing his job properly - I started to think, 'Bugger me! I've done everything by the book. What more do you want?'

'No, it's here at home,' I said indignantly. 'I'll bring it in if you need to look at it.'

'Yeah, I want to have a look at it, and I want to talk about what's going on at the house. When can you come in?'

'I'll have a shower and be there within the hour,' I said, and then hung up.

'What was all that about?' said Sue, sensing my fraying nerves and giving me a soothing cuddle.

'Bloody Boss wants to see my notebook! He's getting real toey about the search. Bob Broad's been in his ear and told him that we'll be in the shit if we do too much damage to the place.'

'Don't they know that you haven't had your days off, and you need to have a break?' she said as she stiffly sat upright, even more indignant than me. I'd hate to have been in Bob Broad or the Boss's shoes if Susie got hold of them.

'Yeah, they know. I'll take my notebook in, have a chat, square things away and come home. Tell you what, though; I'm putting in a claim for overtime.'

Showering did nothing to stem my state of shock. Whilst the water made me feel almost human again, dealing with death all day had started to make me feel like a zombie, and I was feeling particularly upset by the lack of support. 'Why am I putting myself through all of this?' I thought, and then reminded myself why. I was doing it for the Strachans. I was doing it for Jean.

When I arrived at the station I went straight to Clemson's office, where I found Bob sitting opposite him. I wished Mick O'Connell had been there, because then none of this would have happened. As soon as I walked in, I sensed how badly Bob wanted the search to end, but there was no way that was going to happen, not if I could help it.

'Take a seat, son,' Clemmo said, as if I was a troubled schoolboy and he was the principal.

'Great!' I thought to myself. 'They're talking to me like I'm a rookie. I'm stuffed.'

Bob wouldn't look me in the eye, and I knew he'd been sitting there all morning telling the Boss why the search should end, but I'd made my promise to Jean Keir and her family, and I wasn't going to break it. I opened my notebook to the relevant pages.

'There, Boss. That's what I got from the informant.'

Clemson read it, and straightaway I could see the concern on his face; Broad had done his job well. 'So what makes you believe this bloke?' Clemmo asked as he flicked through the notebook. 'Eleven years of gut instinct, that's bloody what!' I wanted to say, but instead I refrained, and simply put on the broken record.

'Keir told the informant that Jean had rung him two years earlier. Keir told us the same thing in the interview. There's no way Riley could have guessed that. That being the case, I believe the rest of what he said. He was shit scared of the other prisoners finding out he was talking to the cops, and so he took a huge risk. I could read it in his body language; he had severe reservations about telling us what he knew.'

Suddenly, I heard heavy footsteps pounding down the hall, and then Jim Szabo appeared in the doorway. 'Sorry, Boss,' he said, through laboured breathing. 'Pete, I've got some important news. That bone we found went to Glebe, and Dr Oettle has identified it as a human finger bone. It looks like we might've found her.'

My eyes immediately found their way to Bob Broad, who didn't return my stare.

'You bloody ripper!' said Clemmo as he jumped up from his chair like he'd won the lottery. He threw his arms in the air, and his smile went from ear to ear.

'I guess you don't have any more concerns about our search warrant, do ya Boss?' I said. I wasn't a petty man, but I just had to serve that one up to Bob Broad.

'Not at all, my boy. Keep going, and do what you need to do out there. You were on rest today, weren't you?'

'Yeah, I *was*. I take it I'm recalled to duty now?'

'You sure are.'

I hoped, considering the break in the case, that Susie would understand.

'This will be a cancelled rest day from the time you got called at home this morning. Is that okay with you?'

'Sure is, Boss.' I rose from my chair, and knew I should just leave without saying anything, but I couldn't help myself. 'Looks like I'll be calling the Coroner to let him know what we found, Bob.' I looked back to Clemson, whose smile was now even wider.

'I'll keep you updated on what's happening, Boss. And I'll call the Coroner at Westmead to let him know what the go is.'

'Yep, good work, son.'

'Up yours, Bob,' I thought. 'Question my work ethic will you? Well, karma just gave you a hefty kick in the arse!' With that, I left the office, leaving Bob to explain himself to Clemmo.

I headed straight for my desk, needing to sit down for a minute. I was having trouble thinking straight. I just couldn't believe it. All the disappointments, all the setbacks, all the negative comments and attitude had completely gotten me down, and now I couldn't comprehend that we'd actually found her. I'd held out for this moment for so long, and now that it had actually arrived, I wasn't sure what to do.

Lost in everything else, I'd completely forgotten about Susie. As I picked up the phone, the receiver felt heavy, and my heart sank because I knew I had to tell her that I wasn't coming home on time. I'd done it so many times, and she'd been as good as gold, but I doubted she'd be so understanding this time.

How strange is life? Now I had double the excitement. Here I was about to have the second of the greatest blessings a man could ever have and, at the same time, I was just as excited about the developments in the case. My family life was going to suffer, but I had a job to do. I'd made my choices and, whilst it tore at me, what option did I have? Besides, I knew that if Susie went into labour, I'd drop everything.

I put the receiver back down. Wanting my mind clear before I spoke to Susie, I picked it up again and phoned the Westmead Coroner's Court, glad to get John Hiatt, because he was an old-school-style magistrate who understood police work. Hiatt, the police rugby league team's most fervent supporter, knew that sometimes things didn't go by the book, but as long as the job was done properly, and pretty much by the book, there was no drama.

'Good morning, sir,' I said politely. 'We've just received information about a bone we found during a search warrant executed at Tregear regarding the Keir matter. We're searching for his first wife.'

'Ah, yes. What have you got for me?' Hiatt said.

'Forensics has confirmed that the bone is human.'

'Righto then, are your people still at the scene?'

'Yes, they are. I'll be heading down there shortly to meet up with everyone and make sure everything is on track.'

'I want you to wait until I get my pathologists out there. You know Dr Ellis and Dr Little? I want them to oversee things. Keep me in the loop, and let Homicide know what you've got.'

'Will do, sir.'

After I hung up, I called Susie to give her the good news about finding the bone, and the bad news that I would be late again.

Optimism surrounded Wilkes Crescent when I arrived. The news had already filtered through to the boys, and you could sense that every man wanted to get on with the dig, none more so than Steve Wye.

The media had been listening to the boys discuss the news on police radio, and as I made my way to the backyard, I was confronted by numerous journos shoving microphones and tape recorders in my face as they asked me dozens of questions. I simply said, 'No comment.'

The Forensic Pathologists turned up, were escorted through the media throng by a couple of uniformed officers, and came straight up to us. I immediately took them to where the bone had been found.

'That's where it was found, Dr Ellis,' I said. 'The hole was about 18 inches deep and about the same in width. You can see that it's between two brick piers, and there's a fruit tree a few feet away.'

'That tree could be a drama if we need to get in for a closer look,' Dr Ellis said. I couldn't help but think that, as he stood next to the big orange tree, Dr Ellis was a deadset doppelganger for Don Burke of *Burke's Backyard*, although to be fair, I don't ever remember Channel Nine doing an episode called *Ten Easy Steps on How to Find a Dead Woman*.

'Okay. We'll trim it back for you,' I said to Don…I mean, Dr Ellis. Without need of an invitation, Steve was suddenly cutting back branches like a man possessed. I took a look around the yard and realised that the media were perched on Max Wormleaton's fence behind me. Although we couldn't let them onto the premises, I was actually rather glad to have them filming; it meant we'd have everything we did on tape when the time came to give evidence.

We started using the Kanga hammer to break the soil, but didn't find anything, so we shifted to looking between the two piers and further in from the edge of the house. It was getting darker and darker, so we whacked light poles all along the fence. Jim Szabo and another detective were alternating, one using the hammer while the other used a shovel. At one point, Jim turned some soil over and as soon as he'd done so, the other detective became very animated.

'Have a look at this,' he said as he held up a lightly coloured object, just like a gold-panner holding up a small nugget.

Dr Ellis moved in closer, examined it, and then showed it to Dr Little. 'I think you may have found something here,' he said.

Szabo and the other detective continued their digging duet, and soon uncovered more lightly coloured objects. Dr Ellis and Dr Little were a godsend because, due to Keir's burying habits, there was all kinds of crap, like little pieces of concrete, and we had no idea how to distinguish one object from another. Every time we found something, we'd show Dr Ellis, who would examine it and say, 'No, that's not human,' however, we did occasionally find objects where he'd say, 'Yes, this looks more promising.'

Night had well and truly settled in when Dr Ellis suggested we finish up. He came up to me as the last of the chequered blue-and-white police tape was wrapped in a triangular shape around the fruit tree. 'I'll need to examine what we've found more carefully back at the mortuary, but it's looking promising,' he said.

It was getting late, and it didn't seem like we were going to find anything more, so we finished up and headed back to the station for the customary pizzas and debriefing. I could feel it as soon as I set foot in the station; the mood in the office had changed completely. Scepticism and dejection had given way to a new sense of hope. All we needed was Dr Ellis's confirmation. I sat back, slice of pizza in hand, satisfied; the sacrifices had been worth it.

Susie had been quite angry when I'd been recalled to duty, but had calmed down by the time I got home. When I explained the reasons for the recall, she became almost as excited as the boys. She said she still wished that I'd been at home, but that she understood.

'I hope now you can give the family some peace,' she said as she kissed me goodnight.

I lay back, but couldn't sleep, the projector screen replaying everything over again, but then suddenly the scene changed to a courtroom. There was a jury, an even mix of six men and six women, and the foreman stood and delivered a 'guilty' verdict. In the next scene, the judge was passing sentence as Thomas Keir stood in the dock. The movie ended with the Strachan family embracing each other.

The next morning, we returned to the site at 9 am and continued to dig, locating another two lightly coloured objects. I hadn't been at the site for more than an hour or so when one of the boys came up to me and told me I had to call Dr Ellis urgently. I rushed back to the station and rang him, eagerly anticipating what the doctor had to say.

'Pete, they're human. The first one I've identified is the proximal phalanx of the right thumb, the second is the left capitate or wrist bone, the third is the proximal phalanx of the right big toe, the fourth is the left patella, the fifth one is the proximal phalanx of one of the right-side fingers. All of them are from an adult.'

I started fist-pumping with my free hand and before I'd even said anything, the other boys in the office knew the results. Better yet, Dr Ellis would later confirm that the latest two objects were also bones. The sixth bone was the left third metacarpal, and the seventh another finger bone from the right hand.

Seven bones. Seven reasons to see Keir behind bars. Seven steps closer to justice. Seven pieces of their daughter for the Strachans to bury.

The job was, however, far from done. I rushed back to the site and told the rest of the boys the good news. With this, a lot of the fellas now expected to find Jean's body, but I wasn't so sure. We needed to conduct a more thorough dig, but before we did, I needed to contact Mr Hiatt to update him. I drove back to the station and phoned him, and he said that he'd ask a structural engineer to come down and have a look at the house to see, because of the fire damage it had sustained, whether the place was salvageable. If not, we could lift the house off its foundations to conduct a more effective search. I had to laugh, because in the space of a few days I'd gone from being in trouble for damaging some floorboards to now being on the brink of tearing the entire house off its foundations!

When I'd finished speaking to the Coroner, I went back to the house and found Muzza.

'Hey, Muzz, I just spoke to Mr Hiatt. He wants a structural engineer to come in and make a judgment on the place. If it's rooted, we can lift it off the foundations. I'm thinking that there's not much more I can do here now, so I'll start my two weeks leave tomorrow. Can I leave it with you to organise everything? Unless we find something major today, there's no point me being here when Sue's about to have the baby. I think it's time for me to spend some time at home.'

'Yeah, Pete. I've got it. You need to be with your wife, mate,' Muzza replied.

Shifting to my impending joy, my mind switched to what I would have to do for my family over the next few weeks and months. I'd just started to walk out of the yard when I stopped and turned back to Muzza with a puzzled look on my face.

'Muzza,' I said, 'We've only found small bones. What happened to the rest of her? She was obviously here at some point, but I reckon Keir's dug her up and put her somewhere else. I'll bet she's in that missing drum.'

'Yeah, but the question is, why did he need to dig her up again?' Muzza replied.

'I dunno,' I said as I walked around examining our excavation work, 'Unless…'

'Unless what?'

I'd just had another epiphany. 'Unless Keir had to get rid of the body because of the smell! Remember the statement from the tenant, Denise Wilkes? She said there was a "God-awful stench", a "rotten meat" and "real dead smell" in her son's bedroom. She also said her dog would bring clumps of dark hair from under the house, and on a number of occasions the dog had bones in the backyard that she hadn't given to it. If Keir knew the dog was digging up Jean, he wouldn't want to bring his new wife here and have her complaining of bad smells. Maybe that's why he got rid of Wilkes. We find the drum, we find the body.'

Despite readying myself to go on leave, I had to go back to the station and make sure all the paperwork was squared away. Consequently, I didn't get home until late that night, whereupon I rushed inside to give Sue the good news that I wouldn't be going back to work for two whole weeks. Needless to say, she was absolutely thrilled.

While I was away, the boys continued the dig, and the entire area between the two brick piers had been excavated to a depth of a few feet when the pathologists decided we probably weren't going to find anything more. Most of the beat cops were returned to normal duties, with just a few fellas remaining to go over everything with a fine-tooth comb.

Although I was on leave, Mick Lyons rang me a few days later. 'So why do we just have these small bones then, Pete?' he said. 'Muzz said something about the drum. If he's put her in the drum, why would we find the bones?' he asked.

My break from the case hadn't lasted long. 'Mate, I reckon that when he's dug the body up he hasn't noticed these small bones being dislodged. If it was something big, like a femur, he'd have noticed, but he's just missed these small ones. They were all found in the same area, so it makes perfect sense. Think about it. He would've been in a bloody big hurry, and probably wouldn't have thought to stop and check for smaller bones.'

'Sounds feasible enough,' said Mick.

'That statement from Riley is vital now,' I said. 'He didn't want to sign it until he got legal advice. I think we should pay him another visit.'

'Yeah, mate,' said Mick. 'I think you're right. Where's your notebook? Is it in your drawer? I'll give it to Muzza and he can go down to the gaol tomorrow and see if he can get Riley to sign it.'

'Yeah, mate. It's in the top drawer. Just get Muzza to put it back when he's finished.'

The next day, Muzza arranged for a structural and civil engineer to inspect the house. Mick Lyons hadn't found anything more, so he decided, pending what the engineer had to say, to conclude the dig. Meanwhile, Muzza went to Long Bay to speak to Riley. Riley walked in to the interview room, so Muzza told me later, still obviously apprehensive about what he'd get from us, and from having told us what he had.

'Good morning, Mr Riley,' Muzza said.

'Mornin'.'

'I have some information that may interest you.'

'Yeah? Like what?'

'The information you provided to us proved to be correct. We've located seven small bones under the house.'

Muzza later told me that Riley had seemed relieved to now be getting what he wanted, but seemed equally disgusted as he signed the notebook. When Muzza asked him about it, he said it wasn't because he was being a 'grass' or a 'dog', but because it meant that Keir had been telling the truth about what he'd done to his first wife.

CHAPTER 11

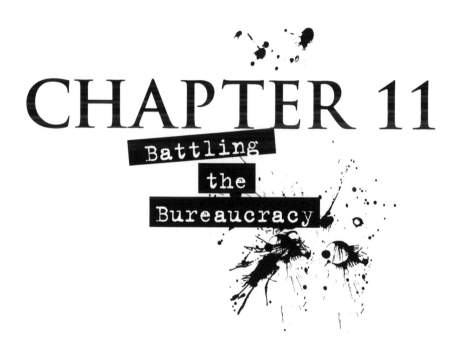

Battling
the
Bureaucracy

Riley's agreeing to sign the statement was a huge relief. It was tremendous to know that we'd soon have Keir on Jean's murder, as well as Rosalina's. It was like a refreshing afternoon storm at the end of a long, hot day. The case was almost done, and I could turn my attention fully to my family. I began to allow myself time to truly take in the miracle that was about to occur, the arrival of my second child. My world was all blossoms, but I still had mixed feelings about the find, because I'd expected to find an entire body, not just a few small bones. Jean Angela Keir had touched my life and, no matter what happened in the future, she would always be a part of it. I'd never met her, but I was somehow drawn to her. I imagined that she must have been magnetic, and luminous, and this was what had made Keir so infatuated and infuriated; but she didn't deserve to die because of her personality or beauty!

I couldn't get it out of my mind. Where had Keir put the rest of her body? I kept in touch with Mick every few days, hoping he'd eventually tell me that they'd found the rest of her. I'd been on leave for about a week and then, on the 14th May, he phoned me.

'Hi, Pete. How are things with Sue?'

'She's okay, but still pregnant, mate. The little bugger is either very lazy or just doesn't want to come out. It's driving her insane. How are things at work?'

'Well, I don't have real good news about Riley. You know the bail application? Well, he gave you the wrong date. I typed up a letter of comfort for the 10th, but the hearing was on the 9th. He was refused bail.'

'Shit, he gave me the wrong bloody date!' I said as my grip tightened on the phone. 'Have you spoken to him and explained what happened?'

'No, but I've left a message for his solicitor to ring me. Mate, it's just one of those stuff-ups. Not much we can do about it now. Perhaps we can make another application when it's all cleared up. Don't worry about it, mate. We'll sort it out. Your main concern is Susie.'

'Yeah, mate, I know. Mick, I hoped we could keep this bloke on side, but I reckon that until we smooth things over, we've got Buckley's.'

All of my conjecture and solutions to the problem eventually proved to be a moot point, anyway; Riley was convicted, and had to serve his sentence. After his release from jail, he moved north with his new partner and kids to start life anew. That was it. He was gone, and we were never going to receive his help. For now, however, apart from the seven bones, we were back to square one. So be it. *Che Sera Sera*. I had more important things to worry about.

In the early hours of 17 May 1991, I was suddenly woken by a hefty slap on my back. 'My waters just broke!' Sue screamed, continuing to thump me. 'I think we'd better call the hospital!'

I leapt out of bed and rang Baulkham Hills Private Hospital. Sue's contractions had started, and before I really knew what was going on she was dressed and making her way out the door carrying her pre-prepared bag of toiletries. I snatched Ash up in my arms, dressed her in a nightie and beanie, and then rang my parents, who were going to take care of her. I then called Sue's parents, who lived on the Central Coast. We rushed to the hospital, and Sue was admitted to the labour ward where, a few hours later, Jenna, our beautiful second daughter, was born.

Fortunately, the delivery went smoothly and Sue was fine, but I spent a few more weeks at home just to make sure everything was sweet, although I felt an irresistible urge pulling me back to the case. I know I should have been content at home with my wife and newborn child, but I simply couldn't sit there and be happy about what I had when I knew what someone else had lost. Jenna had her whole life ahead of her, including the chance to achieve so many wonderful things, but Jean Keir didn't.

I went back to work on 2 June. Mick Lyons briefed me straightaway, and I kicked back into work mode almost as if I'd never left.

'I've been concentrating on getting statements relating to Rosalina's murder,' said Mick, 'so I can prepare a brief for the prosecutors. Your main focus is still Jean.'

I immediately rang Dr Ellis and asked him what he could tell me about the bones.

'Well, they all have the same appearance, which is consistent with them having been buried in the ground for a similar length of time. They're not very dry either, which tells me they've only been in the ground for a short period, perhaps a couple of years, or maybe only months.'

'Sweet, that all fits with our time frames,' I said.

'The other thing is,' Dr Ellis continued, 'there aren't any duplicated bones. This would be consistent with them all coming from the same person. From the look of them, they're from an adult human.'

'I don't suppose you could give them a sex and a name, could you?' I joked.

'We're pretty good down here!' Dr Ellis laughed, 'But not that good! You'll need DNA testing if you want that kind of evidence.'

Over the next few months. Mick and I worked our butts off. We took every statement and chased up every piece of evidence regarding Rosalina's case, no matter how small, while I also continued my lines of inquiry into Jean's murder. Even though we'd found the seven bones, it still wasn't enough to charge Keir. We had to prove she wasn't alive, which was made all the more difficult because Keir was still maintaining that she was. The best piece of evidence, apart from the bones, that we discovered was when we checked the medical records at Nepean Hospital and confirmed that Jean's blood type was O Positive, an essentiality for the DNA testing. Mick obtained statements from Rosalina's family members who were living in Australia, including Christine Strachan, and we put together a strong circumstantial case that Keir was the last person seen leaving the house and the only person seen going back in.

There had been no sounds, no screams, and so it seemed impossible, considering the time frames, that an unknown person could break into the house, confront Rosalina, strangle her and then go out the back, find cans of petrol, douse the room, set it alight and then get out without being seen by any of the neighbours. The whole series of events seemed impossible. If there'd been another assailant, surely the neighbours, particularly Max Wormleaton, would've said they'd seen a suspicious character in the backyard.

After Keir was committed to stand trial, Mr Hiatt, the Senior Deputy State Coroner, said to me and Mick, 'The only way you'll lose this one is if the jury leave their brains at home.'

With the Rosalina case pretty much squared away, we now focused all of our attentions on Jean's murder. We reinterviewed Christine, who told us she'd gone to the 'Salvos' (The Salvation Army) and asked them to help find her daughter, so Mick contacted their Missing Persons Unit and got a statement from a Major. She told us that she'd placed a picture of Jean in *War Cry*, with an accompanying article. The publication had gone out Australia-wide, but nothing came of it. Common sense said that if Jean was anywhere in the country, she would've made contact with her mother to allay any concerns, not just make phone calls to the man she'd chosen to leave.

In the middle of all of this, Mick O'Connell retired. It wasn't like you could begrudge him his well-earned rest, and we didn't, but it was the last thing we needed in the middle of two big murder cases. Mick was the glue that held most of us together, and we always felt confident of getting things done with him there.

Detective Sergeant Tom Sharp took his job. He was another old-style copper, and also a Vietnam Vet. He was a stocky bloke with short, combed-back yet thinning, white hair. Unlike Mick, he was a deadset stickler for the rules, and as soon as he took over he called us into his office for a briefing on Jean.

'You know you'll have to prove she isn't alive,' was the first thing he said.

'Yeah,' Mick replied. 'We've also got to get some blood from her parents, once we find out where we can get the bones DNA tested.'

'Have you had any luck with that?' Sharp asked.

'We're waiting to hear back from Dr Ellis. I'll follow it up and let you know,' I said.

'You'll also have to make inquiries with every government department in New South Wales and across Australia to prove she hasn't accessed anything like Medicare or Social Security.'

'Yeah,' I said. 'I'll arrange with police in different states to do their own checks, and to make sure she hasn't obtained an interstate driver's licence. I'll tell the interstate coppers there'll be a free trip in it for them to come here and give evidence; that should mean things get done a lot quicker.'

Sharp laughed, and we started to feel more confidence in our new Boss.

'You'll have to liaise with Homicide and the Coroner. I don't want anything even remotely out of place. There's no way I'm letting this bastard walk!' he said vehemently.

'Yep, no worries, Boss,' I said as Mick and I walked out of his office.

'You do the police checks and I'll sort out the government shit,' Mick said. 'Hopefully there won't be any record of Jean being alive.'

It wasn't like Mick was being callous or uncaring in saying that. It would've been bloody fantastic if Jean *was* alive. Then we could get in touch with her, tell her to contact her mum and put all of this to rest. However, we knew that she wasn't.

'Well, are we expecting her to be? If she's alive, she's going to have a hell of a time getting around missing a kneecap and a toe,' I said as I sat down at my desk. It was a complete pain in the arse doing all the checks, one of the most menial tasks in police work, but it had to be done. Besides, we wanted Keir so badly it kept us going through all the tedious hours. After a few months, however, we'd found…nothing.

It was mid-October 1991 when the phone rang. I was busy filling out my duty book and didn't really pay much attention.

'You're fucking joking,' I heard Mick say. 'Are they aware that this is a murder investigation?'

My ears pricked up and I flicked Mick a worried look.

'Yeah…so why isn't it in the public interest? Yeah…nah…I don't really agree. Okay, I'll let our boss know.' Mick hung up the phone.

'What's wrong, Mick?'

'Fuck ol' Daisy, it's the bloody Federal Health Department. They're not going to provide us with a report. They say it's not in the public interest!'

'That's a load of bull! It's a murder, for God's sake. How much more in the public interest do they want?'

'Well, there's not much we can do, but it's going to be a big problem, 'coz we need to know if Jean's accessed Medicare.'

'We'll see about that,' I said as I reached for the phone book, absolutely furious with the bureaucratic bullshit. There was no way we were going to come this far and let some bureaucratic idiot stand in our way.

'What are you gonna do, mate?' Mick asked.

'I'm gonna ring the friggin' NSW Health Department to get the Federal Health Department's number in Canberra, and then I'm gonna ring the Minister for friggin' Health and find out why they won't release the info.'

'I wouldn't do that, mate. You'll end up gettin' your arse kicked.'

'Don't worry about that, Mick. What are they gonna do, sack me?'

'Well, yeah, mate, they just might.'

'Too bad! We haven't come this far to fall at the final hurdle.'

Within seconds, I was on the phone to Canberra. Mick just rocked back in his chair and watched on in disbelief. Even if he'd wanted to stop me, he knew he couldn't. 'Good afternoon, my name is Detective Peter Seymour from Mt Druitt Police in Sydney. I want to speak to the Federal Health Minister or someone in his office.' Mick nearly fell off his chair; I don't think he thought I'd really do it. 'Yes, I'm investigating the disappearance of a young woman by the name of Jean Angela Keir, who we believe has been murdered. I've just received information that your department is the only department or government agency in the whole bloody country that won't provide us with the information we've requested. I've just got off the phone from the Senior Deputy State Coroner of New South Wales, Mr John Hiatt, and he's instructed me to ring your office and find out why our murder investigation is not in the public interest. Also, he wants me to report back to him with the name of the person to whom I speak. Can I have your name, please?' I looked over to Mick, who was chomping on his nails. I smiled and gave him the thumbs up. 'Yes, I'll hold,' I said.

I winked at Mick and placed my hand over the receiver. 'Don't panic, mate. He's going to speak to someone and get back to me.' Just as I finished speaking to Mick, the man came back on the phone. 'I want it as soon as possible,' I said. 'You're the only one we're waiting on.' There was a brief pause. 'Thank you very much. I'll let the Coroner know. Just send it through to New South Wales Police Headquarters and they'll forward it to us.' I hung up the phone, looked at Mick and gave him another wry smile. 'You see, Mick. I told you everything would be fine.'

'What did they say?' he asked, still incredulous at my audacity.

'We'll have the info by the end of the week.'

I sat back in my chair, satisfied with what I'd just managed to achieve. 'Hey, Mick,' I said, staring at the ceiling before turning to give him an even bigger grin. 'Do you reckon I should ring the Coroner and let him know I just dropped his name to Canberra?'

'Ah…I think that would be a good idea,' Mick said sarcastically. 'I still reckon you're gonna get your arse kicked over this, especially going over their heads in town.'

I rang the Coroner and told him exactly what had happened, while Mick leant forward in his chair, watching on intently. 'Yeah, no worries, sir. I'll let you know as soon as we get it. Yep. Yep. Bye.' I looked at Mick with a contented smile. 'You see, Mick? That wasn't so hard now, was it?'

'What did Hiatt say?'

'He said, "Good job! Let me know when you get the information." He wasn't worried about it at all.'

'I think it's coffee time,' Mick said as he rose from his chair. I could see he thought that my arse kicking was a certainty, but by the end of the week, we had the report, signed off by the Minister himself, and my arse remained intact. The report that had caused all the fuss read as follows:

Jean Angela Keir has not accessed Medicare and we have no records of her since the date of her disappearance.

CHAPTER 12
A New Father?

The following week, Dr Ellis rang and told us we should take the bones to Melbourne for DNA testing. Later that day, we met him outside the Coroner's Court at Westmead just before we went into Keir's Committal proceedings, and he confirmed that the forensic labs in Melbourne were the most advanced in Australia and that they should be able to provide us with the evidence we needed. All three of us walked into the courtroom and sat on the edge of our seats as we watched the court proceedings commence against Keir for Rosalina's murder. Thankfully, he was committed to stand trial on 14 November 1991. Keir was told, as he stood in front of John Hiatt, that there was sufficient evidence against him, and that his bail would continue until his trial began and he was put before a jury.

Mick and I continued our discussions with Dr Ellis as we walked from the Court. We decided to arrange with Penrith Forensics to photograph the seven bones before they were taken away. This was a must, because we needed photographic evidence in case the bones were destroyed during the DNA testing. Dr Ellis left, and Mick and I approached Keir's solicitor in the adjoining courtroom. Mick was the first to speak.

'Will you be available later this afternoon? We want to photograph the bones at the mortuary with you present. Dr Ellis, the forensic pathologist, will be there.'

The solicitor was an older man, and obviously very experienced, but he looked at Mick with concern. 'No, I don't really want to do that, because then I will be a Crown Witness, and I want to be able to represent Tom.'

'What about your son?' said Mick, knowing that he was also a solicitor, and worked with his father.

'No, I don't want him to be a Crown Witness either. We don't want anything to do with being Crown Witnesses,' he said emphatically. There was a tinge of nervousness in his voice, and Mick and I wondered why as we watched him walk away.

'I can't see how he could end up being a Crown Witness if he's present when we photograph the bones,' Mick whispered. 'After all, he'd only be there as Keir's legal representative.'

'He was pretty nervous,' I said. 'I don't think he really understood what was going on. You're right, he wouldn't end up being a Crown Witness, but to tell you the truth, it doesn't matter if he's there or not. You gave him the chance; there's not much more you can do. I'll call Dave Hurst and see what time he can come down and take the photos.'

Mick and I met Dave Hurst back at the Court at a quarter to four that afternoon. All three of us walked across to the mortuary to see Dr Ellis.

'Okay, guys, the bones are on a table,' Dr Ellis said as we walked in to the main area of the morgue. 'I've laid them out so you can photograph them individually and collectively.'

We followed Dr Ellis into the post-mortem examination room, and I was immediately reminded of the first time I'd had to watch an autopsy at the morgue. It had been a tremendously difficult, gut-wrenching experience. Dr Ellis, who'd been practicing back then, had led me into the room and I'd noticed that there were four bodies awaiting autopsies laid out on the stainless steel tables like slabs of beef in an abattoir. The sterile environment, the lifeless forms; it all seemed so final. I felt less upset at seeing the dead bodies when I realised that the mortuary staff were just normal people going about their work in a 'matter of fact' manner. It wasn't a big deal to them, which seemed to bring a sense of calm, and made me realise that death was just another part of life. I found the smell a bit funny at first, but I got used to it pretty quickly. Then I stepped into the area where they do the post-mortems, and suddenly I felt like I was in another world, totally unsure about what I was going to see. Nothing can ever prepare you for that first time, and mine turned out to be a rather strange experience. It was an elderly Polish man who'd hung himself in the shower recess in his room at the nursing home. He was a fairly large man, and had been up there for some hours before he'd been found. Added to this, it had been an extremely hot day, and he was extremely bloated. I stood to one side and watched as Dr Ellis started work. The first part was the worst, because he began by using a circular-bladed saw, a bit like the tool you use to slice up a pizza, to saw open the skull and reveal the brain. I remember thinking how sad it was that this had to happen to a person's body and, funnily enough, I also thought about how painful it would be if the person was still alive!

Dr Ellis then began to open up the chest cavity with a scalpel, and started separating ribs, etc., as he began to take the body apart. The gases were released from the body, and initially I forgot to breathe through my mouth. Up until then, it had been a very sterile smell, not dissimilar to the smell in a school science lab, however the gases that are expelled from the body are vile. It really is indescribable, something I couldn't possibly compare to anything else I've ever experienced. Nothing can prepare you for the first time you see - and smell - an autopsy, no matter how much advice you're given. It leaves an indelible mark on your psyche, and the smell lingers in your nose and mouth, and in your clothes. However, you soon learn to breathe through your mouth instead of your nose. Over the years, as I attended more and more post-mortems, I gradually learned to desensitise myself to them.

When I was a little more senior, I'd have a laugh when I took a new cop to their first autopsy and saw their reaction. Some of the new recruits would put their hands to their mouths as soon as the body was opened up, trying to hold back the rising wave of nausea, and would then rush outside and vomit violently. It never happened to me, but I can totally understand why some people reacted in this way. After all, people sometimes forget that cops are human too, and not just emotionless robots.

Dr Ellis placed the blue surgical matt on which the seven little bones had been arranged on top of one of the stainless steel tables. As I watched Dave Hurst taking numerous photos, I found it quite disturbing; this was all that was left of what had once been a bright, vibrant, happy young girl. 'I don't think I'll ever get used to the smell of this place,' I muttered as I started to look anywhere else except at the bones.

'Believe me, after a few years, you get used to it,' Dr Ellis replied.

'Yeah, I'm sure you're right, but you can keep this job all to yourself, Doc,' I said, just as Hursty finished taking photos.

'I suggest you leave one of the bones here,' said Dr Ellis, 'just in case they end up being destroyed.'

Mick and I both agreed that this was an extremely good idea, especially because it would have far more impact on a jury if they could actually see one of the bones. 'I guess we'll keep one of the finger bones and send the rest,' Mick said as Dr Ellis started to pack the bones away.

The next day, I rang the Victorian Institute of Forensic Pathology and was put through to a Dr Bentley Atchison, who confirmed that they could do the DNA testing.

'I'm a little worried about the bones being destroyed during the testing,' I said.

'It's a possibility, but the testing process shouldn't destroy them,' he replied. 'One thing, though. I'll need you to obtain blood samples from the biological parents of the deceased so I can compare the DNA.'

'That's fine. As soon as we get them, I'll arrange a suitable date to bring the samples and bones down to you,' I said.

I hung up the phone, and suddenly realised that Mick was standing in front of me. I'd noticed the now customary cup of coffee in his hand, but I hadn't taken a good look at his face. 'Good news, Mick,' I said. 'I just spoke with a Forensic Pathologist from Victoria and he reckons they can do the testing, but we need to get blood samples from the Strachans so he can compare the DNA.'

'No dramas. We'll organise it. We'll have to get them to give the blood to the Police Medical Officer and have it all sealed properly.' There was something in Mick's voice that didn't seem quite right, but when he rang the Strachans his tone quickly reverted to his usual professional police voice. I figured he was just a bit tired or something, but then Sharpie called me into his office.

'Yeah, Boss, what's up?' I said as I entered the room.

The Boss sat down at his desk and motioned for me to sit opposite him. 'Pete, I just got off the phone to Superintendent Hopkins at Penrith. The Department is looking at each district conducting their own Investigator's course. Penrith is going to be one of the first ones, so it's important it's done right. Hopkins wants you to run the course, which means you'll have to officially transfer to Penrith.'

My jaw literally dropped in disbelief. Now I understood Mick's strange mood. 'You've gotta be joking, Tom! Can't someone else do it? You know where we're up to with Jean's investigation. Just the DNA tests, and we're nearly done. You can't take me off it when we're so close.'

'That's the other thing,' Sharp said in a more-than-serious tone. 'It's been decided that Homicide will finish things off. We're stretched as it is, mate, and Mick needs to make sure that the Rosalina case is watertight.'

I felt like a grenade, ready to explode at any moment. Everything I'd done on this case, all the tiny details, all the leads, all the time I'd spent away from my family, and now, at the last minute, it was going to be handed to Homicide on a platter. No disrespect to the Homicide boys, but I felt that if I wasn't working on the case, it wouldn't get done right. Worst of all, I felt like I was letting Jean down.

'This isn't right, Tom! How can you let Homicide take over when we've done all the work, especially when there's not that much left to do? So basically what you're saying is that they're going to swoop in over the top of us and take all the glory?'

I'd raised my voice now, like an angry teacher reprimanding a disruptive class, and I'm not sure the Boss was prepared for what hit him, although maybe he was. 'No, no,' he said apologetically. 'It's not like that at all. They'll just tie up the loose ends and liaise with you and Mick.'

'What about the bones? I suppose *they're* gonna take them down to Victoria?' I said angrily.

'No, mate, you can still do that one, but Homicide will finish everything else off.'

By this stage, I was absolutely livid. 'Does Mick know about this?' I figured Mick did know, but I wanted to gauge the Boss's reaction.

'Yeah, I told him a few minutes ago while you were on the phone. He's disappointed, but at least he can concentrate on getting a conviction in the Rosalina case.'

I stood up and leaned in close to the Boss, my hands flat on his desk. 'This is bullshit, Tom, and you know it! So, when do I start at Penrith?'

'The course starts next week, but Superintendent Hopkins wants you up there as from tomorrow to start getting things organised. Look, Pete, at least this is an important course for the district, and they'll be looking at what type of job you'll be doing. It must say something about what they think of you as a detective.'

Sharpie's attempts to comfort me went straight through to the 'keeper as I stormed out of the office. 'I don't give a fuck what they think of me; they can shove this job straight up their arse for all I care!' I said as a parting shot.

I returned to my desk, and as I sat there I must've looked like one of those cartoon characters with steam coming out of their ears. Meanwhile, Mick was sitting at his own desk with his head in his hands.

'Can you believe they're going to hand our job over to the bloody Homicide Squad?' I said as I slumped back in my chair.

Mick looked up at me, his face filled with disappointment. 'Yeah, so Sharpie told you?' he said sympathetically.

'And I have to go to Penrith to do a friggin' investigator's course. The whole thing is a pile of shit.'

'Mate, just to make your day all that much better, Christine Strachan has just dropped a bombshell.'

'Serious? What?'

'You ready for this one?' he continued. 'Clifford's not Jean's biological father.'

'What do you mean, "Clifford's not Jean's biological father"?'

'Mate, the man who impregnated Christine was not Clifford. Apparently, it was some bloke called Gaspar Baan. Christine was pregnant with Jean when she and Clifford got married, and Clifford agreed to raise her as his own.'

'Farken' hell! I wonder how many people in the family knew that one? Mate, we'd better find this bloke quick smart and get a blood sample or we're well and truly stuffed. Homicide are taking over, I have to go to Penrith, and now this. Can this day get any better?'

Mick tried soothing my extremely frayed emotions. 'Pete, I'll organise to get blood from Christine, and then I'll track this other bloke down, I swear. I'm not going to let Keir walk. I promise I'll let you know when it's all done. Sharpie said you could still take the bones down to Melbourne, so that's something.'

'I don't give two shits about going to Melbourne, Mick. I'm completely pissed off they're letting Homicide take over when we've done all the work.'

'Well, as Sharpie said, they're just going to do the small things, and see if there are any more witnesses. It's just that we'll be working with them from now on,' Mick said.

'Fat lot of good that does me when I'm stuck over at Penrith! I didn't even ask Sharpie how long I was supposed to be there for.'

That afternoon, I spoke to Superintendent Hopkins, and I'm sure he knew, after I'd got off the phone, exactly how I felt about the whole thing. I went home absolutely reeling. I walked into the house and kissed my wife, sorely needing the comfort and warmth of her presence, but she immediately pulled away. 'What's happened?'

'You wouldn't believe it if I told you. They've taken us off the Keir investigation and given it to Homicide. On top of that, I have to do a friggin' investigator's course at Penrith; they're transferring me. I just can't believe it.'

'Sit down and have a beer,' Sue said, always knowing exactly what I needed. I sat down, while she went to the fridge, grabbed a beer and brought it back for me. 'Why are they doing this?' she asked as she sat down next to me.

'I don't know. Sharpie reckons we haven't got the staff to finish off the inquiries, and that Penrith really want me to do this course.' I savoured the flavour of the beer as it slid easily down my throat. 'How are the kids?' I asked, wanting to take my mind off the day's events.

'They're good. Jenna's asleep, but she'll be up soon. Ash is in her room.' I put my beer down, got up and went into Ashleigh's room.

'Hello, sweetheart,' I said as I walked through the door.

'Daddy!' she squealed as she leapt to her feet and ran to me, still carrying her Cabbage Patch Kids doll in her hand. I swept her up in my arms and cuddled her tightly, just like I would have imagined Clifford Strachan would have done to Jean when she was young. Then it hit me; Jean would have picked her son up like this too, but she would never get to do it again.

'How's my little girl?' I said.

'Good,' she replied as she kissed me on the cheek and then held her doll up.

'You have to kiss my doll too.'

I did so, even though it felt a bit odd. 'Is that okay?' Ashleigh gave me that nod that only little girls can, so I put her down, left her to play and returned to my beer.

As I sipped on it, I reflected on how much I really did love my family. No matter what was going on, they would always be there to take my mind off things, to remind me of the reasons why I'd been put on this Earth.

That night, I had a more a fitful sleep than at any other time during the investigation. This investigation was the carrot, and I was the horse. Every time I'd get close, it was moved that little bit further out of my reach. The next morning, having little choice in the matter, I made my way to Penrith to start my new job. First port of call was Hoppy's office.

'This is a pilot program,' he began, 'and it will be assessed by the Academy, so we need it to work. That's why I wanted you to run it, because you're one of my most experienced detectives.'

His words were no consolation, however. If I was as good as they were making out, then I should be putting my skills into practice in the field. I tried to console myself with the knowledge that there'd be many cases, like the Keir one, that would be solved because of the knowledge I'd pass on. I knew I had to focus on the bigger picture, but I found it tough.

'Thanks, Boss,' I said. 'I'll look at the subjects they want, and give most of the lectures myself. I'll get guest lecturers in to do the other ones, like the Prosecutors. I'll start organising it this morning.'

Hoppy handed me the course outline, and I returned to what had been my office during my last tour of duty to Penrith. Walking through the desks in the main office, I was greeted by many familiar faces. It was like I'd never left.

CHAPTER 13
DNA Tests

I engrossed myself in the course, initially because I wanted to take my mind off the Keir investigation, but I'd also been picturing myself as a young bloke again, and despite my anger and frustration, I knew most of the constables, and I also knew I had to give it my all for their sake. These fellas deserved the best possible opportunity to become plain-clothes constables and then full detectives. The course went for three weeks, and when it was over we all went to the Penrith RSL for a few celebratory drinks and a feed. I was happy with the work I'd done; everyone had passed. I was returned to normal Detective duties, and although I was now at Penrith, the Mt Druitt boys kept me in the loop. One day in December 1991, Mick phoned.

'Hi, Pete, how's it going?'

'G'day, Mick. Yeah, as good as can be expected. What's up?'

'Good news, I managed to track down Gaspar Baan. I've arranged for him and Christine to provide blood samples to the Police Medical Officer in Sydney. As soon as it's been done, I'll let you know and you can get the DNA testing sorted.'

'That's great news, mate. I was a little worried about whether we were going to find that bloke and get him to agree to give a sample after all these years.'

Later that week, the samples were obtained and brought back to Mt Druitt. I phoned Dr Atchison and arranged for the blood and bones to be transferred down there on the 16th of December. On the morning of the 16th, I made my way down to Mt Druitt station with a small esky in hand ready to transport the material.

'You got time for a cuppa?' Mick asked me when I walked in.

'Yep, it's your shout, but.'

As we made our way to the meals room, it felt rather strange to be back in a place where I'd spent so much time.

'So, how are things going with Homicide?' I asked as Mick handed me a cuppa.

'Yeah, they're going okay. Graham Merkel's a good bloke, and he's been keeping me informed. They're just trying to tie up some loose ends, and to find the service station attendant, but I don't think they'll have much luck there. It's been too long. We were bloody lucky to find that Baan bloke, though.'

'Well, let's hope our luck holds and we get a good result with the DNA tests.'

'So you fly down this morning, drop the bones off and fly back this arvo?'

'Yeah, mate. No overnighter for this one, unfortunately,' I said with a smile. 'I've never been to Melbourne before, so I'm looking forward to having a bit of a look around.'

'Mmmm, should be good,' Mick agreed.

I finished my cuppa while Mick went and unlocked the fridge. He took out four vials of blood, two from Christine and two from Baan, and handed them to me. I carefully placed them in the esky, and then Mick handed me the six bones, each individually secured in zip-locked plastic bags, which I also placed in the esky. I signed off the necessary paperwork, grabbed a set of car keys and headed to the airport. The esky was a standard small white foam job with a blue lid and a little blue nylon cord that was secured at each end, the sort of thing you'd see blokes taking to the footy or the cricket. It felt rather odd to have it sitting on the passenger's seat alongside me, and I couldn't help but keep looking at it. There it was, an entire family, or parts thereof, in one small esky. It was amazing how something so big could be symbolised by something so small.

When I arrived at the airport I went straight to check-in, showed my badge and informed them that I didn't want the esky to pass through the X-ray machine in case it damaged the contents. I also informed them that I needed to maintain physical contact with the esky at all times. To reinforce my point, I lifted the lid and showed them the contents. It must have been a bit of a shock to see human bones so early in the morning!

When we boarded the plane, I threaded my way among the other passengers as they placed their luggage into the overhead lockers, holding the esky close to my chest in the same way I would have held Jenna, very careful not to allow a stray elbow to bump it.

I found my seat, and while the last of the other passengers boarded, I looked around the plane and noticed that everyone was dressed in jackets and jumpers. 'That's odd,' I thought to myself. 'It's bloody hot outside.' The stewardesses did their safety demonstration, and before long we were accelerating down the runway, forcing me back into my seat. After we took off, the plane climbed steadily and then levelled off, and soon after, the captain's voice came over the intercom.

'Ah, good morning passengers, and welcome aboard this Qantas flight. Our estimated flight time is just over one hour. I hope you've all brought your winter clothes, because the forecast for Melbourne today is for cold conditions with heavy rain.'

'Just my luck,' I said to myself, glancing down at my casual jeans and short-sleeved shirt. 'I knew I should've checked the bloody forecast.'

Sure enough, when we landed, in true Melbourne style, the rain was torrential. I made my way to the pick-up area at the front of the terminal, and saw a marked police car waiting. I walked over and introduced myself to the middle-aged man who was standing leaning on the car. 'Good morning, Peter Seymour from Sydney Detectives.'

'G'day, mate. Alex from Transport. I take you to forensics lab. Is not far away.' Alex's heavy accent was unmistakeable, and it became thicker the more we exchanged pleasantries, mostly about the crap Melbourne weather and why I didn't have a coat. It wasn't long before we arrived at the lab, and Alex parked directly out the front. 'I leave you here, and you do what you do. Maybe you like to go to shops before we pick you up. Just give us call and we come.'

I thought about it for all of a second. 'Mate, give me ten minutes. Don't go anywhere. I'll drop this off, and then can you take me straight back to the airport.'

'You don't want look around Melbourne?'

'Mate, I don't have a jacket or an umbrella. You're kiddin' yourself if you think I'm gonna be walking around all day freezing my arse off. I'll just go back to the airport and see if I can get an earlier flight back to Sydney, where it's warmer.'

I made my way inside and met Atchison. He signed off the paperwork and took the esky from me, immediately lifting the lid to see that what he needed was inside. 'I'll let you know as soon as the tests are completed but, being Christmas time, it may take a few weeks,' he said.

'No problems, Doctor. Let's just hope you give us the right result,' I replied.

I made my way back outside, dived into the car, and managed to get onto an early flight home. Sitting on the plane as we prepared to take off, I looked out at the endless expanse of grey cloud, and the rain that was sheeting down, and vowed to check the weather forecast before my next trip south.

Over the next few weeks, Dr Atchison attempted to extract the DNA, but the only successful extraction was from one bone at the Apo B locus. Further attempts to extract more DNA all failed. The analysis did, however, show the presence of allele numbers 35 and 43. Dr Atchison compared it with the blood samples, and found that Baan's blood contained alleles 35 and 37, while Christine's contained alleles 33 and 43. His report confirmed that the DNA from the bone was consistent with having come from the child of Gaspar

Baan and Christine Strachan, the number 35 allele coming from Baan and the 43 allele from Christine providing the match.

On 19 March 1992, I flew back to Melbourne. When I arrived at the lab, Dr Atchison handed me the vials of blood and the bones.

'Unfortunately, I couldn't duplicate my results,' he said. 'If I were you, I'd look at having more tests done overseas.'

'Where do you suggest?'

'Well, the Brits are a fair way ahead of us, but if you want the best DNA technicians, then you can't go past the Americans.'

'Thanks, Doctor. We'll look into it.'

I returned to Sydney, and locked the evidence away at Westmead mortuary. The next day, I rang Mick. 'Dr Atchison reckons we should take the bones to America if we want the best results,' I said. 'You might want to let Merky know so he can get it organised.'

'Yeah, no worries, I'll give him a call,' Mick replied.

We hung up, both of us knowing that we still didn't have enough to charge Keir with Jean's murder, and I began to wonder if we ever would. The discovery of the bones had convinced me that we'd get Keir, but now for the first time I began to have my doubts, so I consoled myself with the knowledge that at least we had him for killing Rosalina.

CHAPTER 14
A Change of Scene

Charging Keir with Jean's murder wasn't the only thing I was having doubts about. The whole transfer debacle had caused me to become rather disillusioned, and I began to think about a career change. My wife and two young daughters had always been my main priority, and I felt like I'd been neglecting them. Moreover, seeing the Strachan family and what they were going through having lost a family member, I started to become more concerned about my own family's welfare. Yes, I still felt those same pangs of guilt, but deep in my heart I felt like I'd done all I could for the Strachans. Besides, I'd spent so much time on the job that it was getting to the point where my girls *had* in one sense lost a family member, and I didn't want them to have to endure that any longer.

Destiny intervened when I saw an old mate, Martin Killen, walking down the hallway past the Detectives' office and into the adjoining Prosecutor's office. Killen had been a D, but had transferred over to become a Police Prosecutor. I got up from my desk and walked into the Prosecutor's office.

'Hey, Martin,' I said. 'What's it like in the Prosecutors?'

Killen looked up from the pile of court papers on his desk and smiled. 'Well, if you don't mind reading through all these briefs and dealing with dopes in court, then it ain't too bad. The best part is there's no shift work and you get to spend every weekend at home. Monday to Friday, nine to five; not a bad life at all.'

'How hard is the course?'

'No harder than the detective's course. Why? You thinking of leaving the Ds and becoming a Prosecutor?'

'Yeah, mate. I've been thinking about it. Seems like the right time for a move, especially now I have young kids.'

It only took me a few hours to make up my mind. I called the Prosecutor's Training Unit to see if there were spaces available. There were, and my mind was made up. I headed straight to Ben Feszczuk's office to tell him I wanted permission to transfer. Ben was the Head of Penrith Ds, and was genuinely surprised by my request, but knew me well enough to know that once I'd made up my mind, there was no changing it.

'Yeah, mate,' Feszczuk said. 'I'll approve it as long as Hoppy approves it.'

I made straight for Hoppy's office. 'Come in, Pete,' he said when I knocked on his door. 'Take a seat, what's up?'

'Boss, I want to ask for a transfer to the Prosecutor's office. I've got two young kids at home, and I think it's about time I spent more time with them. Sue's had it hard enough after that bloke stalking her and ringing her a few years ago. I reckon I owe it to her.'

'Are you thinking of studying law as well, 'coz that's what most blokes who transfer over are doing?'

'No, I just want a change of lifestyle. I've been around the courts long enough, and it just seems like the natural progression.'

Hoppy sat back in his chair and folded his arms, whilst I waited eagerly for his response. 'Pete, you've done more than your fair share over the years, so if this is what you really want, I won't stand in your way. Organise the transfer papers, and I'll approve it immediately. It's the least I can do, mate. All the best.'

'Thanks, sir. I appreciate it.'

Within two weeks, I was in training. Most of the course content was stuff that I was really familiar with, so I didn't find it too hard, and not long after that I was in court. Mick kept me updated on the investigations, and there proved to be one particularly interesting development that Mick wanted my legal opinion on. Graham Merkel had managed to track down a former associate of Keir's, Morian Ward, who would provide us with some rather interesting information.

CHAPTER 15
Three is the Magic Number

Morian Ward was a middle-aged man who had known Keir for about eight years, as they both worked in the upholstery trade. In mid-1990, Keir had rung him to ask him to come around to the house to look at some fabric samples. This was about the time Keir had returned from the Philippines with his new bride, and Ward went to the house about a week later. He knocked on the front door, and Keir answered. Ward followed Keir inside, and straight through the lounge room, but Ward hadn't made it more than a few feet inside the house before he noticed that some floorboards had been pulled up in the hallway and there was a hole about three feet square in the floor. He also noticed a pile of dirt on the floor in the kitchen.

'What are you doing?' Ward asked, a little shocked at the odd scene. 'Looking for buried treasure?'

'There's been a bad smell, probably a dead animal or something, and I'm digging to find the cause,' Keir replied, totally devoid of emotion. With that, Ward had followed Keir through the house, examined the fabric samples and then left, having nothing more to do with Keir.

After obtaining Ward's statement, Merkel took him to the house and asked him to point out the exact spot. The house was still in the same condition as we'd left it, because we never did get the approval from the structural engineer to knock it down. Merkel contacted Mick as soon as he got back to the station.

'Mate, I've just been down to Wilkes Crescent with a bloke who reckons he saw Keir digging holes in his floor, and he showed me the spot. Looks like we might have been digging in the wrong place.'

'You'd better give Pete a call at the Prosecutor's office. I think he'd want to be involved in this one,' Mick said.

It was October 1992, and I was working at the Parramatta Local Court as part of my training when I received the message to phone Merkel. 'Hi, Graham,' I said when I got a chance to return his call. 'What's up?'

'Mate, I found this bloke, Morian Ward. He reckons he saw Keir digging up the floor in his house. We're going for another search warrant, and I'd like you to be there to execute it if we get it.'

'Just try and keep me away!' I replied.

Everything about the investigation now whirled through my mind again. Since being away, I had to admit that my enthusiasm for gaining a conviction had begun to wane, but now it returned in spades. However, I did find it hard to believe that we'd missed anything. We'd covered most of the ground under the house, and I was still sure she was in the missing drum.

I was actually feeling pretty guilty about leaving the Ds, because Christine Strachan had been in constant contact, and I found it incredibly hard to keep telling her that there was still hope. A year had passed since we'd found such promising evidence, and it still remained locked up at Westmead, but I tried to comfort her by telling her that the evidence was continuing to mount, and I promised her that we'd never stop until Keir was behind bars.

The third warrant was issued for 1 June 1992, and thankfully I was granted permission to be present for the duration. Merkel served the occupier's notice on Keir, who asked to be in attendance while it was carried out. This sparked my hope. On previous occasions, he hadn't seemed to give two shits about us digging around his house. The fact that he'd now asked to be present made me think that we were getting a little too close for comfort, so I requested that Steve Wye be brought back in because I knew he was as adamant about the investigation as me.

Penrith Forensics were the first to have a squiz. They examined an area under the house, but couldn't see anywhere that was conclusively where the floorboards had been cut or damaged, so we ripped up the carpet and then some of the floor coverings in the hallway and out to the kitchen where Ward had indicated. Meanwhile, Keir sat in what was left of the lounge room the whole time, watching us intently, his face stony as always. I watched him just as intently, searching, probing for any signs of emotion that would give me a hint of what was going on in his mind. He knew we'd found the bones, and he knew that we hadn't obtained any conclusive results, or else we would have charged him, and it played on my mind that he only wanted to watch because he knew that there was some other piece of evidence that we'd missed, and he wanted to see if we found it.

Then it came to me. I remembered the structural engineer, and I took Merk outside so we could talk in private. 'Perhaps we need to get some more experienced people down here to help, because this will be our last shot; they won't give us a fourth warrant,' I said.

'Who do you suggest?' said Merk.

'Well, Sharpie always said after the second warrant that we could've used the army, because they'd love this sort of thing. He reckoned they'd probably do it for free as a training exercise. At least that would save our resources.'

'Sounds like a bloody good idea. Do you want to make some enquiries and let me know how you go?'

I went back to the station to talk to Sharpie. By the next day, we had a team of army recruits carrying out a grid search under the house. They began by lifting the concrete porch.

It was an eerie feeling working with Keir watching on. He scrutinised every move with that same expressionless look, but on the third day, Keir caught on that I was watching him. His gaze found mine and in my mind I said to him, 'We've got you now. You know we have,' but the corners of his mouth merely turned upwards in a smirk.

In the end, we found absolutely nothing. 'Smug bastard,' I thought.

CHAPTER 15

When we'd finished packing up, I was leaning on the fence when Keir walked through the gate and gave me a quick, self-satisfied look. Every fibre of my being urged me to grab one of the uniformed officer's batons and beat the living hell out of him. 'How do you like it?' I would ask. 'Cowards beat women! You're not a man!'

I watched him drive off, and then looked back at the skeleton that was his house. The house seemed to be in pain, and, in a weird way, it reflected the lives of the people who had lived in it. Like Keir, it knew everything that had transpired between its walls and, like Keir, it knew the truth. But, like Jean, it had been completely transformed by Keir's actions, starting out as something lovely and pure before being stripped down to absolutely nothing. I took my last look at the dishevelled property and felt it only right to visit Christine Strachan. Pausing in her front yard, I tried to collect myself. Blind hatred had consumed me when I'd seen Keir's smugness, and I needed a different persona to talk to Christine; my strength was her strength.

I knocked on the door. She appeared behind the flyscreen and, even through the darkened mesh, I could see the years were taking an unfair toll. 'Detective Seymour! What a pleasant surprise!' she cried when she realised it was me.

'Hello, Christine,' I said, just as chirpily. 'How are you?'

'I'm well, I'm well. Come in. Would you like a cuppa?'

'That would be fantastic. White with two, please.'

'Yes, Peter, I know,' she said with a playful tap on my arm. 'So how's your family going? It must be nice to have two beautiful little girls.'

'Yes, it is,' I responded, feeling a little guilty. 'Sue is doing fine too.'

'So how are things going with your inquiries and the investigation?' she asked as we both sat down in the lounge room after she'd made the coffees.

'Dammit!' I thought. 'This woman's spent so much time with the cops she's starting to sound like one.' I even found myself starting to talk to her in the same fashion.

'Well, as you know, the Homicide Squad are finalising the investigation. We're building a strong circumstantial case against Tom, I assure you. The thing is, Christine, we can't move too quickly on this, and we can't do anything until we're certain we can make the charges stick. If we push too soon, we could jeopardise everything.'

Christine's response was as if she was trying to reassure herself. 'You know, Jeannie would never have taken off and not contacted her family or friends. She'd never have left her son, and I know in my heart she would've contacted me. Tom always kept saying she'd called him, but she would never have left all her possessions, like her dolls. Why would she leave them behind? She wouldn't.'

My heart broke as I watched the tears well in her eyes. 'I know. Things are going well with the investigation, Christine, trust me. We'll find out what happened.'

She smiled that smile again. My reassurances had sparked a glimmer of hope in her eye. 'I know you'll find my Jeannie, Peter, I just know you will.'

Holding back my own tears, I finished my cuppa and excused myself. With my role in the case all but done, I went back to my Prosecutor's training. It was a welcome change of pace being able to spend time with my family, and no longer having to leave my wife at home alone was truly wonderful. Everything seemed so right.

I was at work the next day when I received a message asking me to call my wife rather urgently. I picked up the phone and called her, all sorts of thoughts running through my mind, but I wasn't prepared for what Sue told me. I was going to be a dad again.

CHAPTER 16
Rosalina

The trial for Rosalina's murder began early in 1993. We still had no conclusive results on Jean's bones, but we consoled ourselves knowing that we'd nail Keir on Rosalina's murder. My dedication, tenacity and strong will in relation to Jean's case were more than matched by Mick's efforts on Rosalina's. He'd toiled endlessly, organising witnesses and putting briefs together, and just before the trial began, he told me he was good to go, and that he couldn't think of anything he'd missed. We felt very confident of gaining a conviction, and I was given special permission from the Commander of the Prosecutors' Office to join Mick for the duration of the trial. Joining the Police Prosecutors had been a bit of a blessing in disguise, because I now possessed a more refined sense of the legal system, and Mick was really pleased to have someone who could help him with the legal side of things. It was a massive task organising all the witnesses for each day of the trial, added to which we had to arrange a witness list with the Crown Prosecutor, Chris Maxwell QC, and the Instructing Solicitor for each day of evidence.

The trial was presided over by Justice Sully in the Darlinghurst Supreme Court.

Keir had a Legal Aid lawyer to conduct his defence, and they selected an even mix of male and females with a variety of ages and backgrounds to make up the twelve jurors.

The Crown Prosecutor started the trial with his opening address, which outlined how Keir was the only person seen arriving at and leaving the house on the day of the murder. He concluded, and the Defence barrister then outlined the Defence's case. One by one, witnesses, including Max Wormleaton, took the stand and testified that Keir was the last person seen entering and leaving the house. Numerous fire officers and investigators also testified as to the length of time it would have taken for the fire to take hold and for smoke to start billowing from the eaves. A window of ten minutes now became a critical factor.

The Defence argued that the offender must have seen Keir leave the house and, without being seen by the neighbours, entered the house only to find Rosalina, who was then killed and set alight in the main bedroom.

'There's no way the jury will buy that,' I thought to myself. 'Their defence seems pretty thin.'

I chatted to the Crown Prosecutor after the first session, and felt comforted by his words of confidence. Whilst I desperately wanted to get Keir for Jean's murder, I would be, in part, satisfied if we got him for Rosalina's murder.

The trial ran from days into weeks, with Christine and other family members dutifully attending the court each day. Clifford Strachan came whenever he could to support his wife, but I could see in his face that he couldn't sit there and look at Keir, now firmly believing that this man was responsible for murdering his daughter. Keir showed absolutely no emotions as he sat in the dock day in, day out, writing continually on a pad as each piece of evidence against him was presented. I watched him carefully, wanting to see if anything made him visibly nervous, but he was as cool as a cucumber.

One day, as we walked to the train station, I said to Mick, 'What the bloody hell is he writing on that pad every day?'

'He's probably writing, "Thou shalt not kill"', said Mick, who then laughed heartily.

'Mick, you know how you always laugh at your own jokes? It's not a bad thing, but sometimes they just aren't that good,' I said with a grin.

More and more days passed, and the Crown painted a picture of an obsessively jealous man who had tried to control every aspect of Rosalina's life. Some of Rosalina's family had made the trip from the Philippines, including her mother, Ester Canonizado, and sister, Ella, and Mick and I spent time with them each morning explaining what was going to happen, and telling them not to worry.

The media were always on hand, and often spoke to Ester outside the court. She told the *Sydney Morning Herald*, 'He was her first boyfriend… And for someone who is away from her family for the first time and without any friends in Australia, she would fall in love with anyone who was really nice to her.'[1]

More and more evidence was presented, and all of the witnesses provided the same scenario. Ester's testimony was particularly telling, as she painted a far too familiar picture of her daughter's personal state. Talking to us later, she repeated what we'd heard in court.

'She was starting to get lonely and because she was not allowed to go to visit our relatives very often, she got lonely. She can't go anywhere she wants unless she's with Tom. She's not allowed to go anyplace…And she is really sweet to anybody. Especially our relatives, they have close relationships. But suddenly it was cut off by Tom when they got married… That's why our other relatives were saying that "Oh, Rosalie we have not been seeing you so much. Why, what happened?"'[2]

Ella reinforced what her mother had said. 'It's like she was in hiding. Because prior to her marriage, we had a very good relationship with our relatives there. We come to occasions like birthdays and anniversaries. We always get together in parks, you know, BBQs. And since she got married, it also reached me that she is not allowed to go alone…She called me up several times prior to her death. First she was bubbling that she was buying a car. And the next call she was telling me "you know this guy lost in the dog race, greyhounds, and he lost so much $10,000 or something." And she was so mad and she was telling me "you see this man, I've been working hard. I want to go back. My car will be delivered soon and we don't have money to… He promised me."'[3]

Ella's comments confirmed my suspicions; the bikini-altering incident with Jean hadn't been an isolated one. 'Tom…was very possessive…When my papa…visited them…and my sister was wearing…shorts…Tom covered her legs…In one of my relative's places that they went swimming, he doesn't want my sister to wear bathing suits. He just wants her to be in… long shorts.'[4]

I listened as the Crown further outlined Rosalina's personality. She was twenty-four years old when she died, and highly educated. She and her siblings had all attended university and Rosalina held a Bachelor's degree in Commerce. She was a qualified accountant, and had met Keir at a family wedding in Sydney in 1988 before marrying him in the Philippines in 1989. Upon returning to Australia she'd become a silent partner in his upholstery business, working two jobs just to keep the two of them afloat, and it was she who had given him the money to restart his business. This was confirmed by Ester. 'She tried to build up that upholstery business and make it big along with Tom…she even funded Tom's start for the upholstery business.'[5]

The Crown outlined Keir's many motives for killing Rosalina, detailing their dysfunctional relationship and Keir's obsessively jealous tendencies. They alleged, considering Keir's financial difficulties, that he had killed her to claim the $80,000 from Rosalina's life insurance policy.

The Crown finished up, and the Defence indicated that Keir would be giving a statement from the dock. We weren't surprised. He had his right to address the jury from the protection of the dock, and we knew he sure as shit wouldn't want to put himself up for cross-examination. When Keir stood up in the dock, there was a deathly silence. Every juror turned towards him, leaning forward in anticipation of what he had to say. I was sitting with Christine Strachan, watching on intently.

Just as he opened his mouth to speak, BANG! There was a tremendous clap of thunder directly above the courtroom. It was as if God himself was screaming and yelling. Flashes of lightning illuminated the room sporadically, each burst lighting up Keir's stony face, and the glass in the windows shook so hard I was sure they would shatter at any moment.

Keir tried to speak, but it was no use, and his lawyer passed a flat hand across the front of his neck motioning for Keir to stop. The jurors absolutely shat themselves, and just sat there staring at Keir, their mouths agape. Surely, if any of them had any doubts, this sign from the heavens would sway them; even the Gods didn't want to let him speak. The storm lasted for what seemed like an eternity, but finally relented, and Keir was able to speak. He talked of how much he'd loved his wife, and said that he hadn't killed her. He claimed that someone else must have entered the house because he was at the shopping centre, so there was no way he could have committed this horrible crime.

He sat back down when he was finished and looked at the judge.

Keir's lawyer continued with his line of argument, in particular how the neighbours all thought Tom and Rosie had a good relationship. He referred to the home videos that had been presented in evidence, which showed them content in each other's company, and finished by saying, 'If there was any whisper of a bad relationship between Mr Keir and his wife, you would have heard it.'[6]

All that remained now were the closing arguments. The Crown Prosecutor tried to convince the jury that there was enough circumstantial evidence to convict Keir, and I was certain this was the case. The Crown Prosecutor reminded the jury that Rosalina's family had outlined Keir's obsessive jealously, and how he had several motives for killing her. The Defence reminded the jury that his client loved his wife, and was not in the house, and that this was a random act committed by someone unknown to the police.

The following day, the judge addressed the jury, telling them how to consider the evidence without *actually* telling them how to find the defendant. The jury then retired to consider their verdict. We felt confident that we'd secured a conviction.

Later that day, we received word that the jury had asked the judge for an explanation of 'reasonable doubt'.

'What the hell did they need that for?' I thought.

The concerns now came quick and fast for both Mick and me, but we kept our fears to ourselves. I didn't want to let Christine see my doubts, and Mick certainly didn't want the Canonizados to see his; we needed to be their rocks.

Eventually, the jury filed back into the courtroom.

Keir rose to his feet in the dock as the jury sat down.

'Has the foreman come to a decision?' the judge asked.

'We have, Your Honour,' the foreman said as he stood.

'The jury will now deliver its verdict. How do you find the defendant?'

'We find the defendant not guilty.'

Dozens of jaws dropped in unison, those of the Crown Prosecutor, the Instructing Solicitor, Mick, me and the two families. Sheer confusion covered everyone's faces, and I would never forget the Canonizados' reaction: they felt utterly betrayed.

Keir turned to his parents at the rear of the courtroom and gave them a smile, then found my gaze. I was staring at him through eyes of pure hatred, but he gave me the same blank look as always. I maintained eye contact, wanting him to see it in my eyes, wanting him to know that I wouldn't rest until justice had been done, wanting him to know that he was on borrowed time; I was going to take him down.

I felt numb as I watched Keir leave the courtroom a free man.

Mick and I made the uncomfortable walk outside the court and tried to explain what had just happened to the families. How could we explain it when we couldn't work it out ourselves? How do you tell a family fully expecting justice to be done that this is the biggest travesty of our legal system you've ever seen? How do you tell a family that they cannot have their peace? They were totally pissed off, and I wasn't far behind. In among the hubbub, I managed to call the Coroner's office.

'It's Peter Seymour here. Can you pass a message on to the Coroner: tell him the jury just left their bloody brains at home.'

I put my arms around Christine and held her tightly. I could feel she was trembling uncontrollably. When she spoke, her voice was a mixture of shock and confusion. 'So what happens now with Jeannie's investigation?'

'Don't worry about that,' I said as reassuringly as I could. 'The reason Jeannie's case is taking so long is because we want to make sure we have everything watertight so that the same thing doesn't happen again.' How could I promise that? Rosalina's murder was as cut and dried as they came, and yet the bastard had walked.

Mick did his best to comfort the other relatives, who now had to grieve for a second time, and it was a long time before we were able to leave. By the time we did, we were both mentally exhausted.

I got home at around 5 pm, totally shattered. I'd barely polished off my first beer when I saw the news on the TV. My stomach churned as I watched on in disgust; Keir's acquittal was one of the top stories. This was just the beginning.

As the weeks went on, the more unscrupulous members of the media had a veritable feast as Keir started his own publicity campaign. He taunted the police, calling us idiots and accusing us of orchestrating a smear campaign against him. He made up a flyer and was filmed by news crews handing them out at the local shopping centre and dropping them in letterboxes. He made himself available for anyone who wanted to interview him, and told all and sundry that he knew who'd killed Rosalina and had the evidence to prove it.

My question was always, 'Well if you know who did it and you have the evidence, then why didn't you tell the police earlier?' He kept on about the smear campaign, accusing us of not doing our job properly, and told everyone we were wasting our time because we were never going to get him. He eventually placed an ad in the *Mt Druitt - St Mary's Standard* in 1995 offering a $50,000 reward to anyone who could provide information leading to the arrest and conviction of whoever had killed Rosie. He was quoted in the paper as saying, 'The whole thing has left me quite bitter and angry. My wife's killer is walking around scot-free and the Police are not doing anything about it…I will never get over her until the person is caught.'

Every time I saw him on TV my blood ran cold. I'd sit there in silence and renew my vow: I'd get him for Jean's murder.

I rang the Coroner the next day to discuss what had happened.

'This is why you need to make sure you have all the evidence sorted for the next one,' he said. 'I wouldn't have thought you'd have any trouble getting a conviction with Rosalina's murder, but it just goes to show what juries can be like; bloody unpredictable things.'

'Yes, sir, they are. Anyway, Jean's case is with Homicide now. They're the ones calling the shots, so we'll just have to wait and see.'

I got off the phone still reeling. It was simply inconceivable that we could lose this trial. I couldn't bear a repeat. I was going to get justice for the Canonizados. Keir would spend time in jail, even if it wasn't for killing Rosalina. But what could I do? I wasn't in charge of the investigation anymore.

A Channel Nine reporter, one of the bloody good journos we were privileged to have worked with, Jane Hansen, had been following the case intently, and had also been in court at the acquittal. Keir, in the course of his media campaign, was more than happy to give her two interviews, first on Channel Seven's *Today Tonight* and then on Channel Nine's *A Current Affair*, but I don't think he'd thought it through, probably due to being too wrapped up in his own publicity, smugness and arrogance, because Hansen had organised for a Professor of Human Behaviour to watch the interview, and privately comment on whether he thought Keir was telling the truth.

Keir, who was now a lot greyer than he'd been when we'd first arrested him, started the interview very confidently, but as Hansen pressed him, he couldn't make eye contact. Hansen was obviously an experienced journalist, and as the interview continued she sensed his body language, so she pushed and prodded, becoming far more assertive in her questions, and telling him that it seemed like an incredible coincidence that his first wife should 'disappear' and then his second wife end up murdered.

The interview had started with Hansen asking straight-out about Jean.

'Is she alive, Thomas?'

'Is she alive? Of course she is,' Keir had responded.

'Why would you think she's alive when her own parents think she's dead?'

Keir took several moments to answer, and his gaze dropped. 'Because I've got no reason to believe she's dead.'

'Are you capable of murder?' Hansen pressed.

'Nope,' Keir mumbled, maintaining his downward stare. At the mention of the word 'murder', his expression had actually changed for once, becoming somewhat stern.

'Could you kill anyone?'

'Nope.'

'Is it possible that, on finding out that your first wife was having an affair, you killed her and buried her in the backyard?'

'No, it didn't happen.'

'Is it possible that that made you angry enough to kill her?'

'It didn't happen.'

'Why don't you look me in the eye when you tell me this?'

'I've had a problem with me neck at the moment…in here…I've had a bit of a cramp, and it's hard to sort of turn me head around.'

Realising that she was gaining the upper hand, Keir tried his best to look at Hansen, but he could only do it for a second.

'Like I said, they've got no doctor's reports, no nothing.'

'Well, I'm telling you they're human bones, and I'm asking you; how did they get there?' Hansen pressed.

'Wouldn't have a clue. Wouldn't have a clue at all.'

'Whose bones are they, Thomas?'

'Wouldn't have a clue. The only bones that we know that were found was, um, either sheep, cattle, pig.'

Keir gave a summation of how both his wives had ended up dead, and then Hansen asked him, 'What do you put it down to?'

Keir began breathing heavily, and his Adam's Apple tightened. 'Just sheer bad luck.'

'My oath it was bad luck!' I thought to myself as I watched the interview. 'Bad luck for Rosalina and Jean to have met you at all!'

Afterwards, Hansen spoke to the Professor, who advised that, in his opinion, there was no way Keir was telling the truth. Hansen had gone some of the way towards proving that Keir was not as innocent as he was making out, and ultimately Crown Prosecutor, Giles Tabateau, would successfully argue at the final trial for admission of this interview into evidence. Hansen was to take a personal interest in the Keir cases from that time on, and would also become a close associate of Christine Strachan.

Whilst the world was seemingly falling apart for the latter, my world was coming together. Where one family was grieving, mine was celebrating. On 23 April 1993, Sue gave birth to the third of our lovely daughters, Tayla.

CHAPTER 17

Jan the Man

In 1994, I became a full-time Prosecutor at the Westmead Coroner's Court. John Hiatt retired, and was eventually replaced by Jan Stevenson, who was finally sworn in as the new Deputy State Coroner towards the end of 1996. Jan was your real no-nonsense woman, and was also what you would call a 'power dresser'. Her glasses enhanced her eyes which, when you looked into them, said, 'Don't mess with me just because I'm a woman.' She had short blonde hair and was always immaculately dressed, a woman who commanded respect and simply wanted to make things right within the community she served. She was one of those Coroners who made it a priority to discover the truth. I remember an inquest into the death of a talented sportsman who'd been working as an electrician on a building site and was killed in a tragic accident. During her summing up at the conclusion of the inquest, I could see Jan becoming emotional as she addressed the family, telling them what a tragic loss it was, and how much he had meant to so many people. As Jan struggled with her words, I jumped up and interrupted her, referring to a small part of the evidence, which I knew she was about to deal with anyway. It was the only thing I could think of to give her the break she needed to regain her composure. She knew what I was doing, and allowed me to speak, as I was the Sergeant Assisting the Coroner in the inquest, and she later thanked me for giving her the break she needed. Jan and I developed a close bond, and I will always be grateful that I worked with, and for, her. I reckon she could have run for Prime Minister, and would have had a bloody good chance of being Australia's first female leader.

It was, however, strange working for a woman at first. The police force can be a bit of an old boys' club, and that's what I'd been accustomed to. Nevertheless, I'd never been one to not give someone a fair run because of their gender, in fact I made it my goal to make her feel as welcome as possible.

Westmead was just that kind of place to work. It had a small, yet friendly, tight-knit staff. Among them were the two cops whose job it was to accept the paperwork from the investigating officers every time a new body was brought into the morgue. Down the hallway was a large whiteboard where the names of the deceased persons were written.

Every day, I had to go past it, and every day I was magnetically drawn to it, because in the bottom right-hand corner was an area where the unsolved murders were written. One entry read, 'Human remains; believed to be those of Jean Angela Keir.'

The bones had been removed from Westmead and taken to the long-term storage facility until a decision could be made. I was still inwardly seething that the whole thing seemed to be taking so bloody long. The only thing that I knew had been done since I'd obtained the DNA confirmation in Melbourne was that Sergeant Dayment had taken them to be examined at the Sydney University Department of Anatomy and Histology in 1997. One of the scientists there had concluded that the bones belonged to an individual of sixteen years of age or more, and if the bones were female, the height would have been between 155.6 cm and 168.8 cm.

Jean Angela Keir was 165cm.

Late one afternoon, I was sitting at my desk when I heard a voice say, 'Hello, little buddy.'

I turned to see the Hulk-like figure of Detective Senior Constable Alan White, bearing his usual larger-than-life grin. After exchanging the usual pleasantries about our families, etc., Whitey asked the question I knew was coming. 'How's the new Coroner then?'

'Yeah, she's bloody fantastic, mate.'

He shot me an odd look. I don't think he thought I'd be so enthusiastic about a female boss. 'So what's on the agenda today then, mate?' he said.

'Not much, mate,' I replied. 'The Coroner wants to clear up the unsolved murders from the whiteboard. There's one in particular I want to talk to her about.'

'Which one?' Whitey asked as he walked across and examined the board.

'The one that says, 'Human remains; believed to be those of Jean Angela Keir.' That's the one I investigated when I was working as a D at Mt Druitt. We need to get those bones to America for DNA testing, but for some reason they won't take them. It's really pissing me off.'

'Why don't you tell the Coroner what's going on and get her to order them to get it done. She can do that, can't she?' Whitey had a way of always bringing things down to their simplest form, a way of pointing out the bleeding obvious.

'I'll run it past her and see what she says. She hasn't read the brief yet, because it's technically still under investigation. Worth an ask though, I reckon.'

'Well, little buddy, I've got some 'real' police work to do, so I'll leave you with it. Let me know how you go.'

'Yeah, no worries. We'll catch up for a beer soon,' I said.

A few minutes later, Jan came to my desk. 'Hi, Pete. You ready to talk about those unsolved murders?'

'Yes, Ma'am,' I responded enthusiastically. I followed her down to her chambers, and when I entered the room, I noticed that the unsolved murder files were already on her desk.

'Ma'am, there's one case in particular that I'd like to discuss with you.'

'Okay, which one is that then?' she said, looking over the files. I could tell she was intrigued by the obvious passion in my voice.

'The one about the human remains believed to be those of Jean Angela Keir. I worked on the investigation, and the bones need to be sent to

America for testing, but for some reason no decision has been made and the bones are still here.'

'I think you'd better fill me in on the whole story,' she said.

I proceeded to outline everything, right down to the most minute details: the original case with Rosalina, the testimony of people like Jean's son and Wormleaton, the picture of the relationship between Keir and Jean, the story of the affair, Riley's testimony, the digs, the DNA testing, Keir's acquittal, everything.

Jan sat and listened intently, her hands clasped together on the desk in front of her. At several points, she made comments as to the bizarre nature of the investigation. When I'd finished, she sat back in her chair, or should I say it was more like one of those slumps that people do when they're like, 'Shit, is that all then?'

She sat back upright and leant towards me. 'So we're at the stage where all we're waiting for is to send the bones to America. If they achieve a result, I take it Keir will be charged with the murder?'

'That's about the strength of it, Ma'am.'

She looked me square in the eye. 'Right then, I want you to call Homicide. Tell them I want to see the investigators and their boss. I not only want you to tell them that I want to know why the bones haven't been taken to America, I also want you to tell them that the bones WILL be taken to America.'

I looked across the desk, barely able to conceal my elation. 'With pleasure, Ma'am.'

I stood up and started to walk out of her office far more pleased about the investigation than I'd been in a long time, but just as I reached the door she said, 'You'd better be right, Seymour. Those bones had better belong to Jean Angela Keir.'

'Ma'am,' I said, turning back with a look of feigned shock on my face. 'Have I ever let you down before?'

'No, but I've never stuck my neck out before based solely on someone's words. However, for some reason, I trust you. I don't really know why, but I do.'

'You can trust me, Ma'am. I'm an ex-detective.'

'Yeah, that's what worries me!' she said, whereupon we both had a good laugh.

CHAPTER 18

Tests in America

I went back to my desk and looked up Homicide's number. For the first time in years, the roller-coaster seemed to be slowing down. Maybe it might even come to a halt soon, and I'd be able to get off. Then again, maybe not. No-one was available to talk to me. I left an angry message that I was to be called *urgently*, making sure to tell them that I was calling on the Coroner's behalf. Sure enough, one of their senior officers called back soon after. After I got off the phone, I walked down the hall to tell Jan what they'd had to say.

'I just spoke to one of the Homicide Bosses,' I said. 'I think he pretty much shat himself about the urgency of you wanting to see them. Either way, they'll be here for a meeting with you on Friday at 10 am. Is that sweet?'

'Sure is! Did you tell them to bring something yummy, like a cake or something?'

'No, I didn't...but I guess that could be arranged.'

Jokes aside now, Jan spoke very seriously. 'Now Pete, you're sure there's nothing else I should know?'

'No, Ma'am. I swear. The bones are the last thing I need done. I know you're going out on a limb, and I really appreciate it.'

She looked at me earnestly. 'You know, you made me feel so welcome when I came here, and I won't forget that. I know you're an honest bloke, and you're a lot like me, except for the bloke part.' She let out a hearty laugh. 'What am I talking about? We're nothing alike. If I go down, Seymour, you're coming with me.'

'I appreciate that, Ma'am, but I assure you, we won't be going down on this one.'

Later that day, I got a phone call. It was Rod Dayment from Homicide. 'Pete, how's it going? I heard the Coroner wants to see us on Friday and wants to know why the bones haven't been taken to America. She hasn't got the shits with us, has she?'

Sensing his concern, I played along. 'Mate, she ain't real happy. The bones have been lying around for years, and the Americans are the leading experts in this kind of stuff. She wants to conclude as many unsolved murders as possible, and the DNA testing is the last thing that needs doing. She wants to know when it's going to happen.'

'Mate, we're making inquiries with the Americans, and it looks like they'll be able to do it. I might have to provide them with an overview of our investigation in return for them pushing it up the list for us, though.'

Whilst I had all the time in the world for Rod, who was a bloody top bloke, I hated the way he said 'our' investigation. No it wasn't; it was mine and Mick's.

'That's good news, Rod,' I said. 'I think the Coroner will be very happy.'

She was, and so was I. I got to work that Friday with a new spring in my step; it might be over, once and for all. It was 9 am when the Coroner came to my desk.

'I think we might have this meeting in the courtroom, at the bar table. It might reinforce to them what the hell we're working for here. It's a bit more imposing in there, and it might make them feel a bit more uncomfortable. Hopefully they'll tell us what we want to hear.' I loved her accompanying grin; knowing yet cheeky.

'Ma'am, I like the way you think. I'll open the courtroom.'

The Homicide blokes got there just before 10 am. Geoff McNevin, the Boss, was accompanied by Rod Dayment and Neil Tuckerman, who was assisting Rod with the investigation. They walked into the Prosecutor's area, adjacent to the courtroom.

'G'day, Pete,' Rod said as he walked into the room.

'G'day, Rod. How's things?'

'Good, thanks, mate. You know Geoff, don't you?'

'Yeah. G'day, Geoff,' I said, shaking his hand.

'And this is Neil Tuckerman,' Rod continued.

'G'day, Neil,' I said, and shook his hand too, before turning, very casually, to pick some papers up from my desk. 'The Coroner wants to see you in the courtroom. There's more space in there. I'll take you in and let her know you're here.'

I led them into the room, switched on the lights and indicated the chairs where they were to sit. 'I'll be back in a minute,' I said, and headed for Jan's office.

When I arrived, I paused at the Coroner's door for a moment and watched her reading a court document. A couple of gentle knocks on the door got her attention. 'The Homicide boys are here, Ma'am. I took them into the courtroom, and they're awaiting your presence,' I said with an overly exaggerated polite tone.

'Oh, isn't that nice,' she responded, with an equal measure of sarcasm. 'I guess I'll just have to join them. Are they nervous?' Her smile told me she hoped they were.

'A little. It'll be interesting to hear what they've got to say.'

She rose regally from her desk and, walking with the grace and poise of a head of state about to sign a peace treaty that was totally in our favour, followed me down the hall. As she entered the courtroom, the Homicide boys moved to rise from their chairs.

'Oh, no,' she said. 'Don't get up; this will be an informal chat.'

I was sure that the mention of the word 'informal' scared them even more. She made her way to the chair opposite them, and I introduced her. She looked McNevin square in the eye. 'I understand that the bones relating to the Keir case have been tested in Melbourne without any conclusive evidence being obtained. Is that correct?'

That was one of the things about Jan Stevenson. She'd do things so calmly and so politely, while still commanding absolute respect. She wouldn't do anything too dramatic, but boy, all and sundry knew not to mess with her. Her personality was certainly impacting on McNevin, and he clasped his hands together as if he was praying to the Big Fella upstairs for salvation.

'Yes, Ma'am. That's right. We're looking at taking the bones to America, but we're waiting on further approval.'

'Okay,' she continued. 'Now, as I understand it, police were told by a forensic scientist in Melbourne some years ago that the Americans were the leaders when it came to DNA testing. My concern is why the bones haven't been taken there already. I take it that this is the last line of investigation?'

'Yes, that's right,' Rod Dayment interjected, trying to look as comfortable as possible in a difficult situation. 'The problem is the cost factor, and whether the Americans could guarantee a result if we took the bones over there. They've also been very busy, and we've had to wait.'

The Coroner could sense that McNevin was her man, so she clasped her hands together and leant in closer to him. 'Right. Well, as you know, the police investigate these matters on *my* behalf, and I can direct inquiries in any way I see fit. So, I want you to tell me when these bones are going to be taken to America. I don't want to hear about costs or time or anything like that,' she said, looking at Rod Dayment. 'I just want to know when they're going to be taken over there.'

'Ma'am, I will give you an undertaking that the bones will be taken over there,' said McNevin.

She shot him a look that would have made Stalin shiver. 'Mmmm, that's fine, yes, but I want to know how *soon* you can get them over there. There has been far too much time wasted on this case already, and this matter needs bringing to a head, not the least for the deceased's family, who must be under enormous stress waiting for these tests to be conducted.'

'I'll make the necessary calls and get back to you with an answer,' McNevin said rather nervously.

'Yes, thank you. I expect that this will be in the *near* future?'

'Yes, Ma'am, it will.'

'Right,' she said, quite chirpily. 'Well, I think that is all for the morning, gentlemen. Let Peter know when this will take place. Now, my understanding so far leads me to believe that if the DNA testing is successful, then Mr Keir can be interviewed straight away. Am I correct?'

'Yes, Ma'am, that is the case,' said Rod. If we get the results we're looking for, we'll be in a position to re-interview Mr Keir and charge him with Jean's murder.'

'I look forward to this matter being finalised *soon*,' said Jan as she once again rose regally from her chair and extended her hand to McNevin. 'Nice to meet you.'

'Yes, nice to meet you too, Ma'am.'

Jan shook hands with Dayment and Tuckerman, and we all walked from the courtroom.

I escorted the boys to the exit. 'I'll give you a call as soon as we get in touch with the Americans and sort things out,' Rod said as he shook my hand.

'No worries, Rod,' I said. I went back to the Coroner's office with a huge smile. The only time I'd had a bigger smile was on the three occasions when Sue had told me she was pregnant, and the three subsequent occasions when my beautiful girls had been born.

'Well, how do you think that went?' the Coroner asked me as I walked into her office.

'I think it went very well. I kinda got the feeling they couldn't wait to be out of there.'

'As long as they get the bones over there, then I'm happy. Let me know as soon as you hear something. Chase them like a greyhound after a rabbit if you don't hear from them in a few days.'

'Yes, Ma'am, will do. Hey, thanks for doing that,' I said with genuine gratitude.

'That's quite okay. As I said, I've never stuck my neck out like that before, but for some reason, I trust you. I don't know why; I must be losing my marbles.'

'No, Ma'am, your marbles are in the bag. You won't be disappointed. You just wait and see.'

'I hope so. You'd better be right about this, Seymour.'

I went back to my desk with a tremendous feeling of satisfaction, like the one you get from a hot chocolate on a cold day, or a beer after a hard day's work. All the moments of doubt seemed to drift away like leaves on the wind. For the first time in a long time, I felt like I could face Christine Strachan without having to weave a web of sometimes hollow promises.

The call came a few days later; the bones were to be taken to America. Approval had been given to hand the bones to scientists at the United States Department of Defence. Rod Dayment left on 16 September 1997, and arranged to have some holidays whilst the bones remained in storage in San Francisco. After that, they would be taken to the U.S. Armed Forces DNA Identification Lab in Rockville, Maryland. Whilst he was over there, Rod was to give a presentation to their law enforcement officers about how the Keir case had unfolded up to the point where he'd brought the bones over, with one bone being left in Australia in case the others were destroyed. I was happy the case was finally moving again.

Nancy Koszelak was the scientist who did the testing. Her work focused on obtaining mitochondrial DNA sequences from the remains of American soldiers who were believed to have died in the Vietnam, Korean and Second

World Wars. Whenever the Americans found a body or some remains believed to be from a missing G.I., it was Nancy's job to conclusively prove that those bones belonged to a deceased serviceman. Her lab had developed special expertise in extracting DNA no matter what condition the bones were in, especially bones recovered from difficult terrain. She was doing successful DNA tests on bones that could have been in some remote Pacific jungles for nigh on sixty years, pretty amazing stuff really; precisely the kind of expertise we needed to prove that the bones were Jean's.

She performed the tests late in October 1997 using the two biggest bones, the left kneecap and the right big toe, choosing bones from either side of the body for the best results. She analysed one bone at a time, sanding back the entire internal and external surfaces to make sure there were no contaminants. In order to be entirely sure, she washed the bones in ethanol first. She then extracted mitochondrial sequences from both bones, and found that they matched. The bones definitely came from the same person, but the real question was, did they match the genetic sequences from Christine Strachan and Gaspar Baan?

Eventually, she was able to confirm that the sequences matched. The bones were consistent with having come from a child of Christine Strachan and Gaspar Baan.

One thing I'll say about the American scientists is that they were very thorough, leaving nothing to chance. Despite the fact that Nancy had proven that the mitochondrial DNA matched Jean's, she passed the blood and bones to Dr Demris Lee, who was the Technical Leader of the Nuclear DNA Section. This section dealt primarily with recent death investigations, where individuals had perished in aircraft mishaps, explosions, gunshots or bombings. Ms Lee conducted her tests on 20 November.

Complete nuclear DNA profiles were obtained from both the bones and the blood, the profiles being based on nine chromosomal markers plus a sexing marker. The two bones were identical. The bones came from the body of a female, and matched the blood samples perfectly. There was no doubt about it; the bones belonged to Jean Angela Keir.

I was in my office preparing a brief in relation to a fatal motor accident when my phone rang.

'Is that Officer Seymour? This is Officer Lyons.'

'G'day, Mick!' I said. 'How are things?'

'Bloody good, mate! I just got off the phone to Rod Dayment. The bones match the blood samples. Rod's organising for the bones to be brought back to Australia. He's just waiting for the Yanks to do their report. Once he gets back, he'll get Keir in and interview him.'

'I take it that means we have enough to charge him with Jean's murder?'

'Yeah, mate, this was all we were waiting for. Looks like we've finally got him.'

I couldn't believe it. Almost a decade in the making, and at last, we could charge him. We'd finally reached the climax; the story was to have a happy ending. I didn't know how to feel. I didn't know what to think. I wondered where Keir was. Was he on another publicity mission? 'Well, mate, you'll be getting a lot of publicity very shortly,' I thought. Lost in my own world, I almost forgot I still had Mick on the other end of the phone. 'That's bloody great news, Mick. I'll let the Coroner know. She'll want to know when they're going to charge Keir.' Without thinking about it, I then went into a bit of a ramble about all the proceedings we'd have to undertake at our end.

'Yeah, mate,' said Mick sarcastically. 'I think I'll leave you to sort all that shit out.'

No sooner had I put the phone down than I was in the Coroner's office. 'So, why are you so happy?' said Jan after I'd skipped in there like a cashed-up kid walking into a sweet shop.

'I just got news that the Americans have matched the DNA from the bones. That's all we needed; as soon as the Homicide boys get the report, they'll arrest Keir.'

'That's fantastic news, Pete. I knew I could trust you!'

'I told you,' I said, unable to help myself from being one of those 'I told you so' people. 'Must make you feel good to know you have such good staff.'

'Spare me,' she said. 'Just make sure the paperwork is crisp. I suppose you'll enjoy having this matter finalised in court?'

'Ma'am, words cannot express.'

CHAPTER 19
Locating the Informant

Brian Riley called me in January 1998. He was agitated and concerned. Originally, he'd rung Mick, but Mick had passed him on to me.

'G'day, mate,' I said. 'It's been a long time. How's things?'

'No bloody good!' Riley said bluntly. 'Keir knows where I live.'

'How the hell does he know that?'

'He rang me, and then his bloody solicitor rang me. I can't stay here.'

'Calm down, mate. What exactly did he say?'

'He rang me and said, "Are you the bloke that was in Long Bay seven years ago?" I said, "Nah, mate, you've got the wrong bloke," but I knew he knew it was me, and next thing I know I've got his solicitor on the phone. I have to get out of here.'

'Mate, don't worry about it. It's no drama. He only beats women, not men,' I said, trying to reassure him. 'We'll get you into witness protection.'

'Fuck that! I don't need it, I can look after meself, but I have me missus and kids to think about. Just move me to another house.'

'Mate, I'll make a few calls and let you know,' I said, and then hung up. I couldn't believe it, first that we'd managed to find Riley again, but more so that Keir had been stupid enough to contact Riley in the first place. It pretty much proved that he'd said something, because he was now clearly worried about what Riley might say. Keir was getting desperate, and having thought that we'd lost Riley for good, I wasn't about to let him slip through our fingers again. We'd need him to testify to ensure a conviction. I immediately rang Rod Dayment and told him about the problem. Rod was just as aware of Riley's importance to the case as I was, and organised everything as quickly as he could with Police Headquarters, obtaining approval for $1500 for the switch. I rang Riley the next day.

'Mate, find another place to rent. I'll be flying up there shortly with $1500 for you. If you have any dramas, you ring me straightaway, yeah?'

'Yeah, mate. I'll meet you when you get up here. Just make sure no-one knows where I am when I move.'

I thought I'd better pull at the heartstrings, just to make sure he stayed on side. 'No worries, mate. We'll be the only ones who know where you live. Brian, we need you to give evidence, mate. Your evidence is very important to us, but it's more important for Jean's family, who've had to wait all this time to find out what happened. I'm sure you can appreciate how they must be feeling. You've got a missus and a couple of kids. Imagine if it was one of your kids that had gone missing.'

'Look, Detective Seymour,' he said, slowly and decisively, 'I *will* give evidence, don't worry about that. Just keep Keir away from me, or I won't be *alive* to give evidence.'

Over the next couple of days, arrangements were made for me to fly up north to meet with Riley. I needed to get a statement from him about Keir contacting him, give him the relocation money, and get the details of the cellmate who'd first told him about Keir's admissions, because up until now, that person's identity had remained unknown to police.

At around the same time, the Homicide Ds got the reports from the Yanks that said the bones were *conclusively* from a child conceived by Christine Strachan and Gaspar Baan, and Rod Dayment rang me.

'Pete, how ya goin', mate? It's Rod Dayment. We're arranging for Keir to come into Penrith station with his solicitor on 20 February so we can interview him about Jean's murder.'

'Beautiful, mate. Make sure you nail him, ay?'

'Will do, mate. Will do.'

Keir arrived with his solicitor on the 20th and, after a lengthy interview with Rod and Tuckerman, was taken to the charge room and formally charged with Jean's murder. Rod rang me straightaway. 'He's down in the dock as we speak, mate.'

'Did he make any admissions?'

'No, none at all. He reckons she's still alive, and still maintains he's spoken to her since she disappeared.'

'Well, it must be hard for her to be getting around missing various finger bones and a kneecap. Surely a jury can't stuff this one up.' I was suddenly agitated at the possibility and annoyed that Keir hadn't confessed and taken the need for a jury out of the picture. We had massive amounts of evidence against him, so he must have known we were going to get him on this one, but who knows what goes on in the mind of a psychopath. Maybe he'd so convinced himself as to the validity of his lie that he actually believed it. He'd got away with murder once, so he must have been convinced that he could do it again.

'Let's hope not,' Rod replied. 'Anyway, Pete, I'll get back to the charge room and make sure he's processed properly.'

'Yeah, mate. Hey, listen, thanks for keeping me in the loop.' I put down the receiver, and then lifted it up again and dialled a number I'd come to memorise. A familiar voice answered.

'Hello, is that Christine?'

'Yes, is that Detective Seymour?'

'Yes, yes it is. How are you, Christine?'

'Oh, you know, living day by day.'

'Listen, I have some good news. The test results came back positive. We've finally charged Tom with Jean's murder.'

There was an extended pause; she obviously hadn't been expecting news of such magnitude. When she eventually spoke her voice was faltering. 'I...I...I can't believe it! After all these years! I just can't believe it is all over!'

'Christine,' I said, not wanting her to get her hopes up too high, 'there's a long way to go yet. We'll put a brief together, and hopefully the jury will be in no doubt this time. I'm confident we'll see justice done, but you just never know with juries. We saw that with Rosalina's case.'

'I know, but I also know you guys have done everything you can, and we will get the result we're all hoping for. I just know it.'

'At least we're still in contact with the prison informant, and after all these years, he's still prepared to give evidence. It's a huge bonus.'

'I'd like to meet him one day and thank him myself,' Christine said.

'You'll get that chance when we go to court. I'll let him know that you want to meet him.'

Keir, being on trial again for murder, was obviously refused bail, and was remanded into custody at Penrith Local Court. The bones returned to Australia on 9 March, and I flew up to meet with Riley on the 23rd. After arriving at the airport, I rented a car and drove straight to Riley's new address. It had been seven years, but I recognised him straightaway. He was still slim, and still wore his black hair in the same fashion, just above his collar.

'Brian, good to see you again, mate,' I said as he opened the front screen door.

'G'day, Detective Seymour, good to see you too.'

'It's Peter, mate. Don't worry about the "detective" bit.'

I walked inside the small, three-bedroom fibro place and immediately realised that no-one else was home. Seeing the way I was looking around the room, as if I was expecting to find someone, Riley sensed what I was thinking. 'Yeah, I sent the missus and kids away,' he said. 'I've spent a lot of time putting my past behind me, and I didn't want them around to hear all of this. D'ya want a cuppa?'

'Yeah, cheers, mate. Just white with two sugars will be fine,' I said as I sat down on the couch. 'So, you've settled in okay?'

'Yeah, it's fine, as long as Keir doesn't find out where I am,' Riley said as he disappeared into the kitchen.

'Don't worry about that. If you have any concerns, any concerns at all, just ring me and we'll sort it out. You did the right thing by calling us; it means we can take care of it all. Although there is one thing that's bothering me.'

'Yeah, what's that?' Riley asked as he came back into the living room with the cuppas in hand.

'Well, after you gave me the info, you gave me the wrong hearing date for your bail application. We did up the letter of comfort for you, but you never got it, and you got convicted. I'm just wondering why you still want to help us.'

'Peter,' he said, making a point of using my name as he handed me the coffee, 'what he did was wrong. You don't do things like that to women. Even the blokes inside don't take real well to anything done to a woman or a kid, you know. I did my time for something I wasn't guilty of. I know I ain't no saint, but I have to do what's right for that woman he killed.' I studied Riley as he spoke. His voice was sharp, but it had a soft edge.

'I spoke to Jean's mum the other day,' I said. 'I told her you were still prepared to give evidence against Keir. She really appreciates it, mate. She said she can't wait to meet you so she can thank you personally, and she told me to tell you that what you're doing means a lot to her and her family.'

Riley smiled broadly. 'Well, it's the least I can do. Actually, I'd love to meet her, but I guess we'll just have to wait until the court hearing for that to happen. I'll leave you to do the intros.'

'Yeah, mate, no dramas,' I said as I leant across the coffee table and handed him the cheque for $1500. I also pulled out my portable typewriter, plugged it into the socket and set the paper up. 'I'll just show you the original statement you gave us, and the second statement you gave the detectives when they came to confirm the first one. Have a read through them and check that they're right while I try and fix this bloody thing.'

Riley read through the statements and then placed them on the coffee table in front of the typewriter. 'Yeah, mate, they're spot-on.'

'What I need is for you to confirm that you gave me that original statement, and the reason why you didn't sign it initially.'

'It was because I told you I wanted to get some legal advice, and because I was concerned for my safety because I was still in jail.'

I typed as he spoke.

'Yeah, I remember the day Joe Perkins came up to me and told me all about it. I remember feeling a bit sick about the whole thing, but I knew I could use it.'

I wanted to ask Riley about Perkins, seeing as we didn't know much about him, but I let him speak as I typed. I'd clarify things when he was done. It never paid to interrupt a witness when they were talking.

'After I spoke to Keir in the yard, it was probably a coupla days later when I saw something on the news about him, so I went back to him and said, "Mate, you're on the news." I can't remember if he said anything back, but I remember that I didn't want anything more to do with him. What I'd seen on the news was on Channel Ten and it showed you blokes diggin' up around Keir's house.'

'What happened after that?'

'I didn't hear anything else until about a year ago, when I got a letter through Probation and Parole from Wilson Solicitors wanting to talk to me about a police interview I'd done. I remember wondering how the hell they knew about it. I was a bit pissed at you guys, 'coz someone must have leaked the info. Either that or Keir had realised that he'd only told me and Perko, and he'd figured that one of us must have mouthed off. From the sound of things, he should've gone down for killing his second wife, so I never expected to hear from him.'

'Yeah, the jury left their brains at home on that one,' I said.

'Yeah, sounds like it,' Riley continued. 'Anyway, I asked me Parole Officer what to do. He said to ignore the letter, so I did. I got another one about six months later, and I ignored that too. Two months ago, I got a phone call, which was answered by a friend of mine. Me mate told me about it when I got home later that day.'

'Then what happened?'

'That same arvo, the phone rang again and when I answered, a bloke says, "Brian?" I said, "Who's that?", and he says, "Tom," so I said, "Tom who?" He says, "Is this Brian Riley? You've been in gaol, you've been down Junee?" I said, "Who's this?", and he says, "Tom, Tom Keir. Were you in Long Bay Gaol Remand seven years ago?" I said, "Nah," and he says, "You've never been in gaol?" I said, "Nah. How did you get my number?" and he says, "Through Telstra." I was concerned, so I said, "I think you've got the wrong bloke, mate. Don't ring here again," and he says, "Yeah, no worries." I hung up the phone and contacted me Parole Officer straightaway.'

'What happened after you spoke to your Parole Officer?' I said.

'Later that afternoon, I received a call from a guy who said he was Keir's solicitor. I was still very concerned, so I said to him, "You've been trying to track me down. Tom rang me this afternoon. I don't want him ringing here again. How did he get my phone number?" The solicitor said, "We got it through Telstra. Tom shouldn't have rung you." I was still trying to dodge things, 'coz I didn't like what was going on. I chatted to him for a bit, then hung up.'

'Did it surprise you when Keir spoke to you in gaol in 1991?'

'Nah, not really. He appeared reasonably calm until I told him I knew where the body was. When he started shaking, I knew I'd hit the nail on the head. I knew that Perko had told me the truth.'

I finished typing, removed the sheet of paper from the typewriter, handed it to Riley and asked him to read it. He did, and nodded to signify that everything was right. He made us both another cuppa, and we talked about the upcoming trial.

'How long do ya' think this will take?' he asked.

'I don't know, but it should be a bit quicker, because he's been refused bail,' I replied, and then leant forward. 'Mate, you mentioned "Perko", Joseph Perkins. Are you sure he's the guy who gave you the info in the first place?'

'Yeah, mate, positive. I think he's up in Queensland at the moment, but you blokes won't have no dramas tracking him down. I don't know if he'll talk to you, but it's worth a shot. He might not be much bloody good to you though; he's a bit of a junkie.'

I left Riley's place knowing that sooner or later I'd have to provide him with more money to relocate again as a precaution against either Keir or his lawyers finding him.

As Riley had predicted, we didn't have much trouble finding Perkins, as it turned out that he was serving time up north. Detective Tuckerman was sent up to Queensland to speak to him, whereupon he took a statement confirming what Riley had said, and then arranged for Perkins to be brought down to Sydney under police escort.

We'd confirmed the seven bones to be Jean's, and we had two key witnesses. All that remained now was the formalities of the trial, and we could finally put Keir away.

CHAPTER 20

The Jury Decides

On 21 May 1998, Thomas Keir appeared at Penrith Local Court and was committed to stand trial for the murder of Jean Angela Keir. The magistrate, as anticipated, refused him bail, and he was taken back to gaol. It wasn't until 10 August 1999, however, that Keir's trial commenced at the Darlinghurst Supreme Court. It had been eleven years since Jean's disappearance.

Justice Adams presided, and the jury was an even mixture of men and women. The Crown Prosecutor was Richard Cogswell.

It felt strange to be back at Darlinghurst after we'd lost the first trial, and I couldn't shake the bad feelings. The room was filled with negativity, as though it was riddled with ghosts and we were stuck in purgatory. Try as I might, I had trouble convincing myself we wouldn't lose again, that the insurmountable evidence wouldn't be enough or that the jury would, once again, leave their brains at home. Nevertheless, I dutifully set my mind to organising all the witnesses' statements with Mick, Rod and Neil. I comforted myself in the knowledge that I *had* done everything I could do to secure a conviction; the rest was out of my hands.

Christine and Clifford were just as dutiful. Every day, they trudged up the hill from the Museum train station to the court, and every day they'd have to run the media gauntlet. The *Daily Telegraph* had dubbed the case *A Husband on Trial*, which didn't really show a great deal of imagination, but being the ongoing saga that it was, there was tremendous interest in Keir's trial, and a run-down of the evidence that had been presented appeared in the papers every day.

I entered the witness box early in the piece so that the bones and video evidence could be tendered to the court, along with the photographs of the crime scene. The TV footage of the searches of Wilkes Crescent was played for the jury, and I made the appropriate comments about what we'd been doing and what we'd been looking for.

The bones were tendered to the court, still intact apart from small incisions where the DNA had been extracted. I wondered how Keir felt, looking at his wife's bones as they were brought into the courtroom. I hoped he felt scared. I hoped he felt sickened. I hoped the realisation of what he'd done had finally dawned on him. I hoped he knew we had him. Then again, he probably wouldn't have, because he'd totally convinced himself of his innocence, and that Jean had run off with another man. 'She hasn't gone far, mate,' I thought to myself. 'She's here, right in front of you.'

All seven bones were placed in front of the jury so they could see part of the human life form that had once been Jean Angela Keir for themselves. They passed the plastic bags containing the bones among themselves, and it was clear that the act of holding human remains in their hands was having a huge impact.

I spent the best part of two days in the witness box, most of the time being cross-examined by the Defence barrister. He tried his best to pick holes in my version of events, but I knew exactly what had happened, because it was stored in my mind like a videotape. Every time he tried to question me, or ask me if I'd gotten something wrong, I'd simply say, 'No, that is incorrect.'

Christine Strachan was the next to take the stand, and the Crown Prosecutor, Cogswell, began. 'Now, I want to ask you about Jean's nature, personality and the sort of person she was at the age of 17 or 18. Around the time that she was married, what sort of personality or nature would you describe her as having?'

'She was a very happy girl,' said Christine. 'Basketball was her life, she loved sports. She got into soccer once, but I told her "no" because I was scared.'

'What about socially, in terms of friends?'

'Yes, she had friends at school, Shona, Fiona, a lot. She had quite good friends.'

'How would you describe her personality?'

'Very bubbly, very happy, always joking, the type of girl that never took anything seriously. She was happy.'

'After she married, in the period after her marriage to Tom, which you told us was in August 1984, over the following two, three years, did you notice a change in her personality, in how had she evolved in terms of personality?'

'Well, she wasn't as happy as she was before, because she said to me that every time she did something he always put her down. She's like, "I can't do nothing right." I mean, everything was wrong, and there were a lot of things she used to tell me that I just couldn't make sense of. Jean wanted to go back to basketball, and did for a bit, but Tom thought the clothes were too revealing. He even asked me to change some tank tops her sister-in-law had given her.'

'Did anything happen in the relationship between her and Tom between the time they married and February 1988?'

'Yes.'

'In how the relationship was going?'

'Jeanie was always stressed, very stressed. She was…like I said, she said to me, "Mum, he doesn't treat me like a wife. He treats me more like a piece of property, a possession. I can't do this. I can't do that."'

'Did she say this to you more than once?'

'More than once.'

'Do you recall when it was that she first said that to you after the marriage, that is, in between August '84 and February '88?'

'Oh, it was just after her son was born. It had already started, even before her son was born, but she was persevering. Towards the second and third year, though, she just couldn't handle it any longer.'

Christine gave evidence on how Jean had complained to her that Keir would not speak to her for weeks on end, and that when Christine confronted him at work about it, he would deny it. She also said that after he and Jean had been married, he didn't want to go out and socialise, and Jean wasn't allowed to go out with her friends, such as Shona and Fiona. Christine said that she'd told Keir that Shona and Fiona were nice girls, and his reply had been, 'Fiona's not a nice girl.'

Christine then painted a picture of her beloved daughter, of her hopes, her dreams and her aspirations. She spoke of the special bond she'd shared with her daughter, and of what a caring mother Jean had been to her son. She spoke of her heartache at losing her daughter and, more importantly, of the toll Jean's disappearance had taken on the family. She also spoke about the trip to Culburra.

'Tom came to the house and said, "Jeannie rang me last night. She was crying. She misses her son. She wants to come home." I said, "That's funny. She never rang me." I was happy about her coming home though. I said to Tom, "All right, can you wait a minute? I'll give you her birthday card and present. That might perk her up a bit. I'm surprised, though. You told us that you weren't going to pick them up until the weekend."

'Tom said, "Well, she rang me, and she's very upset, and she misses her son. She wants to come home."

'The present was some clothing and a prayer plaque, and the note in the card said,

"When you get back we will talk. If you are willing to divorce Tom, your father and I will stay with you. We will always be with you. Don't worry about Tom taking your son either. Tom has to prove you're an unfit mother to do that."'

As if everything she'd already said wasn't enough, when she started to talk about the sheer torment of not knowing, I could see it was having just as big an effect on the jury as the bones. The jurors listened intently and many were moved to tears by what Christine said. Maybe, just maybe, they'd brought their brains.

One by one, the witnesses came and went, each one of them portraying a picture of Keir's obsessive and psychopathic behaviour when it came to Jean. As Jean's friends took the stand, and memories of Jean came flooding back, they revealed new information that even we hadn't heard. Fiona Chalmers testimony was particularly disturbing.

'Jeannie started to look very sick, and I could see that she was deteriorating physically, getting very skinny and hollow around the eyes, and becoming very depressed. Jeannie always seemed to have bruises near the top part of her thigh. She told me she wanted to leave Tom, but she couldn't because he would kill her. There were at least three times she said that.'

'You have already told us that one of them was when you were at her house at Tregear. Do you recall the two other occasions when she said that to you?' Cogswell asked.

'Yes, we were coming home from a restaurant after having lunch one day and we were having a serious conversation about how to. I was asking her why she stayed when it was clear that she was very unhappy and depressed. She said in all seriousness that it wouldn't make any difference where she went, he would find her and kill her, that she didn't want to involve us. She told me that if she went missing, I would be the first person he would come after.'

'What about the third occasion when there was reference made to her being killed; do you remember where that was?'

'We were with my sister, Shona, and we were having a serious discussion about ways of...of helping her to get away from him, and she said it wouldn't make any difference where she went, he would track her down like a dog.'

'Did she say what he'd said he would do if he found her?'

'I think he said he would chop her up and feed her to the dogs.'

Fiona then spoke of other things Jean had said. 'God was pulling her one way and the devil was pulling her in another, and she was just... um...I know that when I was talking to her, in a way I could see she was...like, I could just hear in her voice that she...she was really losing it at that point, and I said to her to...to...to...that she needed...that something bad would happen in that house, and that she needed to leave.' Fiona also stated that Jean had repeatedly said, 'My life's in God's hands.'

When Court resumed the next day, Cogswell asked Fiona to clarify some parts of her statement.

'The matter we were discussing,' Fiona said, 'the last conversation when Jean said she feared he would kill her, when she was talking about being pulled in different directions. She was talking about inside her house, talking about God, and about being pulled in one direction, and she was saying that the Devil was in her house; the dilemma wasn't inside herself. The Defence made it sound like she had a dilemma inside herself, and we were talking about that, but I called her up to tell her that she had to get out of that house, that something bad was going to happen there, and that's when she said, "I feel the Devil's pulling me, and God's here." I said to her, "God's with you, and you're going to be okay," and she replied, "I can see God's here, but I can see the Devil here too, and I don't know who's going to win."'

Fiona's sister, Shona, told a similar story about how much Jean had wanted to leave Tom. It was late in 1987 and, after playing basketball one day, Shona and Fiona had raised the subject of Jean leaving Tom once more, and Jean had started punching the car and had said, 'I just want a fucking life! He's making me crazy! He's sending me mental!'

The Crown continued to question Shona about Jean's disposition. 'You have said she didn't seem to be her normal self. Did you notice anything about her appearance on this occasion when you came down from Inverell?'

'Yes, she was always thin, but she was thinner, her hair was a little unkempt, and her eyes just didn't seem to have the usual spark.'

Another member of Jean's family, Catherine Moore, a close cousin, had been at the house in Wilkes Crescent watching videos one night, and she told the court that Tom had said, 'Yes, if I can't have her, nobody is going to have her.' Catherine also related two incidents at a beach on the Central Coast late in 1985. Peter Boros, who was Jean's cousin, and about the same age as her, had put some suntan lotion on Jean's back. Catherine said that Keir had threatened to kill Boros, because he had touched Jean.

Jean's Godfather, Colin Page, then took the stand and recalled his last conversation with Jean.

'What did Jean say?' said Cogswell.

'She was unhappy with the relationship with Tom, and said that she felt restricted. He used to try and control what she wore, and prevented her from seeing her friends, and didn't want her to get her licence and didn't want her to get a job. If she went out without a bra, which was the fashion then, I suppose, he would hit the roof.'

'These are the things that Jean told you?'

'Yes. She said he was jealous and possessive, and didn't like to see her talking to other people, other boys, men.'

'Did she say anything else?'

'Yes. She said she was frightened of him because she...sometimes they would be fooling around, wrestling, and all of a sudden he would get very serious and get her in some sort of a choke-hold and say, "This is how easy it would be to kill you if I ever caught you messing around with someone else." And she also said there was something else...'

Colin Page dipped his head and brought his hands to his eyes as if trying to hold his tears back.

'Mr Page?' Cogswell asked.

'I'm sorry.'

'Did she tell you something else?'

'Yeah. She said that there was something she knew about him that frightened her, but she wouldn't tell us what it was. I asked her several times, but there was some dark secret that she knew about him that she wouldn't reveal.'

'Is that what she said?'

'Yes.'

Page confirmed that this was the last time he had spoken with Jean, but that Tom had telephoned him not long after Jean had been reported missing.

'What did he say to you?'

'He was telling me how Jean had left and gone off with this Carl.'

'To the best of your memory, can you recall what Tom said to you in that call?'

'Yes. He said he'd been looking for her, and he'd tracked this Carl down, found out where he lived and followed him and watched him. He said he belonged to some religious cult, and that he had a reputation for being involved in the disappearance of young girls, but he couldn't find her.'

'Did he say anything about what he thought might have happened to Jean?'

'Well, he thought she'd gone off with this Carl fellow, and then he discussed his fears about people disappearing when they got involved in this religious cult or whatever it was.'

Heather, Jean's sister, was also asked to give evidence about Culburra.

'What was her emotional state at that time?' Cogswell asked.

'It was shocking. She was really depressed, really down, she wouldn't take her sunglasses off, she was real thin and white in the face, real pale.'

'You told us you had a long conversation with her?'

'Yeah.'

'What was that about?'

'It was about Tom and Jean and their relationship.'

'Can you tell us as much as you can remember of what Jean said during that conversation?'

'She was a bit worried about him, like, she was very worried.'

'If you can remember either the words she used, or if you can't remember the exact words, the gist of what she said?'

'She was just…she asked me if I could…if I knew anyone in Queensland that would look after her. I told her she should have worked it out with him. Like, I said that, you know, "You're married. You should work things out." She said she couldn't, she'd tried, and she'd had enough. She just felt restricted. I don't know.'

'Did she say what her plans were, or what she wanted to do?'

'She wanted to leave Tom. I don't know, she was just real upset. I just kept telling her she should try and work things out. I didn't understand too much about the nature of what was going on there, but it didn't sound too good. She just wanted to get out. She was scared of him.'

'Did she say why she was scared?'

'Because he kept threatening her life…we talked about everything, mate, like everything. We talked a good lot of hours. I can't remember, I can't recall everything that we said, but in general it was about getting away from Tom. He wouldn't let her do anything, she wasn't allowed to, in my words, breath properly without him coming down on her.'

The Defence tried once again to paint the picture that Jean and Tom's marriage was like any other marriage, but Heather remained adamant that Tom had slapped Jean and had threatened to feed her to the dogs. 'He used to say that a lot of times when we were there.'

Heather also stated that she thought she'd heard Tom repeat his threat about cutting Jean up and feeding her to the dogs when he'd come to collect her from Culburra. Later in the trial, Heather was asked to describe the events that had transpired when Tom had come to Culburra to get Jean.

'I seen a couple of bags out the front and Tom arguing with Jean, saying he was taking her home, and Jean was fighting. She didn't want to go.'

'You said that you saw Jean and Tom; what was happening?'

'Tom was trying to grab Jean and drag her into the car.'

'How was he doing that?'

'Just with his arms around her waist, picking her up, arms and legs all over the place. Just, yeah, trying to get her forcefully...'

'Can you describe the physical movements of Tom and Jean?'

'Yeah, he picked her up around the waist, and she was just all arms and legs. He's just picked her up around the waist and dragged her that way, dragged her to the car.'

'Did he put her in the car?'

'He threw her in the car.'

'How did he do that?'

'He like opened the door, and she had her legs sort of like on the door and on the side of the car, and he's thrown her in the passenger side and then he's locked the door and quickly run around to the driver's side. And she's jumped out, and he's chased her around again and grabbed her and put her back in the car.'

Heather's boyfriend at the time, Peter Bullock, took the stand, and was queried on his opinion of the relationship between Tom and Jean, and whether he'd seen or heard any threats Tom had made.

'Was there an occasion in late '87 when Tom said something about disposing of a body?' asked the Crown.

'Yes.'

'What did he say?'

'Virtually to feed her to the dogs...'

'Feed the meat to the dogs?'

'Take the meat off the bone, feed it to the dogs and then get the bones, put them on the grinding disk, turn them into fertiliser and throw it over into the paddock.'

'Was any reference made in that conversation to starving?'

'Yes.'

'What was that?'

'Starving the dogs and then feeding the meat off the body and the bones to the dogs.'

The Defence questioned Bullock as to whether he was intoxicated at the time of hearing this, having picked up on the fact that not only had Bullock not mentioned any of this in his statement but that, on the whole, he was a dishonest character who had stolen cars and given false names to police. Bullock admitted that he'd been drinking, and that he was no saint, but he was adamant that he was not intoxicated at the time of hearing these things.

Peter's sister, Lisa, also testified that she had heard Tom say, 'Cut the flesh off and feed it to the dogs, grind the bones and throw it as fertiliser down in the bushes and burn the hair.'

As if all of what was being presented to the court wasn't emotional enough, one piece of Peter Bullock's evidence was truly heartbreaking. He recalled the incident at the caravan park. 'As I've gone back to the caravan, I seen Tom with Jean, dragging her towards the car.'

'Can you describe exactly what you saw Tom doing?'

'He had Jean by the arm, and Jean was like throwing her little arms around and that, and kicking her legs to try and get away from him, I'd say. She asked me to help, but I just turned around and said, "Youse are married, I'm not getting involved."'

'What do you remember in terms of what Tom was doing to Jean physically?'

'He just had her by the arm, and was just sort of walking her to the car, while she's like throwing her arms around, you know, virtually like an elastic band. She was just throwing her arms out. She was a tall, skinny girl. She has no weight on her. She was just like virtually saying, "Let me go," you know?'

Bullock then leant forward, his tattooed hands clasped firmly together, and I could see that he was trying to stop them from shaking. He paused and bowed his head. When he raised it again, I could see the tears welling up in his eyes. He took a deep breath and looked at the jury. 'That was the biggest mistake I've ever made in my life. If I'd of stopped him when Jean was screaming out for help, she'd be alive today, but I didn't, and now she's dead.'

The sight of this burly man, who looked like a typical bikie with his bushy beard and tattoos, his voice shaking and low, the tears dripping down his cheeks, clearly shook the jury. I was an experienced detective who'd seen it all, and even I shed a tear.

The other key person we wanted to give evidence was Carl Neiding. Neiding's part in the whole saga whilst small, was rather important because for years Keir had tried his hardest to convince everyone that Jean had run off with him. Mick Lyons had interviewed Carl back in 1988 and we were satisfied that he had told us everything he knew, and that when he dropped her home on that fateful February night it was indeed the last time he, or anyone else, had seen her. We knew this was the case, but we needed the jury to believe the same.

Neiding took the stand and described how one day, prior to August 1987, he was walking through Hyde Park on his way to do some shopping. He noticed a pretty girl walking in the park and, on his way back, saw her again sitting by the fountain. They fell into conversation, whereupon he discovered Jean's name, gave her his number and they then went for a walk in the Botanical Gardens and had a cup of tea.

Afterwards they sat on the grassy bank and, noticing the tears welling in her eyes, he put his arms around her and said, 'What's wrong? What's up?'

'Nobody has ever held me like that before,' she replied. He proposed they go to Bondi beach, Jean consented, and after wandering around and talking a little more, they went back to his flat and had sex.

As Neiding continued to give evidence, he painted a picture of Jean's desperation to turn the brief encounter into a relationship and his own desire to avoid involvement in a complicated situation. Jean's calls started a week after their initial meeting.

'Her calls would usually come pretty late at night and I would try and listen to her, be kind of helpful, but she would say things like she wanted to move in with me, that she was in love with me, all kinds of things like that.'

Neiding outlined how she'd said she wanted to get out of her marriage and while he tried to listen and give her support, he told her a relationship was impossible and she should 'forget it'. At her request, he met with her briefly three weeks later. Jean desperately tried to convince Carl to continue the relationship but he refused.

Soon after the second meeting, Carl told how he came home one night to find Tom sitting outside his flat. Tom talked to Carl about his troubles with Jean and asked Carl to talk to her and try and 'straighten her out'. Carl said he rang Jean and told her that Tom was with him and that she should try and sort things out. Soon after the visit Carl said he decided to, 'pull myself out of the equation' by moving out of the flat and going overseas for a short period.

A couple of months later, after returning from overseas, Carl said that Jean started to call him again, before one day turning up at his unit unexpectedly.

'Suddenly Jean shows up at my door and tells me the story that she was down in Nowra and that Tom went down and picked her up and she was coming back and, you know, she jumped out of the car or something at a gas station and hitchhiked back to Sydney. Maybe she didn't have anywhere to go or something like that, and so she came around to my place.'

Again determined to stay out of the situation, Carl said he encouraged Jean to go back to Tom and, 'talk it over, work out what you want to do with him' and when she finally agreed, dropped her home. He said Keir had invited him in but he politely declined. He watched Jean walk inside and, like he'd told us, informed the court that this was the last time he saw or heard from Jean; once and for all refuting Keir's claims that she had ran away with him.

The trial continued for many weeks and, with each new day, I felt confident that the evidence was mounting. Keir maintained his stone-faced composure and continued to write in his notepad, but I knew we'd get the conviction we so desperately desired, especially when Christine gave more evidence about Tom's actions after Jean's disappearance.

'Did you have a conversation with Tom afterwards about what you'd done with the neighbours?' Cogswell asked her.

'Yes.'

'What did you say to Tom?' I said, 'I asked the father of the girls next door, because they used to play with Jean when they where young, and he said that none of them saw anything,"

'Is that what you said to Tom?'

'Yeah, I said to him, "None of them saw anything."'

She then said than Tom had rung her a week later regarding the supposed phone call from Jean.

'What did you say?'

'I said, "Why would she be ringing you? She should be ringing me." I said, "Did she ask about her son?" and he said, "No, she never asked about her son." I said, "Did you mention to her that her son is, you know, missing her?" and he said, "We didn't talk very much," or words to that effect. It was like he didn't really want to get…'

'I'm not asking about that. Was anything said in that call about Jean coming back?'

'No. There were two or three phone calls, and I don't remember which phone call it was, but I said to him, "If she rings again will you tell her to ring me? It's unusual…she always used to ring me," but he told me, "She said no, she doesn't want to ring you. She said you're a bitch, and you're siding with me all the time."'

'Is that what Tom said she'd told him?'

'Yes. I said, "What about her son?" and he said, "She doesn't want anything to do with her son anymore, and she told me to remarry, because her son needs a mother."'

Christine also told the court about another rather bizarre phone call. 'Around November or December, something like that, there was a phone call from a very young girl, and she was saying, "This is Jen, this is Jen."' I said, "Who is Jen?" and she said, "Your daughter, Jen." I said, "My daughter, Jen?" I was just wondering about it, when she said "Yeah" and hung up. When Jeannie used to ring me up, it was always, "Hello, Mum." All my daughters say that; "Hi, Mum, it's me."'

After the lawyers had finished with Christine, and with Keir, the Crown brought in the scientists who'd been flown from America. Their evidence, I was sure, was going to remove any calmness from Keir's demeanour. They described, in the most precise of details, the DNA testing process. Charts and diagrams were produced showing how the DNA from the bones matched the blood samples. The Defence barrister tried his best to suggest that the bones had been contaminated, but the scientists shot him down every time.

Dr Ellis took the stand first. 'Bone 1 was a finger bone from the right hand, and this was the bone that had originally been examined by Dr Oettle. Bone 2 was the proximal phalanx of the right big toe, which, in common parlance, is the base of the right big toe. Bone 3 was probably the proximal phalanx of the right thumb, or the base of the right thumb. Bone 4 was the left patella or knee cap. Bone 5 was the capitate bone, which is one of the bones in the left wrist. Bone 6 was the third metacarpal, which is a bone at the base of the middle finger of the left hand. Bone 7 was the proximal phalanx of one of the right fingers, the base of either the index, middle, ring or little finger.'

'You also say that. "They have an appearance consistent with them having been buried in the ground for a similar length of time?"' Cogswell continued.

'Yes.'

'What do you mean by that?'

'The surface appearance, the degree of wear, or the fact that there wasn't any wear, the colour, the extent of dirt, or lack of dirt, was virtually identical for all of the bones, which would suggest that they had probably been in the ground, if not for exactly the same time, then certainly for a similar amount of time.'

'You go on to say that, and this is at the time of your examination, "They are not very dry, suggesting burial for only a small number of years or months."'

'Yes.'

'What do you mean by that?'

'Bones that have been buried for ten or twenty years or more become very dried out, and become very white, chalky. These bones did not look like that. It is by no means an accurate assessment. It is not suggested that I know how long they were buried for, because I don't, but it does suggest to me that they weren't there for twenty or thirty years. They were there for far less time than that.'

'You go on to say, "As no duplicate bones are received, the collection is consistent with but not definitely originating in one person."'

'Yes.'

'In paragraph 10 of your report you note that from the size of the finger bones you made a rough estimate that the person would be of small to average stature, and was probably an adult. Is that right?'

'Yes. I guess it is a matter of rough assessment on the basis of experience. Based on the fact that I'm six foot tall and I can tell how big the base of my finger is, for example, these bones are smaller than mine, and therefore likely to come from an individual who would, at least in terms of the hand, have smaller hands than mine.'

The two American scientists, Nancy Koselak and Demris Lee, were next to take the stand, and in the context of the trial, they were sensational. The Defence did their best to discredit the scientists' testimony, but these two women were the world leaders in their field and, confident in the soundness of their methods, were unflappable. In return for their assistance, after they'd finished giving evidence, we took them out for a day on Sydney Harbour. It was the least we could do, and it provided a welcome break from the intensity of the trial.

Back in court the next day, Riley and Perkins were due to give their evidence. Riley had been put up in a hotel not too far from the court and, on the first morning he was due to appear, he arrived early and tracked me down. 'Pete, I'd like to be introduced to Jean's Mum.' I took him over to meet Christine.

'Christine, this is Brian Riley. He's the one who gave me the information on where to find Jean.'

Christine started to cry, and held out her hand to shake Riley's. 'Oh, it's so lovely to meet you! I want to thank you so much for helping the police to find my daughter, and to find out what happened to her.'

'That's okay,' Riley said as he took her hand, lowering his head in embarrassment like a shy child. 'What Tom did was very wrong, and I'll do whatever it takes to see justice done. I just hope I can help. Nobody has the right to treat any woman like that. I just wanted to meet you, and say I'm sorry for what happened to your daughter.'

Riley let go of Christine's hand and moved off, wanting to be by himself. I could see, as he stood there, that he was mentally preparing himself so he would get everything right when he took the stand.

'Christine,' I said, 'he was a crook, and spent a bit of time in jail, but he's doing the right thing now and trying to get his life back on track. I think giving evidence is a big thing for him.'

'Yes, he's not a bad man,' she said. 'I'm really happy I got the chance to meet him and thank him personally.'

Just as she finished speaking, the Court Officer appeared in the doorway and told us we were due in the courtroom. We all went inside feeling like today was the day.

Riley spent a number of hours in the witness box. I knew he was going to be cross-examined about his criminal history by the Defence barrister, who was a bloody good lawyer, and gave Riley an absolute grilling. I could see it was starting to take its toll on Riley when the Defence barrister accused him of making up the story because he wanted reward money from the Government, or wanted his sentence reduced. Riley was like a soldier fighting to hold on to a strategic position while the Defence barrister rained down shell after shell, but to his credit, Riley stuck to his evidence, not faltering even slightly. I was certain that meeting Christine had given him the extra lift he needed.

Perkins appeared the next day, but was by no means as convincing as Riley. His constant drug use had made his memory sketchy, but he was able to provide enough details to corroborate most of Riley's evidence.

The Prosecution called their last witnesses, and then the Defence took its turn.

There weren't many witnesses Keir could call, but one of them was his son. The son's evidence, it was clear, was given very much under the influence of Keir and Keir's parents. He spoke as if he'd been coached, in much the same way as when Mick and I had first interviewed him. He said that he'd seen his mother at the local swimming pool, but at the time of the alleged sighting he was only three, so little weight was given to what he had to say. He also talked of alleged sightings over the following years, but little weight was given to those either.

We waited to see who the Defence barrister's next witness would be and much to our surprise, it was Keir himself.

'Mr Keir, can you please tell us about your relationship with your wife?' the Defence barrister began.

'Yes. I loved my wife very much. Our marriage had its troubles, but we were sorting things out.'

I was very interested to see what he had to say about the night Carl had dropped Jean home, which was what the Defence barrister had now started to question Keir about.

'What happened after they arrived?' the Defence barrister asked.

'I walked down the driveway or front footpath and walked down the... because I had the front door open so I could see any cars coming up the street immediately. I actually met them as the car pulled up. Jean got out of the car and I went to give her a kiss and she gave me a peck on the cheek as she was walking past and said "Hi" with a big smile on her face, and started walking into the house. I went around to the driver's side and thanked Carl for bringing Jean home and invited him in for a coffee.'

'Did he go in?'

'No. He said he had some things to do in the morning, and said it was too late as it was a long drive back to Bondi, but he said thanks for the offer and that he'd catch me later, and off he went.'

'When you went inside your house in Wilkes Crescent, what happened?'

'Jean was sitting on the lounge first up, and we had a cup of coffee and sat there talking about things, just the stupidity of the evening with her taking off, and other bits and pieces. She said, "Look, that's it. I just needed to say one last thing to Carl. That's it. It's all been said, now he's out of my life for good," and stuff like that.'

'Did you speak to Christine at all after Jean returned?'

'Yeah. Christine phoned up and I told her that Jean was home. She said, "Good, put her on the phone," but Jean gave me a signal to say "I don't want to talk to her," so I just said to Christine, "Jean's already in bed." I knew it was going to be bad if Christine came over…they would have had a slanging match. All the good work would be undone with her interfering, so I just told Christine she was already asleep.'

'Did Jean tell you she was going to go anywhere in particular?'

'When she said about needing more time away and everything, I said it wasn't a drama. She says, "Well look, I want to go and talk to a friend of mine in Campbelltown, get a bit of advice from them and other things." I thought to myself, "I'm not going to start any argument about that," because everything was running along nicely, so I said, "Yeah, no problem, go."'

Keir also told the court that after her 'disappearance', Jean had rung him and told him to find someone else, because their son needed a mum, but then when he'd told her about Rosalina, she'd started screaming and become upset. It was something the judge didn't buy, and neither did I.

The Defence barrister and Keir continued to paint a picture of a man who truly doted on his wife, a man who would do anything for her, and they did a pretty good job, too. I'd thought that putting Keir on the stand was a pretty big mistake, but they managed to pull it off, and as a consequence the weight of everything Bullock, Riley, Perkins and Christine had said was slightly diminished.

However, the Crown Prosecutor was having none of it and proceeded to use the Defence's arguments against them. Cogswell immediately focused on the fact that Keir did indeed dote on his wife, and it was this doting that had led to Keir's jealous and psychotic tendencies, thus, providing the reason why Keir had killed his wife.

'Mr Keir,' said Cogswell, 'We have heard from several witnesses that you would become enraged when your wife spoke to any other man, including one instance when she hugged her own cousin. Is this true?'

'Yes. I'm her husband. Of course I will be jealous of other men.'

'Isn't it also true that you would alter your wife's clothing if you thought it was too revealing, including one instance when you altered her bikini?'

'Yes, that is true, but it is my right as a husband. What husband would want his wife getting about in really tight clothes?'

What Keir was saying was gold; he was digging his own grave. I looked at the jury to gauge their reaction, paying particular attention to the female jurors, and I could see they didn't like what they were hearing.

Keir didn't spend a lot of time in the box and, to be frank, Cogswell, as his name would suggest, had turned the cogs really well. All in all, it would've been better for Keir not to have taken the stand.

The Prosecution and the Defence closed their respective cases, and Justice Adams then directed the jury on how their deliberations should go. Adams was a big man with a hefty white beard, and Christine had jokingly referred to him as 'Santa Claus' throughout the course of the trial. He was very specific with his instructions, telling the jury to be careful with Riley and Perkins' evidence, especially when assessing its credibility. He also addressed them about how they should assess the DNA evidence.

It was midday on 17 September 1999 when the jury retired to consider their verdict. As they filed out of the courtroom, some of the jurors glanced at

Keir, who'd stood up in the dock to face them as they left. As we got up, Mick whispered to me:

'So whaddya reckon? D'ya think we'll witness a hanging here today?'

I laughed. 'Mate, the best thing that could have happened was Keir giving evidence. I don't think he went over too well, especially with the female jurors. I'm feeling very confident.'

Mick and I walked outside with Christine and Clifford and the rest of the family and I spent the next hour and a half talking to Christine and some of the other family members in the waiting room. There was a little old lady selling coffee and tea and biscuits for a small donation, and I bought Christine a cuppa and suggested we walk outside to talk in private. I was waiting for her reply when the message came through; the jury had reached a verdict. We quickly made our way back into the courtroom. The media had gathered, both inside and outside the courtroom, all of them hanging on the verdict, most of all Jane Hansen. The same sickly butterflies I'd felt with Rosalina's case now filled my stomach, because the deliberations had been far too quick. I relayed my fears to Mick.

'Mate, that was a quick deliberation. What do you make of it?'

'I don't think they could've made their mind up that quickly if they were thinking he wasn't guilty. They'd have to think long and hard to find any reasonable doubt. I think it's good for us. It means they all made their minds up a long time ago. I guess we'll soon find out.'

The judge entered the courtroom and called for the jury to be brought in. As they entered the room, Keir stood up, but none of them made eye contact with him. They sat down, and I noticed a few of them looking towards the back of the room, at us and the family. My adrenaline surged like never before, like a jolt of electricity pulsing through my body. I was so nervous that they were going to deliver the wrong verdict. No, they couldn't possibly do that; the evidence was too damning. But then, we'd thought that about Rosalina's murder. I tried to calm myself and remain positive; surely there couldn't be two miscarriages of justice?

The judge broke the silence. 'Has the jury reached its verdict?'

The foreman stood. 'We have, your Honour.'

'How do you find the defendant, Thomas Andrew Keir, on the charge of murdering Jean Angela Keir?'

'We find the defendant guilty.'

My heart skipped a beat, indeed I think it might have even stopped for a few seconds. The word 'guilty' resonated in my head. I knew I'd heard it, but I had a hard time actually believing that everything that had happened over the last eleven years had finally come to a head. I held my hand out to Christine. She squeezed it tightly, and I could feel her trembling. I looked at the jury, and gave a nod of appreciation to those who returned my glance.

Then I looked at Keir. The rock-like façade had disappeared, replaced by a slight frown. The papers reported that he looked stunned, but I don't think that's really apt.

The judge thanked the jury for the important work they had performed, and then dismissed them. Keir was remanded in custody to await sentencing on 29 February 2000, and the Defence barrister then walked to the dock and whispered into Keir's ear. Soon after, he was led away, and the court began to empty.

Every detective that had worked on the case went over to the Crown Prosecutor and Instructing Solicitor to thank them for their hard work and to congratulate them on their victory. We then went outside with the family, but hadn't taken more than a few steps when the media absolutely swamped Christine. The poor woman was trying to come to terms with the realisation that justice had finally been done, and that she finally knew for certain what had become of her daughter, and now she was being absolutely overwhelmed, although she held up pretty well.

One reporter asked her, 'What was it like hearing the word "guilty"?'

'Beautiful! Wonderful! We've waited eleven years for this,' Christine replied.

She was also quoted in the *Daily Telegraph*, on 18 September 1999, as saying, 'I think watching his face during the guilty verdict that was sentence enough for me…Jean loved her friends and family and would never have abandoned her son.'

Jane Hansen interviewed Christine afterwards. 'After eleven years, what does this verdict mean to you?' Jane asked.

'A helluva lot. That at last they will know that she didn't run away with another man and left her son. That her son will at least know that she did love him and that we were the ones telling the truth and not his father. He doesn't look guilty. I don't think that man even has a conscience. Whatever he does, he reckons he's done the right thing.'

Meanwhile, back outside the courtroom, after the media frenzy had finally died down, Christine came over to us. 'I cannot thank you enough for what you have done,' she said with what was obviously heartfelt sincerity.

Clifford came up and shook all our hands. He was a man of few words, and all I got out of him was, 'Thanks for everything.'

The detectives decided that we would all go across the road for a few celebratory drinks with the Crown Prosecutor and Instructing Solicitor. I made my way over to the family and asked them if they wanted to join us. 'Of course,' Christine said. 'That would be lovely.'

Part of me felt really good that we could have a quiet, pleasant drink together, and that Keir wouldn't get to experience that feeling in a long, long time. As we started to make our way across the road Clifford stepped up and said, 'I want to be the first one to buy you fellows a couple of beers,' but Christine lingered, looking at me.

Eventually, she came over to me and said in a quiet voice, 'Can I speak to you quietly for a minute?'

'Of course,' I said as we let the crowd move on ahead of us.

Christine took hold of my hand. 'You know, Detective Seymour,' she began, 'years ago, after Jeannie disappeared, I went to a friend of mine who is a clairvoyant. I asked her about Jeannie, and she told me something had happened to her, but wouldn't say what. She told me about a detective who was tall and thin with brown hair. She said he'd be the one who would never give up, and would make sure the truth came out. She said this detective would make sure justice was done. I know now that she was talking about you.'

Her eyes pierced me as she spoke, and I shuddered as a cold wave passed through my entire body. I could see the tears in her eyes, so I embraced her, my eyes beginning to get a little watery as well.

'I've had a lot of strange feelings,' I said to Christine. 'Now I know that Jean has been here with me throughout the entire investigation, willing me on. But I only did my job, Christine. There were a lot of us involved; it was a real team effort. It doesn't matter who did what, though; justice was done. Unfortunately, I never got to meet Jean, but I feel like I know her after all these years. I'm just happy knowing you can get on with remembering Jean the way she was, instead of not knowing what happened to her.'

We headed across the road and climbed the stairs to the first floor of the hotel, where we were met by Clifford, who immediately asked us what we wanted to drink. I'd never really seen him smile, but as he made his way to the bar, you couldn't wipe the smile off his face. We joined the family at the tables, and sat and drank. We talked of the trial, the highs and lows, the times when we were sure he was guilty, and the moments when we thought the jury might be swayed, but most of the talk was about Jeannie herself. The family reminisced about all the wonderful times they'd spent with her and, before Mick and I left, Christine invited us to attend Jean's memorial service. I told her we would, and that we'd call her to get the details.

As Mick and I walked back to Museum station for the last time, he said to me, 'Well, we came here today to witness a hanging, and that's what we got.'

I laughed again. 'We sure did, Mick, but it's hard to believe it's all over after all these years. It's a shame he got away with Rosalina's murder, but at least we got him for one of them.' With that, I went home to be with my family.

As I walked through the front door, I wore the same grin as Clifford's. I'd rung Susie earlier to let her know that justice had finally been done, and she'd told me she was cooking my favourite, a baked dinner, to celebrate. As I sat there eating my dinner, I looked at my three daughters. It was a strange feeling. I was horrified to think that anything like what had happened to Jean could happen to my daughters, but I also felt relieved knowing that there would be people like me who'd never rest until justice was done. Ash was almost twelve now, and my two youngest girls had been born during the investigation. It felt like a chapter in my life was over, and now the next one was about to begin.

Just as we finished dinner, the evening news came on and I saw the footage of the Strachans being interviewed. 'They needed to hear that guilty verdict,' I said to Sue.

She leant over to kiss me. 'I think you needed to hear it as well.'

CHAPTER 21
Jean's Memorial Service

Christine and Clifford arrived home that afternoon to find a note saying that their neighbour had accepted on their behalf a bunch of flowers and an envelope that had been delivered at about eleven o'clock that morning. After Christine had collected these from the neighbour, she went inside and opened the envelope. Inside, there was a letter.

Dear Mrs Strachan,

Over the six weeks of the trial I felt I really came to know Jean. I think all twelve of us developed a bond with your family as we all learned of the anguish and pain you have endured since the loss of such a beautiful person.

I hope you will take some comfort from the swift and unequivocal nature of our verdict.

I send you these flowers as a token of appreciation for the strength you have shown over the last eleven years. You have shown resolute determination and perseverance to see that justice is done. I believe this to be an inspiration to us all.

I hope you will also accept them as a tribute to Jean. She paid the ultimate price for her individuality. Jean had dreams and aspirations to better herself and the future for her son. All of us have such dreams in life and we will learn to treasure these all the more for knowing Jean.

CHAPTER 21

I am thankful for having known her; she will always have a special place in my heart.

Kind Regards,

Juror.

Christine told me later that she held the letter in her hands and trembled, and her heart quivered as she held the letter to it. Everything, all the emotions, the fear, the anger, seemed to drain from her from knowing that a complete stranger felt so strongly about her daughter. Throughout the trial, she'd collected all the newspaper articles and kept a scrapbook. The juror's letter would now take pride of place within the collection.

Jean's memorial service was held on 25 September at the Holy Family Parish in Emerton, the suburb next to Tregear. Hundreds of people milled around outside as they waited for the service to begin, a testament to the fact that, after so many years of absence, Jean Keir could still touch so many people's lives.

Father Hanna, who conducted the service, was the same priest who'd married Tom and Jean and baptized their son. It must have been a bizarre situation for him, having once seen Jean and Tom smiling at one another, the love sparkling in their eyes, standing in front of Jean's family preparing to deliver Jean's eulogy. In another strange twist of fate, I'd discovered that I'd attended school with one of the Hannas!

Although Christine invited both Mick and me, Mick was unable to make it, which he was rather disappointed about.

I arrived just as Father Hanna asked everyone to take their seats, and tried to remain inconspicuous. I'd done my job, and I was merely here to pay my respects. As I tried to slink into a pew at the back, Maria Boros caught sight of me out of the corner of her eye, stood up and motioned for me to come up and sit in the second row, behind Christine and Clifford. Everyone in the church saw it, and there was no way I could refuse, so I shyly made my way down the front, trying to remain unnoticed. However, I felt the weight of every pair of eyes upon me. As I sat down, I realised that my view from the back had been rather obscured, and I could now see that there were pictures of Jean on the altar, and it really hit home how young and innocent this girl had been when her life had been brutally and cruelly snatched away. I'd seen pictures of her before in the course of investigating the case, but something broke inside me when I saw all her special personal items laid out in front of the pictures. As the song says, only the good die young.

Father Hanna made his way down to the family members, shaking their hands individually with that prolonged grasp that only a priest can manage, before returning to the microphone and beginning the service.

'Today we gather with Christine, Clifford, Heather, Fiona and Len. We are also mindful of Jean's son, who cannot be with us today, and we pray for Tom's salvation. We must try to integrate into our lives the lost, and sometimes forgotten, memories of the wonderful gift of life and love that was Jean Strachan. Whenever we come to celebrate and remember, as we do today, we all have a way of carefully putting our spirit, our soul and our body back together again. This is an essential part of life; reshaping and recalling. It is the work of an artist. We are all the artists and creators of our lives if we can but put ourselves into the heart of the great artist that is God. We truly remember. In coming here and celebrating the life of Jean Angela Strachan, we do so using a mosaic of signs and symbols that tell us of this wonderful and courageous woman of faith, a daughter, a mother and a victim of a violent death, taken from us long before her time. On the table, you will find photo albums, trophies, the marriage booklet, the son's baptism certificate, a candle, some small crosses and the baptismal water in a shell. What you will not find on this table are reminders of the many years, days and nights of isolation and loneliness. You will not find the struggles, the waiting, the watching, the wondering and hoping that something will change or happen. You will not find on this table the symbols of dedication, tenacity nor teamwork of the media, police, detectives, scientists or the forensics and judicial people that did such a sterling job in search of the truth. The life of Jean Angela Strachan has changed, not ended. Her life and her light will shine forever in our midst. Her remarkable family will always carry her memory and spirit with them. She called them to get to know her anew over these past eleven years. She has brought the entire community together through her death. What a rare gathering she has designed for us. She dared us to stop, to be still and listen, to listen to each other and explore the intimacy of the pain of it all. Now she dares us to explore and keep vigil yet again, knowing the peace and rest that is now hers forevermore will one day be ours. May Jean continue to rest in peace. Amen.'

I bowed my head, and could feel the emotions welling up inside me. I was particularly pleased that Jean was being referred to as Strachan, and not Keir, as if that final hold he'd had over her had been removed. Maria took my hand and smiled at me. Through a teary haze, I watched Leonard take the stage.

'Together, we are gathered to celebrate the life of Jean Angela Strachan...

'In fact, we have been celebrating her life and remembering her, even more so, over the last few weeks. Volumes of legal transcript now describe her life and the person she really was; active, fun-loving, caring, close to relatives and friends, a true innocent by nature. Those volumes describe her undying love for her son, her carefree persona and her deep-seated want to please all those around her. It is these qualities by which we will always remember her.

'From my own point of view, I remember the occasions when she would come to my aid when I needed help. She listened when I needed to talk, and she would always manage to spring me when I was stealing a drink of milk straight from the bottle. She was a valued member of her basketball team, respected by coaches and players alike...

'The close bond she formed with her friends at school continued through her marriage, and through all the bad times. The strengths of those friendships have become even more evident throughout the last few weeks, and even today. The support Jean's friends have given the family, in my view, is unparalleled. Jean left us eleven years ago, in suspicious circumstances, shrouded in doubt and mystery. It is only now that we can say goodbye and, in a way, be glad that she can now rest in peace. Justice has been done.

'I would like to extend my gratitude to the detectives. They went that extra mile in circumstances that were not easy, and displayed unequalled dedication. Although they never knew Jean in life, their investigation led them to know who Jean really was, the type of person that Jean was. Their presence here today and their show of support indicates that the world lost a very special person back in 1988.

'Each one of us who knew her has a memory of Jean and a story to tell. Some are saddening, but most are good. Keep those memories close, and feel relief, as I do, that she can now rest in peace.'

There was a profound silence as Leonard made his way back to his seat, his head bowed. After a few moments, Father Hanna resumed the service. He called Shona McDonald up, and she told some funny stories about her and Jean. When she'd finished, Father Hanna concluded the service. As everyone began to rise from their seats, I moved into the aisle and tried my best to keep out of the way as the family mingled, but Maria noticed me standing on my own, my hands placed respectfully in front of me.

'You need to come and join us,' she said. 'You're part of this family now.'

I gave her a shy smile as she grabbed me by the arm and led me over to Christine and Clifford. Once again, Christine gave me that smile of hers, and embraced me. 'Thank you for coming,' she said. 'It means a lot.'

'I wouldn't have missed it for anything. It was a beautiful service and I think Jean would have loved it,' I whispered into her ear, not wanting the others to hear the tremor in my voice. They asked me to join the family gathering, but I declined, telling them I had things to do, and that those kinds of things should really be left to the family.

As I went to leave, Christine said, 'You know, I always wonder about that large bone I found in the backyard when I was helping Tom to clean up before he moved in with Rosalina.'

No sooner had she said it than I stopped her. 'Christine, don't go wondering about that. It may not be what you think. I'll keep in touch with you, and let you know when Tom will be sentenced. Thank you for inviting me to the service; it was very special.' I hugged Christine once more, shook Clifford's hand and turned to Maria.

'Thank you for everything you've done,' she said as she held my hand.

'I'm just glad we got the right result,' I said. 'Take care of Christine, and I'll see you at the sentencing.'

I turned and walked towards the huge doors at the back of the church. They were splayed wide open and, as I moved towards them, I could see the rays of sunshine beaming down onto the carpet. I stopped and turned back to see all the people inside the church talking and hugging, some of them still wiping the tears from their faces. I turned again, and as I headed towards the exit, I bowed my head. 'Now you can rest in peace,' I said to Jean.

I emerged from the church and walked to the top of the steps, the blinding sunshine causing me to stumble a little, and then stood there for a few moments before looking up to the sky and saying, 'Well, Jean, my job is done. It's all over.'

SEVEN BONES

CHAPTER 22

Sentencing

On 29 February 2000, Thomas Keir was sentenced to twenty-four years imprisonment with a non-parole period of eighteen years.

The Defence barrister had a forensic psychiatrist take a history of Keir after his conviction, and the psychiatrist gave evidence at the sentencing that Keir maintained his innocence, and couldn't understand how the jury had reached their decision. The psychiatrist concluded that Keir didn't constitute a danger to the general population if released in the future, but would constitute a danger to any woman with whom he formed an intimate relationship.

'His risks with intimate relationships must be considered to be reasonably high. The history indicates that he became particularly obsessed in this relationship; he may have developed a case of morbid jealousy, but I cannot confirm that. The history does indicate that concerns about certain aspects of his wife's behaviour were unhealthy and probably extreme…

'He potentially does represent a risk to the other person in the context of an intense emotional relationship, particularly if that person chooses to leave him at some stage.'

Justice Adams, in his final findings, said, 'It is convenient to say that, quite apart from other matters, the account of these conversations does not ring true to me. Why would Jean Keir ring the man from whom she had run away rather than her family and friends, even if not her mother? Why did she not at least wish to speak to her son? The comment "she had split with Carl" implies that she had continued a relationship with Carl Neiding. I do not believe this to be fact…it is difficult to think of a rational explanation for Jean Keir being prepared to inform the accused that she had had a child, not his, but not to inform her family and friends…I do have some difficultly following why Jean Keir, who had left the accused and told him to find somebody else because her son "needs a mum", would start screaming and shouting down the telephone at an indication that they would be divorced.'

Adams also said something very poignant to those seated in the court. 'It has sometimes been suggested that "domestic" murders comprise a less heinous class of crime than murders where such a relationship is absent. I do not accept this point of view. The deliberate infliction of lethal violence is as culpable whether the victim is a spouse or a stranger. I add that it is apparent that there are some men in the community who consider that marriage gives them the right to control the lives and welfare of their wives and to punish them when they do not comply with those demands. Those men should be warned that the law will not stand idly by and permit them to commit crimes of violence; however justified they think they might be. Nor should they think that such attempts at justification will be met with sympathy. To the contrary, the assertion of such a right should be treated as regarding culpability all the greater.'

CHAPTER 23

Prophetic Words

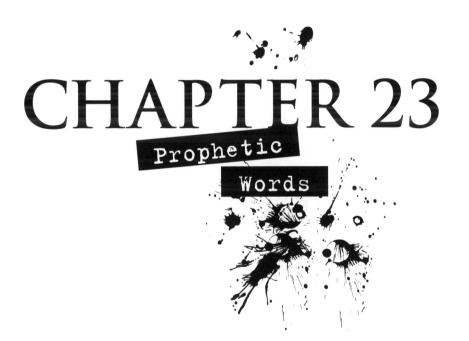

The second trial for the murder of Jean Angela Keir began in 2002.

It wasn't over after all.

Justice Adams had made errors in his directions to the jury on how the DNA evidence should be considered. As it happened, the statistical evidence about DNA results, and how a jury could use it, was subject to rather complicated and subtle rules of law. Adams, when summing-up to the jury, had informed them that the chance that the bones were not Jean Keir's was 1 in 660,000. Now, those might seem like pretty large odds, but it still leaves some possibility that the bones did not belong to Jean, no matter how big those odds are. I mean, as the little signs on the pokies say, 'Your chance of winning the maximum gaming prize on any machine is 1 in 1,000,000,000', but people do still win them. People's chances of getting struck by lightning or attacked by a shark are probably pretty similar, and yet people still do get struck, or eaten. Therefore, whilst it was most probable that the bones were Jean's there was still an element of doubt.

In the appeal against the conviction, Keir's appeal barrister said that what Adams needed to say was, 'If you take a randomly chosen member of the community, the chances of that individual matching the DNA characters of the bone fragments is 1 in 660,000.'

The appeal barrister also focused on the fact that the judge had given hefty weight to the DNA evidence, and not the 'sightings' of Jean Keir, therefore the Defence had not been able to give a fair side to their story. However, the key defence witness who'd seen Jean happened to be Keir's mother. Keir's lawyer, as was his right, argued that dismissing the sightings and focusing on the DNA 'effectively deprived the accused of the chance that the jury might have looked at the sightings as evidence as grounds to acquit.'

All of this allowed Keir to appeal.

Everyone, myself included, had to go through the exact same process as the first trial. I could see it was gut-wrenching for Christine and Clifford. They'd said their final goodbyes and had begun to move on with their lives, only to suddenly be brought right back to where they'd started from.

We were back at Darlinghurst again, however, this time the Prosecutor was a tall, thin man by the name of Giles Tabuteau. Over the course of the trial, I came to know Giles as one of the best Crown Prosecutors I'd ever had the privilege of meeting. He had short, wavy hair and wore thin-rimmed glasses. He spoke very eloquently, and was one of those Crown Prosecutors who took the time to really communicate with the Police investigators to make the trial a real team effort. There was also a new Defence barrister, and he fought the case tooth and nail. There were seemingly endless pre-trial hearings that he required before the trial could begin and the jury could even start considering the case. It felt like a war of attrition, which continued on throughout the trial, and the patience of the new judge, Justice David Kirby, was tested more than once. The whole proceedings stretched on for thirteen weeks.

One day, while waiting for the trial to resume, Tabuteau asked my opinion about why only the small bones had been found. I told him about my drum theory.

'That'll do me,' he said, and it was this line of argument that he was to use throughout the second trial. At this point, I was very glad that I'd had my epiphany.

The same witnesses were paraded through the courtroom, including Riley and Perkins, and the stories were told word for word as they had been before.

I think it is pertinent to mention a point of law here. When the Defence barrister asked me about the first time we'd interviewed Keir, I told him we'd pretty much read him his rights, and Mick had said, 'I want you to understand you are not obliged to say anything unless you wish to but whatever you say will be recorded and may later be used in evidence.'

The reason I mention this is because the 'right of silence' is an important one. The judge explained this to the court.

'It is a fundamental right in some countries as it is in our system of government. Every citizen has the right of silence…a police officer told Mr Keir that he had the right not to respond to questions and Mr Keir then exercised that right…it is important that you not use the exercise of that right in a way adverse to him; that is, in order to draw an unfair, unfavourable inference against Mr Keir.'

And he was bloody right to do so; if every bloke who chose not to say something was considered guilty, then the prison system would have prisoners coming out its arse. Just because a bloke doesn't say something does not indicate guilt.

I was called to the witness box, and the Defence decided they were going to question me on how we'd gained the information from the prisoners. Their other line was to question our excavation of the house. When you're in a witness box, you can't recall events as if you were watching them being replayed on TV. You remember what happened, of course, but you can't remember every minute detail. Besides, if a court or jury heard two police officers giving the same evidence, word for word, then they'd soon realise that something was fishy, like a teacher knowing that two kids had cheated on a test.

I'd been giving evidence about the excavation of the house, and I'd forgotten certain details. When I entered the witness box the next day, I remembered several things that had appeared the night before whilst I was watching the projector on the ceiling, trying to get to sleep, running the case over and over again in my mind.

'Did you say dirt was being excavated out of that hole and you were moving it somewhere to sift through it?' the Defence barrister asked.

'Yes…thinking about what you said yesterday, it did cause me concern last night, and then I realised that the dirt, yes, was excavated dirt…all that dirt was not from the hole, but brought out from under the house when we commenced digging.'

'So, in your *troubled* night, you say you have thought about your answers yesterday, where you agreed that all of that soil had been backfill, right?'

It was as clear as a bell that this bloke, in my opinion, was a deadset smart-arse. He crapped on about who was there, and who was in charge, and then came out with, 'Why didn't you photograph the bones *in situ*, where they had been found?'

'They were…' I managed to say before the barrister interrupted me. 'Wouldn't it be a prudent thing to do, if someone says, "Look, I have found what appears to be a human bone," that someone would say, "Well, let's take a photograph of it, where we say we have found it?"'

You can guess what he was trying to infer, that somehow the police hadn't found the bones of Jean Angela Keir, and because we had no case, we'd taken bones from somewhere else and planted them under the house, deciding to put on a show and make it look like we were doing an excavation.

'So you take the bones out of the ground and then you photograph the ground where you have taken it from; is that what you're saying the police decided would be a cunning plan?' he continued.

This bloke was a real knob, and he was starting to get on my nerves. I could see from the looks on the faces of the Judge and the jury that he was starting to piss them off, too. 'Stuff you,' I thought, and decided I wasn't going to let him get the better of me any time he asked me a stupid question.

'Well, I don't know if you would describe it as a *cunning* plan,' I replied. 'Actually, there was no plan, cunning or otherwise.'

I couldn't believe it; the longer the trial went the more of a prick this bloke was making of himself. I guess when you agree to defend a guy who's already been convicted of murder, and allegedly murdered another person, then that's the kind of person you have to be. They were clutching at straws, and we knew it. In fact, Keir would later accuse me of corruption, etc. I was informed of the fact, but was never investigated, so there was obviously no substance to it. It made me quite pleased, actually. I'd matched myself against him, and he had nothing left. He knew I'd beaten him.

Back on the stand, the Defence barrister returned to the main Prosecution witness, Brian Riley.

'Now, back to Mr Riley. He received a letter of comfort…on 10 May 1991.'

'Yes.'

'He has said he will only give evidence if he is allowed to have a pseudonym?'

'Yes.'

'Are you aware that, after the first trial, he was given a reward?'

'Yes.'

'How much was he given?'

'$18,000.'

He continued on, trying to imply that we'd paid Riley for the information. Eventually, he came to the point about Riley still wanting to give evidence after he'd left prison.

I'll stuff this bloke at his own game, I thought.

'He showed interest in this matter even to the point of returning to the court at a later stage of the Crown case after giving evidence?' the barrister asked.

'If I recall correctly, I think it might have been Mrs Strachan who said he'd came back and wished her luck and so forth,' I replied.

I was happy that the jury now knew that Riley had spoken to Christine, and that he was doing this to see justice done, not for the money.

'And he was very happy to get the $20,000, wasn't he?' the barrister said.

'Well,' I said, pausing, 'I would be too.'

I had him. The jury were smiling, and I could see that the judge was having a little chuckle.

The high point, I suppose, was when the Defence barrister started to have a crack at me. He insisted that I'd threatened Riley, and he'd given his testimony under duress. I just stuck to my guns, and the Crown Prosecutor quickly informed the jury that this whole line of argument had never been mentioned previously, and was therefore clearly just an attempt to shift the focus away from the accused. In a last-ditch effort, the Defence once again tried to argue that we'd planted the bones under the house.

Once more, the evidence from the DNA testing was submitted. It was impossible to fly to the two ladies back from the United States, so it was arranged for them to appear by video link-up. Despite the time difference, meaning that they were giving their evidence in the middle of the night, their time, they were equally as unflappable as they'd been in the first trial. Nancy Koszelak, now Scibetta, gave evidence that was identical to that which she'd given in the first trial. She began by explaining the processes of examining the bones in response to questions from Tabuteau. She explained how she analysed the bones one at a time by sanding the inside and external surfaces and she also described how she went about extracting the DNA.

'Can you explain things in terms of sanding? Can you explain the purpose of sanding both the external and internal surfaces?' Tabuteau continued.

'It was a procedure that was validated at my laboratory and it was to remove any external contaminant such as soil or if there was anything else present on the outside of the bone. The inside was also sanded because the inside of the bone contains marrow or spongy bone, which is more susceptible to bacterial degradation, therefore it is advantageous to remove that for further steps along the way.'

'Does that allow you to conclude that it was consistent with these two bones having come from the same identified individual?'

'Probably from the same individual; at least from an individual with a common maternal ancestor.'

'Would you just go on then in relation to what those results showed you?'

'They were complete mitochondrial DNA sequences, and indicated good quality mitochondrial DNA, which led me to conclude that the next step would be to obtain a mitochondrial DNA sequence from the blood of Christine Strachan.'

'How unique are mitochondrial sequences?'

'They're not unique, because they are the same as a maternal relative. Yours would be the same as your mother and her siblings. Yours would also be the same as all of your siblings with the same mother, so they are not unique, but mitochondrial DNA can be used to determine whether there are consistencies and inconsistencies.'

Ms Lee from the Armed Force's Laboratory was the next to give evidence.

'Can you tell us a little bit about the Armed Forces DNA Identification Laboratory, of which you are the technical leader? Can you tell us a little bit about what it does, and in particular, what it was doing back in '97 in terms of identification of human remains?' Tabuteau asked her.

'Yes. I'm actually the Technical Leader of the Nuclear DNA section. Our laboratory actually has two sections, a Nuclear DNA section that works on death investigations for our Armed Forces, and we also have a Mitochondrial DNA section that works on ancient death investigations, such as remains coming back from Vietnam, Korea, and World War II. The Nuclear DNA section's primary focus is recent death investigations, where individuals are deceased from incidents such as aircraft mishaps, explosions, or motor vehicle accidents, as well as military attacks such as gunshot wounds or bombings.'

'Are some of those incidents mass disaster incidents?'

'That's correct. Our laboratory has also provided assistance not only to the military community but also to the civilian community in mass disasters such as commercial airline incidents such as TWA, Egypt Air, and Alaska Air. We helped in identifying human remains of individuals that were aboard those aircraft.'

'Getting back to your earlier references, do some of the casework remains come from burial sites?'

'Yes, they do. Some of the remains come from burial sites, and we have had remains recovered from the ocean floor.'

'In other words, have some of your casework remains come from very harsh environments, and environments where there may be mixed samples, and therefore a high possibility of contamination?'

'Yes, that is correct, particularly in an aircraft accident, where you have hundreds of individuals aboard an aircraft that then hits the ground. You have a great potential for co-mingling or, as you put it, mixed samples. Quite often, in some of our aircraft mishaps remains have been exposed to harsh environments such as fire, because once the aircraft has crashed, carrying all that fuel, there is a post-crash fire. They can also be exposed to chemical contaminants, such as the fuel. So we have quite a bit of experience working with challenged samples.'

The Defence barrister cross-examined Ms Lee about any possible contamination.

'Were you concerned about contamination as a result of those observations I've taken you through and to the fact that you were unaware of the specific examinations that had occurred previously?'

'I was concerned that there was a possibility of contamination. I'm concerned on every occasion, on every skeletal remains case that I work on, that there could be some form of contamination.'

What I'm suggesting to you is that those bones could then reflect the DNA of the material that have come into contact with... and, in effect, become a reflection of the bone's DNA by way of contamination.'

'But DNA is a – it does not exist naked. In nature it is protected by a nuclear membrane.'

'Are you saying it can't permeate other items such as bones?'

'DNA itself?'

'Yes.'

'In order to obtain the DNA sequence, or DNA profile, as a nuclear DNA analyst I would first perform an extraction procedure to get that DNA to come out of the material that it was in. If you're asking me if cellular material could stick to a bone, yes, cellular material could stick to a bone.'

'And so couldn't that cellular material, by way of its contact with the bone, allow DNA to pass into the bone?'

'I don't know if it could pass into a bone or not. All I know is that in this case, and whenever I handle skeletal remains, I sand the exposed surfaces, the external and internal surfaces, to remove the potential.'

The Defence barrister pressed Ms Lee on this point. 'I'm asking about the combination of those three. Small sample, small quantity of DNA, and PCR used to amplify the DNA. If you combine those three conditions, is STR susceptible to contamination?'

'Yes, it is susceptible to contamination, but we would be able to detect the contamination using our controls.'

'If the specimen that you were extracting the DNA from had been denuded from DNA but contaminated by coming into contact with other DNA, you would not detect it as a contaminant, would you?'

'Coming into contact with what, specifically? Are you talking about coming into contact with a person's hand?'

'Anything that contained DNA that wasn't the DNA inherent in the DNA, or the sample originally.'

'Given our protocol, we actually sanded off the exterior of the bone as well as washing the bone in ethanol, and so if there was an external contaminant of the bone, that would be removed before we extracted the DNA.'

'I understand that, and I understand you had high standards for removing the possibility of contaminants in the laboratory back in 1997, but what I am asking you is if it is possible or plausible even, that if a specimen that had been denuded of any DNA came into contact with another specimen, such as a hand, or a scalp, or dandruff, that DNA could be transferred to the degraded specimen? Would you accept that proposition?'

'It is plausible. It is plausible that it can be transferred to that sample, that's correct, but in order to obtain the DNA profile from that bone, it would have had to have actually penetrated that bone because of the clinical procedures I've mentioned.'

'And it's possible that DNA could have penetrated a specimen?'

'Not from a touch of a hand or from dandruff, as you suggest.'

Despite the Defence's best efforts to insinuate that the DNA process was flawed due to the contamination of the bones, it had no effect. The Judge accepted that their testing methods were sound, and Ms Lee came to the conclusion that, after her testing, 'Based on DNA results, the bone samples were consistent with being from an offspring of the two blood samples.'

Justice Kirby began his summing-up.

'I begin by reminding you of certain principles of law. They are fundamental to our system of criminal justice. The first is that every accused person is presumed innocent until his or her guilt is proven. The accused Mr Keir has the benefit of this presumption. He is presumed innocent. He is entitled to have you return a verdict of not guilty unless you find the Crown has proven his guilt. At no stage in this trial is there any onus upon Mr Keir to prove that he is innocent of murder because his innocence is presumed. In respect of all issues, the onus is upon the Crown to prove his guilt. The onus never shifts from the Crown. Mr Keir has no obligation to disprove any part of the Crown case against him. Indeed, the onus rests upon the Crown from the start of this trial until the end.

'The onus is in no way affected by the fact that Mr Keir has given evidence before you. Mr Keir was not obliged to give evidence, he could have remained silent...

'The second fundamental principle is that everything which the Crown is required to prove must be proved to your satisfaction beyond reasonable doubt...The Crown, to succeed against Mr Keir, must establish his guilt beyond reasonable doubt...

'You have heard the evidence of Christine Strachan, the mother of Jean Keir, and you have no doubt seen Mrs Strachan sitting in the back of this Court throughout this trial, as well as other members of her family. It is natural that you should feel sympathy for her. Likewise, you have seen the son of the accused, after he completed his evidence, sitting in the back of the Court, and other members of his family. It is natural that you should feel sympathy for him, and for them. However, when you determine the issues in this trial you must put that sympathy to one side. It has no place in your evaluation. Your task is to reach an objective view of the evidence.'

'Let me say something about the process of fact finding...A vital part of your function will be to reach conclusions on what evidence you accept, and what evidence you find reliable and credible and what evidence you believe you can act safely on....

'Before you can convict Thomas Andrew Keir of murder, you must be satisfied beyond reasonable doubt:

1. That Jean Angela Keir is dead

AND

2. That her death was caused by an act of Thomas Andrew Keir on or about 9 or 10 February 1988

AND

3. That at the time of carrying out that act, Thomas Andrew Keir intended to kill her or to cause her grievous bodily harm, that is, really serious bodily injury...

'The offence of murder is defined in various ways. Here, the issue is relevantly uncomplicated. There are no issues of self-defence and other such issues that sometimes arise...

'Jean Angela Keir is dead. Let me pass on to the second element, that her death was caused by an act of Thomas Andrew Keir on or about 9 or 10 February 1988…Are you satisfied beyond reasonable doubt that the accused did something to harm Jean Keir…If he did, are you satisfied that whatever he did caused her death…

'Here, the evidence does not establish the precise act which caused death. However, you must be satisfied that whatever that act was, it was accompanied by an intention either to kill Jean Keir or cause her serious bodily injury.'

The jury was certainly satisfied that all these conditions had been met, and Keir was convicted for a second time on 17 September 2002.

We breathed a collective sigh of relief, but no sooner had we exhaled then we needed to inhale once more. The Internet has many uses, but when it comes to a court of law, it can cause real problems. It emerged that some of the jurors had researched Keir online during the trial, and had found out what had happened to Rosalina. Keir's lawyers found this out, and Keir immediately lodged an appeal and obtained another new barrister. The Appeal Court granted the appeal and ordered a new trial.

For the third trial, there was another change of Defence lawyer, and this time Keir elected to go judge-alone, with no jury. Giles Tabuteau continued on as the Crown Prosecutor. He told me that he thought he should agree to do so, because the history of the case was so unusual. I was happy with that, and so was Christine. Now, you would have thought that, with the history of the jury either being on Keir's side, as in the trial for the Rosalina case, or messing things up in the second trial for Jean, the Defence would opt to have a jury again, but perhaps they thought their luck might have run out.

The third trial was held in front of Justice Campbell in 2004. He stared across the courtroom as he completed his deliberations, and we could see that he was ready to announce his verdict. Fortunately, he decided not to read out his findings, which amounted to nearly 300 pages, only the verdict. His findings, meanwhile, were handed out in booklet form for all concerned to read if they so desired, and the last paragraph reads:

'It is my view that the only reasonable inference to be drawn from these circumstances, taken together with the other findings I have made, is that the bones are those of Jean Keir, that she is dead and that her death was caused by an act of the accused on or about 9 February 1988. I am satisfied that the Crown has proved beyond reasonable doubt that Jean Angela Keir is dead and that her death was caused by an act of the accused on or about 9 February 1988… The above views and findings lead to the conclusion that the accused is guilty of murdering Jean Angela Keir on or about 9 February 1988 at Tregear in the state of New South Wales. I so find.'

Keir looked at his barrister with that same stone-faced façade, and with a slight frown, nodded his head.

Afterwards, Christine said, 'He's my grandson's father. I have to forgive him, but he's in gaol, and he's going to pay for what he did to my daughter.'

Keir launched yet another appeal in the middle of 2007, but this time, the conviction was upheld.

He was sentenced to twenty-two years in gaol, meaning that he would possibly remain in gaol until 19 February 2020, but at worst, with parole, he'd be free on that same date in 2014.

CHAPTER 24

Resting in Peace

Keir's nine lives had run out. He'd always maintained that he could commit the perfect murder, but he was wrong. His threats to Jean within earshot of family and friends had come back to haunt him like a ghost in purgatory. However, the stress of the trials had begun to take its toll on us.

'This bloke's like fucking Santa Claus. Every year, he keeps coming back,' I once remarked to Mick during one of the more stressful days when I had to ring Mick to tell him that there would be a third trial.

I'd lived and breathed this case since it had begun with the Missing Persons file way back in 1989. It had taken just short of twenty years, but we had our conviction. There were so many highs and, of course, so many lows. So many nights I'd lain in bed trying to visualise where Jean's body was; now I could switch off the projector once and for all. Well, maybe not, but at least I could play a new movie. In the darkest hours, as I lay there, I'd come to the point where I found myself asking Jean, out loud, for some kind of sign.

I remember one night, during the most intense parts of the investigation I'd barely gone to bed one night when I heard a female voice call:

'Peter.'

I rolled over and instinctively replied, 'Yeah?' thinking that it was Susie, but no-one was there. I sat bolt upright in bed and scanned the room. The only thing I could see was the slivers of moonlight flickering through the curtains as they moved in the breeze. I went and checked on my daughters. 'It can't have been them,' I thought. 'They wouldn't call me "Peter".'

I went back downstairs. 'Did you just call me, Susie?'

'No, darl,' she replied. 'I turned the TV down so I wouldn't disturb you. Is everything OK?'

'Yeah, fine, no worries,' I said as I walked back upstairs.

This was the first of three occasions on which I heard a young woman's voice call my name. Later in life, I would come to know a medium called Robyn Caughlan, an Indigenous woman who is a brilliant artist and fashion designer. I confided in Robyn about the young woman's voice. Robyn knew nothing about Jean, but said, 'There's a young woman who is reaching out to you. She'd died, and she was contacting you. You were trying to find this woman, and she was letting you know you were on the right track, and that you should never give up.'

I confided in Robyn that my dreams were often filled with the colour red. 'Red, in a dream,' she said, 'symbolises danger, but it's a reference to the young woman, because it also symbolises blood.'

I finally told Robyn about Jean. 'She's the one coming to you in your dreams. I'm telling you, she'll continue to contact you, in some way, until this is all over. She wants the truth to come out. When this is over, only then will she leave you alone.'

After the third trial, in 2004, I was sitting at home with Susie one evening. 'You know, Keir always said the cops were stupid, and the only way they catch crooks is if the crook is stupid enough to open their mouths about what they've done. The funny thing is, that's exactly how we got him. If he'd kept his mouth shut, then we'd never have found the bones. I guess that's Jean's way of getting back at him.'

'Well, it's all over now,' Susie replied. It took up a large part of your life, and your family's too, but at least you were able to get her family some closure.'

'I don't believe in closure,' I said as I kissed my wife. 'All we did was give the family answers. To me, closure means that it's finished, and there's nothing else left, but memories of Jean will always be there. So there's no closure, only answers.' I paused for a moment.

'You know what? Until we find that bloody drum and the rest of Jean's body, this job will never be finished.'

EPILOGUE
To Detective Peter Seymour
from Christine Strachan,

The following letter was sent after Thomas Keir's final conviction, but before a final order could be obtained to return Jean's belongings to her family as a result of the lengthy appeals process.

To me, Peter, you are fantastic! You believed from day one. When you first came to my house for Rosalie you thought that Jean had come home and had been finished off. When Cliff and I told you that it was her who had been strangled you and the other detective sort of looked at each other in shock. You said to me then that you would take on Jean's case and would start putting out feelers.

Then you all started excavating.

When I saw you at court you told me that Tom wanted to see his son but that they couldn't let him.

You also told me that you had seen Fiona and Shona. You told me that after you had heard their story that you was going to speak to Tom. When I spoke to you at court I could tell you really understood what had happened.

At about that time, I had gone to see a medium and she told me that there would be a dark-haired detective who would be really passionate about finding Jean and would stop at nothing until he did.

Every year I would ring to find out what was happening.

I would always ask what was going on and, I guess, I became really pushy at times. I was really upset that every time I would ring I would have to talk to a different detective, Merkel and all the other ones. I would always think: 'What are they doing? Why do I always have to speak to a different detective?'

I just really wanted to know what happened to my daughter.

I was told by Rod Dayment that they couldn't do much and that he didn't think they had a very strong case.

I was so pushy. I just wanted them to push everything through and to have an end to it all.

Peter, you said they would put out their feelers for the DNA testing and try England and the United States.

Although I became upset and was really pushy, all of the detectives were very helpful and understanding and I would get so upset that I would have to apologise throughout the case. It must have been hard on them too. All I wanted was justice for her; I just wanted someone to pay.

I think I have to start writing letters to the media, to the Parliament, to anyone just so I can get this finished.

It is twenty years on and all I have left of Jean is her bones, her dolls and her letters and because the case is still going I can't get any of it back.

I feel like I am in the lurch. My husband has passed away and I am not well with things like arthritis and I just want everything over and done with. I am going to have to take matters in my hands. Why won't they just give me back what I have left of Jean?

How many more families have to suffer through this kind of thing?

I just want it over and done with before I pass away too – twenty years is just too long.

AFTERWORD
by Giles Tabuteau

Jean Angela Keir was a happy, optimistic young woman. Twenty-two, married, with an adorable two-year-old son, the future held all the hopes and dreams that any young woman would have at her age – or should have.

Late on the night of 9 February 1988, in her own family home in western Sydney; Jean Angela Keir would suffer a violent and brutal death – at the hands of Thomas Andrew Keir, the man she had married three years earlier.

This book traces the extraordinary saga of bringing Jean's murderer to justice.

Remarkably, Jean was not the only wife of Keir to suffer a gruesome and untimely death in the family home.

Not long after Jean disappeared, Keir began courting, and then married, Jean's cousin Rosalina. But Rosalina, aged just twenty-one, was herself found dead soon after; strangled with an electrical cord in the main bedroom of the very same family home, which was subsequently set on fire.

But in an extraordinary irony, Rosalina's murder gave investigators the key to unlocking the mystery of what happened to Jean. The investigation into Rosalina's death led to the Missing Persons file for Jean's earlier disappearance being reopened - and becoming a murder investigation - thanks to the dogged determination of the main investigating detective, Peter Seymour.

It is through Seymour's eyes - and heart - that this story is told. Written in the knockabout style of a true working detective, this book traces how Keir was finally brought to justice for the murder of his first wife, and how it all started with the discovery of the murder of his second wife.

Although the jury in Keir's trial for the murder of Rosalina acquitted him, in truth Rosalina had not died in vain. It was through her death that the police investigation into Jean's earlier disappearance was reactivated, ultimately resulting in Keir's conviction for murder.

Through her death, Rosalina held Keir accountable for Jean's murder. Rosalina brought Keir to justice.

But the drama of that police investigation, and the three trials, convictions, and appeals, would take no less than fifteen years to play out to their final conclusion.

If every human drama has heroes, then Peter Seymour, and Jean's mother, Christine Strachan, deserve that honour.

Whatever the difficulties and frustrations that murder investigations encounter, and here these seemed at times interminable, as Seymour recounts, it is the story of Jean's mother that will captivate the reader. Her sheer courage, good nature, and infinite patience inspired the investigation and the conduct of the trials over those seemingly endless years.

When I was briefed as the Crown Prosecutor in late 2002, Keir had already been tried and acquitted of Rosalina's murder, and had stood trial for the first time for Jean's murder. The jury in that trial, in the Supreme Court before Justice Adams, had found Keir guilty of Jean's murder, but the conviction had been overturned on appeal, and a new trial ordered.

Following Keir's conviction after the first trial for Jean's murder, Peter Seymour and Jean's mother, Christine, had already been through two lengthy Supreme Court trials. Little did they, or anyone else, know that the agony of another six years of trials and appeals still lay ahead.

I conducted the second trial for Jean's murder, before Justice Kirby. The jury convicted Keir, but that conviction was overturned on appeal as well, after it was learned that some jurors had become aware of the circumstances of Rosalina's death. I embarked on the third trial for Jean's murder, before Justice Campbell, knowing this was probably the very last chance to put Keir behind bars. This trial resulted, once more, in Keir being convicted for murder.

It was, for me, a privilege to know and work with Seymour and his investigating colleagues, and to meet Christine, her husband and family, and her devoted friends.

Most of all, this book reminds us of the two young women who paid the ultimate price, the victims of crimes that are sometimes so blandly referred to as 'incidents of domestic violence'.

Domestic violence is better recognised and addressed today than 25 years ago, when Jean agreed to marry Keir, through developments in criminal law, protective orders available through the courts, and various support services and programs.

Whether our society has done enough, however, to ensure mutual respect in relationships, and the means of protection for those at risk of violence when relationships deteriorate is debatable.

This book provides cause for society to consider these issues, at least for the sake of those who might find themselves in Jean and Rosalina's circumstances in the future.

Giles J. Tabuteau

Crown Prosecutor, Director of Public Prosecutions

Sydney, Australia

August 2010

WRITER'S Note

Peter Seymour was introduced to me by Robyn Caughlan, who came to me and said Pete needed help writing his story. I was only too happy to help.

In our primary phone conversation, Pete outlined the amazing story that you have just read, and I remember driving to Pete's place to collect all the material I'd need to complete the book for him.

It was about nine at night, and it had been raining quite heavily. I was thinking about how I would write the story, when a tremendous shiver ran up my spine, and an overwhelming sense of someone else being in the car with me came over me.

I knew it was the girl in Pete's story. so I made a promise out loud: 'Okay! Okay! I will do my best to make sure your story is told.' With that, the sense of someone else being in the car left me. When I arrived at Pete's house, I told him what had happened. It was only then that he told me that Jean had come to him as well.

A few weeks later, when I was about halfway through rewriting Pete's story, I was sitting out the front of my home having a coffee break, contemplating packing it in for the night when an incredible gust of wind came up from nowhere, and then died.

I looked up to the sky, but there were no clouds, only stars, and decided that would do me for the night. Suddenly, the gust returned, stronger and more ferocious than before, sending leaves and debris flying through my front garden.

'Alright! Alright!' I yelled, 'I'll go back inside and do some more.' As soon as these words had left my lips, the wind died again.

I've now shared in Jean Angela Keir's story, and I'm proud to be the one who has refined it for Pete so that we can both share the story of a remarkable young woman whose life was so cruelly cut short.

I hope you have taken many things from this book, but primarily, I hope you have taken and will keep the idea of the preciousness of human life. We all have but one short moment on this planet and it is up to all of us to squeeze the life out of every day.

Jean Angela Keir could have been so much to so many, but she will never have the chance to fulfil her dreams. You, our reader, will.

ENDNOTES

1.   Macken, *Sydney Morning Herald*, 1993, from N. Saroca, 'Representing Rosalina and Annabel: Filipino Women, Media Violence, Representation and Contested Realities.' *Kasarinlan: Philippine Journal of Third World Studies*, 22, 2002, p. 13.

2.   Saroca, N., '*Violence Against Filipino Women in Australia: Theorising the relationship between the Discursive and Nondiscursive*', Expanding Our Horizons Conference, Sydney, 2002, pp. 16-17.

3.   Ibid., p 17.

4.   N. Saroca, 'Representing Rosalina and Annabel: Filipino Women, Violence, Media Representation and Contested Realities.' *Kasarinlan: Philippine Journal of Third World Studies*, 22, 2002, p. 42.

5.   N. Saroca, '*Violence Against Filipino Women in Australia: Theorising the relationship between the Discursive and Nondiscursive*', Expanding Our Horizons Conference, Sydney, 2002, p. 19.

6.   Macken, *Sydney Morning Herald*, 1993, from N. Saroca, '*Violence Against Filipino Women in Australia: Theorising the relationship between the Discursive and Nondiscursive*', Expanding Our Horizons Conference, Sydney, 2002, p. 13.

ABOUT the Authors

Seven Bones is collaboration between Peter Seymour and Jason Foster.

Peter Seymour joined the New South Wales Police Force in 1980 as an eighteen-year-old. He worked as a general duties officer for two years before gaining the rank of Detective. He worked as a Detective for twelve years at various stations across Sydney. In 1992, Peter moved into the Police Prosecutor's Branch. In 2001, Peter became the Crime Co-ordinator of the Crime Management Unit at St Mary's in Sydney's western suburbs.

In his time as a police officer Peter has investigated several murder cases, including that of Jean Angela Keir. He has also investigated numerous armed robbery, rape and fraud cases. As a Police Prosecutor he was involved in countless inquests into suspicious deaths and much of the evidence he gathered for these cases led to murder convictions.

Peter now works at Blacktown City Council as the Team Leader for Community Enforcement.

Jason Foster is an author, poet, journalist and History teacher at Jamison High School in Sydney's western suburbs. He holds a Masters Degree in History and is currently studying a Diploma in Languages (Spanish). Jason is widely travelled, having travelled through over fifty countries. He has taught in Australia, the United Kingdom, Spain and Argentina.

He has been published all over the world with his work being published in American History magazines, Australian travel magazines and poetry anthologies in the United Kingdom. *Seven Bones*, is his first major true crime novel.

Made in the USA
San Bernardino, CA
16 November 2015